CHILDREN AND YOUNG PEOPLE
'LOOKED AFTER'?

CHILDREN AND YOUNG PEOPLE 'LOOKED AFTER'?

Education, Intervention and the Everyday Culture of Care in Wales

Edited by
Dawn Mannay, Alyson Rees
and Louise Roberts

UNIVERSITY OF WALES PRESS
2019

www.uwp.co.uk

British Library Cataloguing-in-Publication Data.
A catalogue record for this book is available from the British Library.

ISBN   978-1-78683-355-6
eISBN   978-1-78683-356-3

MIX
Paper from
responsible sources
FSC® C013604

Typeset by Chris Bell, cbdesign
Printed by CPI Antony Rowe, Melksham

Contents

List of figures and tables

List of contributors

GEMMA ALLNATT is a Research Development Officer with the Wales School for Social Care Research at Swansea University. She is also a Ph.D. student in the School of Social Sciences at Cardiff University. Her research is exploring the perception and experiences of care leavers in higher education. She is a qualified Social Worker. Prior to commencing her doctoral studies Gemma worked in a statutory childcare team and spent a number of years working in a residential unit. This is where her interest in the educational achievement and aspirations of children in care originated. Gemma has worked on a number of research studies, including the Looked After Children and Education project – Understanding the educational experiences and opinions, attainment, achievement and aspirations of looked after children in Wales.

RACHEL BROWN is a Research Associate with Cardiff University School of Social Sciences, based at the DECIPHer research centre. Her research interests are in substance use and young people, with particular focus on the delivery of interventions in complex settings. Her recently completed Ph.D. explored the utilisation of alcohol by new university students and the development of organisational responses to alcohol issues. She has previously worked in both voluntary and statutory substance misuse services, supporting young people with problematic drug and alcohol issues.

CASCADE VOICES is a collaboration between Voices from Care Cymru and CASCADE, Cardiff University. Care-experienced young people are trained in research methods by CASCADE researchers. The group meets every two months and provides advice and consultation on research projects from initial stages of design through to dissemination of findings. Members of the group have also acted as peer researchers and have facilitated focus groups with other care-experienced young people. Since its inception, the group has advised researchers from universities in Wales and Northern Ireland and the third sector, on a range of health and social care topics.

MARTIN ELLIOTT is a Research Development Officer with the Wales School for Social Care Research. A social worker with 17 years' statutory children's services experience, including front-line management and practice, contracting and commissioning, and strategic development work, his research interests include: children and young people in out-of-home care; children on the edge of care; social inequality and poverty; and services for disabled children and young people. He has a methodological interest in the use of routinely collected administrative data and quantitative methods.

RHIANNON EVANS is a Senior Lecturer in Social Science and Health at the Centre for the Development and Evaluation of Complex Interventions for Public Health Improvement (DECIPHer) at Cardiff University. She is an affiliated Senior Lecturer at the Children's Social Care Research and Development (CASCADE) Centre. She is also a co-applicant on the What Works Centre for Children's Social Care. Rhiannon's substantive research interests include the mental health and well-being of children and young people, particularly the prevention of self-harm and suicide. She has a methodological interest in the development and evaluation of complex intervention, and systematic reviews.

REBECCA GIRLING is a social worker currently working part-time in front-line children's services around training as part of the Great British Rowing Team. She completed her Masters in Social Work, writing a dissertation that focused on the experiences of children and young people in residential care. Prior to this she worked with young people with autism, living in a residential setting. Rebecca also has a degree in Psychology from Cardiff University.

HOLLY GORDON has 12 years' experience as a qualified social worker in Wales. Holly gained a professional doctorate from Keele University and her research explored the identities and perspectives of social workers with environmental interests. Her background is in children's social work, specifically with children and young people who are looked after and care leavers. She has been a trainer-consultant with the British Association for Adoption and Fostering (BAAF) Cymru and the Association for Fostering and Adoption (AFA) Cymru, delivering professional training to social care staff across Wales. Holly is currently employed by the National Society for the Prevention of Cruelty to Children (NSPCC) as a team manager for the Protect and Respect child sexual exploitation service in north Wales

SOPHIE HALLETT is a Lecturer in Social Policy in the School of Social Sciences at Cardiff University. Sophie's particular focus is on children, young people and social care, and her research interests revolve around aspects related to social policy analysis, care and welfare, with a particular focus on youth and young people and exploring the relationship between policy, practice and lived experience. Her specialist interest is Child Sexual Exploitation, and she is the author of '*Making Sense of Child Sexual Exploitation: Exchange, abuse and young people*' (Policy Press, 2017).

JENNIFER LYTTLETON-SMITH is a sociologist of children and childhoods whose research focuses on issues surrounding subjectivity and power. While her PhD explored early childhood and gender, her current research interests focus on participation and well-being for children and young people in care. She is currently undertaking a post-doctoral fellowship awarded by Health and Care Research Wales to examine how the ethos of co-production is being applied in Wales with children and young people in care, and how this interacts with the concept of 'personal well-being outcomes'. She works within the CASCADE Children's Social Care Research and Development Centre at Cardiff University.

DAWN MANNAY is a Senior Lecturer in Social Sciences (Psychology) at Cardiff University. Her research interests revolve around class, education, gender, generation, national identity, and inequality; and she employs participatory, visual, creative and narrative methods in her work with communities. Dawn edited the collection *Our Changing Land: Revisiting Gender, Class and Identity in Contemporary Wales* (University Wales Press, 2016); and wrote the sole authored text, *Visual, Narrative and Creative Research Methods: Application, reflection and ethics* (Routledge, 2016). With Tracey Loughran, she also recently co-edited a book entitled *Emotion and the Researcher: Sites, Subjectivities and Relationships* (Emerald, 2018). Dawn is currently working on a project funded by the Welsh Government to establish a community of practice to improve the educational experiences of children and young people who are looked after in Wales, ExChange: Care and Education.

MINISTRY OF LIFE is run by Tim Buckley, Jonathan Gunter, Michael Ivins and Tom Ivins. It is a south Wales-based community organisation that runs creative and musical workshops, youth clubs and events for young people. Ministry of Life has delivered youth work to disadvantaged and marginalised young people for eight years. During this time it has organised community events, youth workshops and youth clubs, accreditations and artistic outputs. It has employed its existing community and youth networks to draw on music and art to disseminate a message of community cohesion and tolerance in south Wales, by raising awareness of issues of racism and urban railway hazards. Ministry of Life also organised the music and art-based productions for the edited collection *Our Changing Land: Revisiting Gender, Class and Identity in Contemporary Wales* (Mannay, 2016) and research projects at Cardiff University related to children and young people in care.

AMY MUNRO is a qualified Educational Psychologist with over 10 years' experience of working with children in educational and social settings. She is also a qualified primary school teacher. In her recent post, she has been extensively involved in promoting well-being in schools, assisting with promoting 'attachment focused' schools and delivering training to Emotional Literacy Support Assistants (ELSA). In her current post, she is also the Lead Educational Psychologist for children with Autistic Spectrum Disorder.

CLAIRE PALMER is a Ph.D. student in the School of Social Sciences at Cardiff University. Her research focuses on the transition to parenthood for adopters of older children. Claire is an experienced statutory social worker and has also worked in the third sector as a children's advocate. Claire's research interests include the social construction of parenthood and the impact of adoption on all members of the adoption kinship network: adoptive parents, adoptees, birth family members and foster families.

REBECCA C. PRATCHETT is a Senior Lecturer at Swansea University. She has a Master's degree in psychology from the University of Glasgow and is undertaking a Ph.D. at Swansea University. The primary focus of her research is on children in kinship care, with particular emphasis on educational and psychological outcomes.

JOANNE PYE is a registered social worker with over 20 years' experience of working with children and families within the voluntary, private and statutory setting, as both a residential and field social worker. Joanne's areas of research interest focus upon children who are looked after and care leavers, with a particular emphasis on promoting positive outcomes for children within the care system.

ALYSON REES is a Senior Lecturer at Cardiff University, teaching predominantly on the MA in Social Work. Alyson is also Assistant Director of the Children's Social Care Research and Development Centre (CASCADE) at Cardiff University. Alyson has been a social work practitioner for sixteen years, working as a Probation Officer and for the NSPCC in a domestic violence unit. She is a registered social worker. Alyson's research interests centre around foster care, looked after children, incarcerated mothers, child neglect, and domestic abuse. Alyson's current research projects include an evaluation of Fostering Well-being and contributing to a study looking at video interactive guidance.

GWYTHER REES is an Honorary Research Fellow in the School of Social Sciences at Cardiff University. He is currently an Associate Research Fellow at the Social Policy Research Unit, University of York, where he is Research

Director for the Children's Worlds project – an international survey of children's lives and well-being. Gwyther was formerly Research Director at the Children's Society in England, where he undertook and managed research projects on a range of policy issues relevant to young people's lives including young people who run away from home, child maltreatment and child protection.

PAUL REES (Associate Professor) is Director of Swansea University's Centre for Children and Young People's Health and Well-being. He is a qualified and experienced teacher, educational psychologist and clinical paediatric neuropsychologist. He has over 20 years' clinical experience and extensive experience of working directly with children and young people in care. He has carried out research and published on a range of topics relating to the education, health and well-being of children in care. In recent times he has been heavily involved in training social workers. He is a registered Expert Witness with the British Psychological Society.

LOUISA ROBERTS is a Research Centre Administrator at the Children's Social Care Research and Development Centre (CASCADE) at Cardiff University. Louisa was involved with the Welsh Government funded 'Looked After Children and Education' project and worked with Dr Dawn Mannay to further disseminate the findings from this research through the Economic and Social Research Council funded project 'Improving the educational experiences and attainment of looked after children and young people'.

LOUISE ROBERTS is a Research Fellow based in the Children's Social Care Research and Development Centre (CASCADE) at Cardiff University. She is a registered social worker and lectures on the MA Social Work course. Louise's research interests are predominately focused around the experiences of children and young people in or leaving state care, as well as preventative efforts to support families and avoid separation. Louise's current project is concerned with the outcomes and experiences of families where one or both parents is care-experienced. In addition, Louise has led the evaluation of the Reflect service; an intervention to support women who have experienced the compulsory removal of a child from their care. The intervention aims to prevent repeat pregnancies in the short term whilst successive state intervention remains the most likely outcome.

PHIL SMITH is a Ph.D. student in the School of Social Sciences at Cardiff University. His research explores the educational experiences of young people in Pupil Referral Units and the occupational roles and routines of staff who work there. He is a qualified youth and community worker, which is where his interests in marginalised young people and the theory and practice of alternative education traditions stem from. He has a particular interest in, and experience of, participatory and creative research methods with young people, ethnographic methods, informal learning practices, and community engagement projects.

ELEANOR STAPLES is a Senior Research Associate at the University of Bristol, School for Policy Studies. Her Ph.D. critically examined Sure Start, the New Labour flagship early years programme in England. Her research interests include children and families involved with children's social care, gender, social justice, and critical social policy analysis. She has been involved in research with children and young people 'in care' and 'in need', women in prison and their children, and mothers in marginalised communities. Eleanor is interested in producing data in creative, participatory ways with children, young people and their families, and in thinking through power, emotion and participation in research with vulnerable groups.

Acknowledgements

IN EDITING THIS COLLECTION, *Children and Young People 'Looked After'? Education, Intervention and the Everyday Culture of Care in Wales*, there are many people who should be thanked and acknowledged. Many thanks go to all of the children, young people and care leavers that we have worked with across our studies, as practitioners, and through other events and activities: without their inspiration this book would never have been completed. We have also worked alongside key partners who influenced and supported us in different ways, including the Welsh Government, The Fostering Network, and Voices from Care Cymru. The Children's Social Care Research and Development Centre (CASCADE), its team and original founder, Professor Sally Holland, should also be acknowledged for their central influence in bringing together this edited collection.

It is also important to thank all of the individual authors for engaging with the project and offering a set of diverse and thoughtful accounts and reflections, drawing on their extensive knowledge and expertise. Many of the contributors are friends and colleagues that we met through research projects, workshops and conferences. However, we feel that we have come to know the authors more closely through the editing process. We have a deep respect for the research and scholarship of all the authors in this collection, and felt privileged that they accepted the invitation to be part of this book. Overall, the authors' commitment to care-experienced children and young people, and their carefully crafted responses have engendered a valuable set of chapters, and, in reading them, we have gained a wealth of knowledge, and developed a more nuanced understanding of the landscape of the care system in Wales.

We would also like to thank the proposal reviewers for their comments and suggestions; and the team at University of Wales Press for their support, particularly Llion Wigley who was Commissioning Editor for this volume, Siân Chapman – Production and Editorial Manager, Elin Williams – Sales and Marketing Officer, Bethan Phillips – Production Editor, and Dafydd Jones – Editor of the Press. We also acknowledge Sarah Roberts at Cardiff University's Planning Division for her assistance in applying for the university managed University of Wales Press fund to support scholarly publications and related activities in the fields of Welsh culture, history and literature. This funding was essential in publishing this collection. Our heartfelt thanks also go to Katerina Hristova at Katka Photography for her work planning and creating the cover image for this book, and to the models who feature in the photograph, Ffion, Oscar, Taya and Tahlia.

Lastly we would like to thank all our great friends and family. We are unable to acknowledge everyone for their support, but we would like to mention (in alphabetical order) those most involved in our everyday lives, with much love: Adrian, Angharad, David, Ffion, Ffion B., Jamie, Jeff, Jordon, KJ, Liam, Matthew, RDJ, Rhydian, Sherelle, Tahlia, Taya, Tilleah, Tim, Toyah, Travis, Travis Jay and Twm.

1 | Introduction

Dawn Mannay, Alyson Rees and Louise Roberts

Setting the scene

THIS OPENING CHAPTER provides the reader with an insight into the rationale for bringing together this edited collection, *Children and Young People 'Looked After'? Education, Intervention and the Everyday Culture of Care in Wales*. It sets out the aims and scope of the volume, as well as providing an overview of the following chapters and the ways in which they connect to the core themes of education, social policy, practice, research, and the everyday lives of care-experienced children and young people in the Welsh context.

All researchers have stories to tell about why they chose to research particular topics, and the book's editors have been involved in work with children and young people in the care system and care leavers, linked with academic research, consultations, teaching and social work practice (Mannay et al., 2015, 2017; Pithouse and Rees, 2014; Roberts, 2017; Roberts et al., 2016, 2017). This experience has engendered an admiration for the care-experienced populations we have encountered, and, at the same time, a disappointment that, despite social research and policy interventions, they are faced with pervasive educational and social inequalities, which can have consequences for their transitions to the workplace and their sense of security, self and ongoing stability.

A range of valuable work has been undertaken across the United Kingdom, for example, in England (Berridge, 2012; Diaz, 2018; Kenny, 2018; Morriss, 2018; O'Higgins et al., 2015; Sebba et al., 2015; Stein, 2006; Woodhouse, 2018), Scotland (Aldgate and McIntosh, 2006; Hill, 2011), and Northern Ireland (Fargas Malet et al., 2014). Additionally, there has been a sustained international interest in the educational experiences of and outcomes for care-experienced children and young people (see Benbenishty and Zeira, 2012; Brady and Gilligan, 2018; Jackson and Cameron, 2010; Matheson, 2015; Nho et al., 2017). In Wales, there has also been a significant body of work undertaken on, and with, care-experienced children and young people, and this edited collection is an attempt to draw together and showcase these insights in one volume, to consolidate this empirical and methodological knowledge base.

In this collection, we engage with the accounts of researchers working in different traditions, including education, psychology, policy studies, sociology and social work. The volume therefore brings together distinct scholarly traditions, providing an opportunity for reflection across disciplinary boundaries, and shedding new light on common problems and opportunities stimulated by research in the field of social care. The volume also introduces a range of contexts and sites, such as the home, the school, contact centres, educational institutions, and the natural environment. In exposing readers to these different disciplinary practices and research contexts, we hope to encourage them to reflect on how this knowledge can inform their own fields of interest.

We have three main aims in this volume. To this end, we have divided the book into three sections, each hosting five chapters, which respectively deal with education and policy interventions, the lived experiences of care-experienced children and young people, and research methodologies. These themes are inevitably interrelated, but shifting the focus to each aspect has enabled an emphasis on specific elements of the care system. The book aims to provide the reader with an in-depth understanding of all of these important areas, to sketch out a picture of key studies, approaches and recommendations in the contemporary Welsh landscape, and, at the same time, to offer fundamental insights that will be useful for a more international readership.

As documented in the rest of this chapter, each section offers contributions from scholars with a genuine commitment to improving policy, practice and research. The authors also share a respect for the views of children and young people in care. For this reason, we have not used the term 'looked after children' in the abbreviated form LAC. Despite its use in policy documents and related publications more widely, its association with the word 'lack' is problematic – 'young people do not like being referred to as "LAC" as they are not "lacking" in anything' (Children's Commissioner for Wales, 2017, p. 11). Accordingly, this edited collection focuses on what can be done to best support care-experienced children and young people, from the perspective that they are unique individuals with the abilities, aspirations and attributes to forge successful and fulfilling futures.

Education and policy intervention

Within Wales, the United Kingdom, and internationally children and young people in care achieve poorer educational outcomes compared to individuals not in care (Jackson and Cameron, 2014; Mannay et al., 2015; O'Higgins et al., 2015; Sebba et al., 2015). Since devolution, in 1999, the Welsh Government has advanced a number of targeted educational approaches, with existing provisions being summarised in the current strategy for the education of children in care in Wales (Welsh Government, 2016). Educational attainment is not the only predictor of success (Berridge, 2012), nonetheless, poor educational outcomes can have serious consequences for future life chances of care-experienced children and young people (Jackson, 1994). This is particularly salient in the landscape of a competitive employment economy, which places a central significance on the importance of qualifications (Brown et al., 2013). Consequently, this opening section is interested in setting a context for the background of the care population in Wales, and then charting research that explores educational experiences, outcomes, and the interventions put in place that seek to alleviate the educational disadvantages experienced by children and young people in care.

It is important to establish a broader picture of the 'looked after' population in the Welsh context. Accordingly, this section begins with a chapter from Martin Elliott titled 'Charting the rise of children and young people looked after in Wales'. The numbers of applications through the law courts to place children in Wales in out-of-home care have illustrated an unprecedented rise, leading to the claim that children in Wales are now one-and-a-half times more likely to become 'looked-after' than those in England (Drakeford, 2012). These increases have a significant impact on services, and the quality of care and education for children and young people. Accordingly, Elliott presents an analysis of large-scale quantitative data sets to offer a more nuanced understanding of this changing landscape, at the level of the nation, and more locally in relation to the differential patterns illustrated between Local Authorities within Wales.

The following chapter, 'Educational interventions for children and young people in care: A review of outcomes, implementation and acceptability' offers the reader an evaluation of educational interventions and their measurable impacts. Gwyther Rees, Rachel Brown, Phil Smith and Rhiannon Evans reviewed the best available evidence on interventions intended to improve educational outcomes for children and young people who have resided in care. The authors' systematic review identified 15 evaluations reporting on 12 interventions, including the Letterbox Club and Multidimensional Treatment Foster Care for Adolescents (MTFC-A). The chapter demonstrates that the current evidence base is mixed, with existing evaluations being the subject of numerous methodological limitations; and the authors argue that future research must focus on developing theoretically sound interventions that maximise the likelihood of demonstrating effects.

Rebecca Pratchett and Paul Rees then consider the experiences of a particular section of the 'looked after' population. 'Exploring the educational attainment and achievement of children who are "looked after" in formal kinship care', reports on their work with a group of children in formal kinship care aged eight to 18, from two local authorities in south Wales. The evidence base on educational outcomes for children and young people in kinship care remains limited (Leslie et al., 2005), and this chapter makes an important contribution to considering the literacy and numeracy skills of children in 'formal kinship care' settings. The authors suggest that kinship carers' access to birth parents and the continuity afforded by kinship care may have the potential to compensate for other disadvantages that are sometimes observed in care placements; and that this is an important area for further exploration.

This emphasis on the potential for good educational outcomes also features in the chapter, 'Promoting the education of children in care: Reflections of children and carers who have experienced "success"'. In this chapter, Paul Rees and Amy Munro move away from an emphasis on poor attainment and instead consider how 'success' can be defined and promoted. Reflecting on a study involving children and young people in care in one local authority in Wales, and their carers, Rees and Munro examine what 'success' and 'happiness' means for these participants. Children and young people discussed the positive effects of ongoing birth-family contact, open, warm and respectful relationships with carers and the carers' family, positive friendships with peers, basic needs being met, partaking in hobbies and interests, and having someone to talk to and share problems with. For Rees and Munro, 'success' for children and young people in care can only be achieved through an holistic understanding of their needs, and this can only be realised if those who live and work alongside them share a common language and understanding.

In 'Transitions from care to higher education: A case study of a young person's journey', Gemma Allnatt also focuses on 'success' in relation to care-experienced young people who gain a place in university. Allnatt draws on a wider study with twenty-one young people, which considered how support from social services and universities helps those in care to complete their university studies. The study explored participants' subjective views of their journey through the care system and to university. The case study presented in the chapter touches on themes that were common across the sample such as traumatic childhood events, overcoming significant hurdles to get to university and succeed, and continuing chaos and turmoil in personal circumstances. Allnatt provides a convincing argument that current systems of support for students are often disorganised and inadequate, so that the relative 'success' of those who prosper in higher education is often in spite of, and not because of, the help that is made available.

The culture of care and the everyday lives of children and young people

The chapters in this section all draw from empirical research findings. However, rather than a specific focus on education and policy intervention, there is an interest in the more mundane aspects of everyday life and the salience of relational encounters. The chapters all emphasise the profound significance of children's and young people's family and non-family relationships on their lived experiences, development and well-being. Examining how the ordinary becomes troubled and the extraordinary normalised (Gillies et al., 2013), the chapters move across the spaces of the 'home', the contact centre, the natural environment and life course transitions. The authors' present problematic accounts, while at the same time offering a range of nuanced insights that can be drawn upon to improve the lives, and futures, of care-experienced children and young people.

The first space explored is the foster home in Alyson Rees', 'The daily lived experiences of foster care: the centrality of food and touch in family life'. Focusing specifically on children's and young people's experiences, Rees documents the mundane, often overlooked, yet important spaces of interaction and everyday rituals within the home, including touch, food and other practices related to physical nurturing. The home is often seen as a type of sanctuary, which is particularly impervious to forms of research inquiry (Lincoln, 2012; Mannay, 2018), however, in engaging with care-experienced participants, Rees was able to perceive this familiar yet unknown space of 'home'. The risk of abuse allegations mean that the importance of closeness and touch, as a means of reassurance to children within social care relationships, is often devalued (Biehal, 2014). However, Rees clearly illustrates the ways in which these relational aspects are significant in fostering, helping to create, and maintain, a sense of value and belonging for children and young people in care.

In 'The natural environment and its benefits for children and young people looked after', Holly Gordon moves beyond the enclosed space of the home to consider the benefits of outdoor spaces. The chapter reflects on the 'Fostering Outside Play' project, which aimed to improve the mental and physical well-being of children and young people looked after by supporting foster carers and practitioners to provide them with opportunities for play in the natural environment. Drawing on accounts from foster carers, Gordon argues that the natural environment can engender benefits for care-experienced children and young people, and that the potential of this under-used resource deserves further discussion, research and development within social care services for children.

Joanne Pye and Paul Rees return to a more confined setting in their chapter, 'Factors that promote positive supervised birth family contact for children in care'. Supervised contact between children and their birth parents involves other groups, including carers, contact supervisors, and social workers. The chapter explores questionnaire and interview data generated with these key stakeholders, who were involved with the process at a single contact centre in south Wales. Pye and Rees contend that effective communication and relationships supported the promotion of positive supervised contact, but that these were often disrupted by the nature of the tightly controlled environment, a lack of understanding of the process, inappropriate and unrealistic arrangements, and inaccurate or inadequate knowledge around the prescribed roles, related responsibilities and expectations. The chapter underlines the importance of promoting positive contact rather than contact per se, and offers a series of recommendations to inform and improve current practice.

'Yet another change: The experience of movement for children and young people looked after', by Rebecca Girling, considers the impacts of stability and transience. Girling conducted interviews with young people aged between 15 and 17, in private residential homes in Wales, which reflected on their care journeys. Movement and change are part of the culture of care and play a significant role in shaping children's and young people's life experiences. However, Girling's findings illustrate the ways in which change can create a sense of psychological instability alongside the physical movement. For Girling, relationships are key in creating a sense of stability and belonging, or extenuating instability, and she recommends that more attention is given to the relational aspects of placements to improve the chance of success in other areas of vulnerable children's and young people's lives.

In Wales, five times as many young people in state care become pregnant compared to the general population of under-18-year-olds in Wales (Craine et al., 2014), and Louise Roberts considers early parenthood for young people in and leaving state care. '"A family of my own": When young people in and leaving state care become parents in Wales' draws from qualitative interviews with parents and leaving care professionals to explore these transitions. Young motherhood is often a source of pride and respect marking an important transition to adulthood (Gillies, 2007). However, the chapter illustrates how this becomes contaminated for care-experienced parents, who can be stigmatised as a result of their care status and assigned a presumed incompetency. Roberts argues that young people in and leaving care face significant barriers as they transition to parenthood, and that these require effective systems of support, rather than discourses of judgement, to prevent cycles of intergenerational care experience; and enable young people to have a family of their own.

Participatory, qualitative and collaborative approaches

As the chapters in the two preceding sections document, insights into policy and practice can be attained through in-depth qualitative interviews, detailed attention to patterns in data, and systematic reviews of existing studies. Additionally, research with children and young people in the care system, care leavers and those who foster and adopt can also provide useful insights into the associated challenges, successes and everyday realities of participants. The findings of these projects often offer new knowledge and perspectives; however, the research process, not simply its output, is an important area for consideration. Consequently, this section is interested in the 'doing' of research, in particular methodological approaches that work directly with participants and involve participatory, qualitative, reflexive and collaborative techniques.

The relationship between researcher and researched is key to the effective data production (Pole, 2007). Accordingly, in the opening chapter Claire Palmer builds on earlier work stressing the importance of 'locating the self' (Coffey, 1999, p.17), and reflects on relationality and positionality in the research process. 'Positionality and reflexivity: Conducting qualitative interviews with parents who adopt children from foster care', draws on a larger Welsh cohort study focusing on children who are placed for adoption. The chapter reflects on a qualitative aspect of the study that explored the motivations of parents who adopt older children and the processes by which they decided to adopt. Methodological considerations arising from interviewing adoptive parents are discussed, providing the reader with important insights including the impact of the researcher on the setting, the emotional impact of conducting a study, and how researchers can be affected by the process of exploring sensitive topics in the field of social care.

'Sandboxes, stickers and superheroes: Employing creative techniques to explore the aspirations and experiences of children and young people who are looked after', by Dawn Mannay and Eleanor Staples, also considers fieldwork relationships. The authors argue that traditional interview techniques in the social sciences can inadvertently mirror social work practice, and document their introduction of creative methods to enable a more participatory research encounter. Focusing on the technique of sandboxing and emotion sticker activities, Mannay and Staples reflect on how providing participants with the opportunity to lead research activities through the creation and discussion of visual artefacts created a more neutral space where children and young people could engage with research on their own terms. The chapter does not present these techniques as a panacea for shifting hierarchical power relations in the field. However, it does illustrate the ways in which this approach can enable children and young people in care to both communicate their subjective experiences, and offer concrete suggestions for improving their educational trajectories.

In the following chapter, 'A view from a Pupil Referral Unit: Using participatory methods with young people in an education setting', Phil Smith also offers some reflections on his work with participatory and creative research approaches. Resonating with the mainstreaming of a commitment to children and young people's participation in research, the study adopted a mosaic approach (Clarke and Moss, 2001), and worked directly with participants to design and select research approaches that were suited to their individual interests and preferences. The study embedded a number of creative activities within a traditional ethnographic fieldwork design, including drawing, story work, photography, and walking tours. Care-experienced young people are over represented in Pupil Referral Units and this multimodal approach allowed an insight into the everyday experiences of this alternative education setting. However, the chapter also notes the difficulties and limitations of creative and collaborative techniques, providing a useful background for other researchers interested in applying a participatory, mosaic approach.

'Enabling care-experienced young people's participation in research: CASCADE Voices', considers collaboration beyond the fieldwork process, exploring how young people can be actively involved in generating ideas for research applications, informing the conduct and design of research studies, reviewing research tools, acting as peer researchers, and contributing to analysis and dissemination. Eleanor Staples, Louise Roberts, Jennifer Lyttleton-Smith, Sophie Hallett and CASCADE Voices discuss a range of case examples to illustrate what can be achieved in a collaborative partnership between social researchers and care-experienced young people. The chapter demonstrates how the positioning of young people as 'experts by experience' (Preston-Shoot, 2007) can engender effective, respectful and productive working relationships and produce more informed research outcomes.

The closing chapter of the section, 'Lights, camera, action: Translating research findings into policy and practice impacts with music, film and artwork', offers innovative approaches to disseminating research findings. Dawn Mannay, Louisa Roberts, Eleanor Staples and the youth and community organisation Ministry of Life consider ways of moving beyond the standard academic outputs of the report or journal article, and employing art, music and film to engage with wider and more diverse audiences. The authors discuss issues of ethical representation, accessibility, and the practicalities of building relationships across the disciplinary boundaries of social sciences and the creative industries. The chapter argues that although traditional research outputs are useful and valuable, to extend the audiencing of findings and recommendations, and contribute to changes in practice for care-experienced children and young people, more creative and multimodal formats are necessary.

Conclusion

The following chapters are all structured around the central theme of the care system in Wales, its relationship with educational outcomes, the everyday lived experiences of care-experienced children, young people and care leavers, and approaches to research. Despite a proliferation of legislative action in response to differential outcomes, the relative educational, employment and life-course disadvantages of individuals who have experienced the care system remains a pressing issue of widespread national and international concern. The rest of this book reflexively explores the changes and continuities within the political landscape and the geographical areas that constitute Wales. Nonetheless, despite this focus on the local and the national, the chapters each introduce insights, reflections and recommendations about the care system and its impacts, which will be useful for readers across geographical contexts, who have an interest in improving the lives of children, young people, and wider family networks.

The concluding chapter will revisit the aims set out in this introduction and consider the key points from the three sections, linking these to the overarching themes spanning this edited book. It will summarise what the collection tells us about the culture of care in Wales. As well as looking back, the chapter will also look forward, suggesting future academic research and emerging policy agendas from the volume, and considering the future of *Children and Young People 'Looked After'? Education, Intervention and the Everyday Culture of Care in Wales.*

References

Aldgate, J. and McIntosh, M., *Looking After the Family: A Study of Children Looked After in Kinship Care in Scotland* (Edinburgh: Social Work Inspection Agency, 2006).

Benbenishty, R. and Zeira, A. 'On the Verge of Leaving the Care System: Assessment of Life Skills and Needs of Adolescents in Care', *Diskurs Kindheits- und Jugendforschung Heft*, 3 (2012), 291–308.

Berridge, D., 'Educating Young People in Care: What have we learned?', *Children and Youth Services Review*, 34/6 (2012), 1171–5.

Biehal, N., 'A Sense of Belonging: Meanings of Family and Home in Long-term Foster Care', *British Journal of Social Work*, 44/4 (2014), 955–71.

Brady, E. and Gilligan, R., 'The Life Course Perspective: An Integrative Research Paradigm for Examining the Educational Experiences of Adult Care Leavers?', *Children and Youth Services Review* (2018) DOI10.1016/j.childyouth. 2018.02.019.

Brown, P., Hesketh, A. and Williams, S., 'Employability in a Knowledge-Driven Economy', *Journal of Education and Work*, 16/2 (2013), 107–26.

Children's Commissioner for Wales, *The Right Care: Children's Rights in Residential Care in Wales* (Swansea: Children's Commissioner for Wales, 2016).

Clarke, A. and Moss, P., *Listening to Young Children: The Mosaic Approach* (London: National Children's Bureau Enterprises Ltd, 2001).

Coffey, A., *The Ethnographic Self: Fieldwork and the Representation of Identity* (London: Sage, 1999).

Craine, N., Midgley, C., Zou, L., Evans, H., Whitaker, R. and Lyons, M., 'Elevated Teenage Conception Risk amongst Looked After Children: A National Audit', *Public Health*, 128/7 (2014), 668–70.

Diaz, C., *A Study into Children and Young People's Participation in Their Children in Care Reviews and the Role of the Independent Reviewing Officer* (PhD thesis, Cardiff University, 2018).

Drakeford, M., *Number of Children in Care Increasing at a Greater Rate in Wales than England* (Cardiff: Institute of Welsh Affairs, 2012). Available at *http://www.clickonwales.org/2012/11/far-more-welsh-than-english-children-in-care/* (accessed 26/02/18).

Fargas Malet, M., McSherry, D., Pinkerton, J. and Kelly, G., *At Home in Care: Children living with birth parents on a Care Order* (Queens University Belfast: Belfast, 2014).

Gillies, V., *Marginalised Mothers: Exploring Working Class Parenting* (Abingdon Oxen: Routledge, 2007).

——, Hooper, C. A. and Ribbens McCarthy, J. (eds.), *Family Troubles? Exploring Changes and Challenges in the Family Lives of Children and Young People* (Bristol: Policy Press, 2013).

Hill, M., *Scottish Research on Looked After Children since 2000* (Glasgow: Centre of Excellence for Looked After Children in Scotland, 2011). Available at *https://www.celcis.org/knowledge-bank/search-bank/scottish-research-looked-after-children-2000/* (accessed 26/02/18).

Jackson, S., 'Educating Children in Residential and Foster Care', *Oxford Review of Education*, 20/3 (1994), 267–79.

—— and Cameron, C., *Final Report of the YiPPEE Project WP12: Young People from a Public Care Background: Pathways to Further and Higher Education in Five European Countries* (London: Thomas Coram Research Unit, 2010).

—— and Cameron, C., *Improving Access to Further and Higher Education for Young People in Public Care. European Policy and Practice* (London: Jessica Kingsley Publishers, 2014).

Kenny, K., 'The Educational Experiences of Children in Care: A Qualitative Study of Stories Recalled across Five Decades of Local Authority Care Experiences' (PhD thesis, University of Exeter, 2018).

Leslie, L. K., Gordon, J. N., Meneken, L., Premji, K., Michelmore, K. L. and Ganger, W., 'The Physical, Developmental, and Mental Health Needs of Young Children in Child Welfare by Initial Placement Type', *Journal of Developmental and Behavioral Pediatrics*, 26/3 (2005), 177–85.

Lincoln, S., *Youth Culture and Private Space* (Basingstoke: Palgrave Macmillan, 2012).

Mannay, D., 'Ethnography in inaccessible fields: drawing on visual approaches to understand the private space of the home', in S. Kleinknecht, L. van den Scott and C. B. Sanders (eds), *The Craft of Qualitative Research* (Toronto, Canada: Canadian Scholars' Press, 2018).

———, Staples, E., Hallett, S., Roberts, L., Rees, A., Evans, R. and Andrews, D., *Understanding the Educational Experiences and Opinions, Attainment, Achievement and Aspirations of Looked After Children in Wales* (Cardiff: Welsh Government, 2015).

———, Evans, R., Staples, E., Hallett, S., Roberts, L., Rees, A., and Andrews, D., 'The Consequences of Being Labelled "Looked-After": Exploring the Educational Experiences of Looked-after Children and Young People in Wales', *British Journal of Educational Research*, 43/4 (2017), 683–99.

Matheson, I., 'Slipping Down Ladders and Climbing Up Snakes: The Experiences of New Zealand University Students who were Formerly in Foster Care' (PhD thesis, University of Otago, Dunedin, 2015).

Morriss, L., 'Haunted Futures: The Stigma of Being a Mother Living Apart from her Child(ren) as a Result of State-ordered Court Removal', *The Sociological Review*, 66/4 (2018), 816–31.

Nho, R. C., Park, E. H. and McCarthy, M. L., 'Case Studies of Successful Transition from Out-Of-Home Placement to Young Adulthood in Korea', *Children and Youth Services Review*, 79 (2017), 315–24.

O'Higgins, A., Sebba, J. and Luke, N., *What is the Relationship between Being in Care and the Educational Outcomes of Children? An International Systematic Review* (University of Oxford: Rees Centre, Research in Fostering and Education, 2015).

Pithouse A. and Rees, A., *Creating Stable Placements: Learning from the Foster Children and the Families Who Care for Them* (London: Jessica Kingsley, 2014).

Pole, C., 'Researching Children and Fashion: An Embodied Ethnography', *Childhood*, 14/1 (2007), 67–84.

Preston-Shoot, M., 'Whose Lives and Whose Learning? Whose Narratives and Whose Writing? Taking the Next Research and Literature Steps with Experts by Experience', *Evidence & Policy: A Journal of Research, Debate and Practice*, 3/3 (2007), 343–59.

Roberts, L., 'A Small Scale Qualitative Scoping Study into the Experiences of Looked After Children and Care Leavers Who are Parents in Wales', *Child & Family Social Work*, 22/3 (2017), 1274–82.

————, Maxwell, N., Rees, P., Holland, S. and Forbes, N., 'Improving Well-being and Outcomes for Looked After Children in Wales: A Context Sensitive Review of Interventions', *Adoption & Fostering*, 40/4 (2016), 309–24.

————, Meakings, S., Smith, A., Forrester, D. and Shelton, K., 'Care Leavers and their Children Placed for Adoption, *Children and Youth Services Review*, 79 (2017) 355–61.

Sebba, J., Berridge, D., Luke, N., Fletcher, J., Bell, K. and Strand, S., *The Educational Progress of Looked After Children in England: Linking Care and Educational Data* (Oxford Rees Centre for Research in Fostering and Education and University of Bristol, 2015).

Stein, M., 'Young People Aging out of Care', *Children and Youth Services Review*, 28 (2006), 422–34.

Welsh Government, *Raising the Ambitions and Educational Attainment of Children Who are Looked After in Wales* (Cardiff: Welsh Government, 2016).

Woodhouse, C., 'Exploring the Physical Education and School Sport Experiences of Looked-After Children and Young People' (PhD thesis, Loughborough University, Loughborough, 2018).

I

EDUCATION
AND POLICY
INTERVENTION

2 | Charting the rise of children and young people looked after in Wales

Martin Elliott

Introduction

T HERE HAS BEEN an unprecedented increase in recent years in the numbers of applications through the law courts in England and Wales to
place children in out-of-home care and in the numbers of children becoming 'looked after' overall (McGhee et al., 2017). This increase has often
been attributed to the publication of a review in 2008 into the death of
a young child, Peter Connelly (Department for Education, 2008) and the
ensuing media attention, the so-called 'Baby P effect' (CAFCASS, 2009).
From a Welsh perspective, as will be discussed later in this chapter, there
is evidence to suggest that children in Wales are now one-and-a-half times
more likely to become 'looked after' than their peers in England (Drakeford, 2012). Welsh local authorities also have some of the highest rates of
children 'looked after' (per 10,000 children) across England and Wales.
Whilst having overall rates generally much higher than those of English
local authorities, there is also significant variation between local authorities in Wales. Reducing the numbers of children in care has become an
identified goal of the Welsh Government (Drakeford, 2015), therefore the
investigation of both the differences in rates between England and Wales,
and the variation in rates between Welsh authorities is likely to make a
valuable policy contribution.

This chapter is drawn from quantitative research undertaken to explore: the numbers and characteristics of the children and young people 'looked after' in Wales; the higher overall rates in Wales relative to those in England; and the variations in rates of children and young people coming into care between local authorities within Wales. The analyses were undertaken on both publicly available aggregate data and child-level data (data relating to individual children rather than total numbers at a local authority or country level) relating to children 'looked after' as part of an Economic and Social Research Council funded three-year doctoral research study. The chapter will present the analysis of the data collected each year through the children 'looked after' data return (also known as SSDA903), conducted in both Wales and England and reported by every local authority. This annual return provides information on all the children in care in Wales on the census date of 31 March (for example, demographic characteristics including age, sex and ethnicity) and their placements (for example, placement type, legal status and category of need) (Stats Wales, 2014; Welsh Government, 2014a).

This chapter will, firstly, highlight comparisons between Wales' and England's children 'looked after' populations over time, and, secondly, compare the twenty-two local authorities within Wales. The period covered by the data (2003–14) is one for which Wales and England operated within broadly the same legislative framework, albeit one within which organisational structures and policy directions were diverging. The period immediately after the data analysis illustrates further divergence, as Wales enacted its first primary social care legislation, the Social Services and Well-being (Wales) Act 2014.

Quantitative analysis in social work research

There has been a case made for many years that the use of quantitative methods is weak within the social sciences, linked in no small part to a lack of quantitative skills amongst social scientists. For example, in the position statement 'Society Counts' (British Academy, 2012, p. 1), serious concerns were raised that 'the UK is weak in quantitative skills, in particular but not exclusively in the social sciences and humanities'. This lack of quantitative research evidence is reflected just as strongly in the field of social work research in the UK. In the 2001 Research Assessment Exercise (RAE), it was highlighted that 'quantitative work, while sometimes of very high quality is rare and not always good when found' (Higher Education Funding Council for England, 2001, p. 4). By the 2008 RAE report, whilst some improvements were noted in regard to quality, the limited amount of quantitative research in social work was still highlighted (RAE, 2009).

The historic issues identified regarding quantitative analysis skills amongst social work researchers are arguably reflected in the minimal use of readily available data. This was highlighted by Maxwell et al. (2012), who identified a range of large-scale, non-social work specific, longitudinal studies that are readily available within the UK which include information regarding children, young people and their families and their use of social work and social care services, but which were rarely harnessed by researchers (Elliott, 2015). One of the areas where quantitative methods can be used is in respect of the analysis of local authority administrative data.

Whilst there is the noted overall relative paucity of quantitative social work research and related use of quantitative data sources, for research using administrative data such as the SSDA903 there has historically been a very different picture in terms of their use in England and Wales. A number of large-scale research projects, often prompted by government departments or working groups, have been undertaken in England regarding children 'looked after' using such administrative data. For example, Statham et al.'s (2002) study, commissioned by the Department of Health for the Children's Budget Pressures working group, utilised administrative data to look at the numbers of children in care. Whilst some research has been undertaken in Wales, such as the 'In Figures: Looked after Children Research Paper' (2009), conducted by the Members Research Service within the National Assembly for Wales, and 'Research on differences in the looked after children population' (Cordis Bright, 2013), studies which include Wales within their scope or which have a specific focus on Wales have historically been relatively limited. It is unclear whether this was due to a lack of social work academics within Wales with the requisite quantitative skills and interest in using these data for research or limited academic and policy interest in researching service use and outcomes in Wales using quantitative research methods.

Children 'looked after' in England and Wales: A comparison over time

The publicly available data allow a picture to be gained of changes over time. For example, the overall country level rates of children 'looked after' within England and Wales can be compared over a number of years. Calculation of rates per 10,000 of the child population based on the number of children 'looked after' on the census day each year (31 March) allows such a comparison to be made. As illustrated in Figure 2.1, these analyses highlight that between 2003 and 2014, the rates of children 'looked after' in Wales were consistently higher than those in England. Such comparison also shows that the gap in rates has increased markedly during that time. In 2003, the overall rate in Wales was nine children per 10,000 higher than that in England. By 2014 the gap in rates had increased to 31 children per 10,000.

Figure 2.1 shows that the trajectory of rates in these countries prior to 2009 were different. Whilst overall rates in Wales were increasing year on year, in England they had started to decrease. This type of analysis also enables an insight into the impact of particular events on rates of children looked after. For example, Figure 2.1 shows increases in overall rates in both England and Wales from 2009, which demonstrate the aftermath of the publication of the serious case review into the death of Peter Connelly and the subsequent media attention his case attracted, the so-called 'Baby P effect' (CAFCASS, 2009). Whilst the effect of Peter Connelly's death is observable within the rates of children in care in both countries, the rate of acceleration was greater in Wales, which prompts questions about the reasons for this difference.

Similarly, in recent years there has been much made of the statistic, derived from analysis of routinely collected data, that children in Wales are now one-and-a-half times more likely to become 'looked after' than their peers in England. This raises questions about causal attributes, and the extent to which this difference may be related to, for example, socio-economic conditions or the levels and types of services. The ability to look at quantitative data that illustrates differences between countries and changes over time can therefore be the catalyst for discussions about the nature of current social work policy and practice and the potential need for change.

If the rates of children and young people who are 'looked after' per 10,000 of the child population are calculated for all the local authorities in England and Wales it is possible to consider where local authorities in Wales are in terms of intervening in children's lives by placing them in care, relative to others. Table 2.1 illustrates the 10 local authorities in

Figure 2.1: *The rates of children 'looked after' per 10,000 child population in England and Wales*

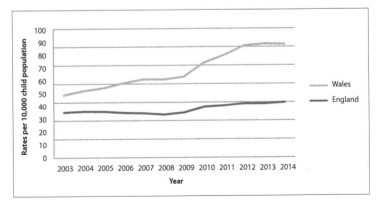

Table 2.1: *The ten highest rates per 10,000 by local authority in England and Wales 2010-14*

2010	2011	2012	2013	2014
City of London	Neath Port Talbot	Neath Port Talbot	Neath Port Talbot	Neath Port Talbot
Manchester	Torfaen	Torfaen	Blackpool	Blackpool
Neath Port Talbot	Blackpool	Merthyr Tydfil	Torfaen	Torfaen
Merthyr Tydfil	City of London	Blackpool	Merthyr Tydfil	Bridgend
Blackpool	Manchester	Manchester	Bridgend	Merthyr Tydfil
Swansea	Merthyr Tydfil	Swansea	Swansea	Wolverhampton
Torfaen	Swansea	Bridgend	Rhondda Cynon Taf	Rhondda Cynon Taf
Croydon	Salford	Rhondda Cynon Taf	Torbay	Torbay
Haringey	Kingston Upon Hull	Kingston Upon Hull	St Helens	Manchester
Kingston Upon Hull	Bridgend	Middlesbrough	Kingston Upon Hull	St Helens

England and Wales with the highest rates of children in care on 31 March across a five-year period; and a high proportion of those in the 'top 10' come from Wales. Between 2010 and 2014, of the 10 local authorities in England and Wales with the highest rates, between four and six of those authorities were Welsh. To put this into perspective, there are 152 higher level local authorities in England and only 22 unitary authorities in Wales. That means that in 2012 over a quarter (six local authorities – 27.2 per cent) of all Welsh local authorities had the highest rates overall.

A further area of comparison between Wales and England is provided at the other end of the spectrum of rates of children in care. Comparison of the lowest rates in each country also provides an interesting insight. In the period between 2010 and 2014 the authority with the lowest rate per 10,000 of the child population in Wales had a rate each year which was over twice that of the equivalent lowest rate authority in England. In fact, in 2013 the difference in these lowest rates was approaching a threefold difference (2.8 times).

During the period 2010 to 2014 there were 174 local authorities across England and Wales (22 in Wales). One English authority, the Isles of Scilly, had no children 'looked after' during this period. With this authority excluded, the remaining 173 authorities can be divided into

Table 2.2: *The number of Welsh local authorities in each quartile by rates per 10,000 (England and Wales)*

Quartile	2010	2011	2012	2013	2014
1st Quartile	10 (45%)	9 (41%)	11 (50%)	10 (45%)	9 (41%)
2nd Quartile	5 (23%)	9 (41%)	7 (32%)	6 (27.5%)	8 (36%)
3rd Quartile	6 (27%)	3 (14%)	4 (18%)	6 (27.5%)	5 (23%)
4th Quartile	1 (5%)	1 (5%)	0	0	0

quartiles to allow investigation of the distribution of Welsh local authorities within these quartiles. Table 2.2 illustrates that rates for Welsh
authorities are not equally distributed across quartiles. With the exception of 2013, over three-quarters of Welsh local authorities have rates per
10,000 which place them within the 50 per cent of local authorities with
the highest rates per 10,000 across England and Wales. Even when 2013
is considered, with 72.5 per cent of authorities placed within the first two
quartiles, the distribution of authorities is still unequal. Conversely, in
relation to the 4th quartile, the 25 per cent of local authorities with the
lowest rates per 10,000, only one Welsh authority is present within this
quartile in 2010 and 2011, and thereafter there are no Welsh authorities
within this quartile, with all authorities being within the 3rd quartile or
above. This illustrates a picture where rates in Wales are skewed towards
the higher levels of intervention when considered in the context of rates
across England and Wales.

Changes in the child population and rates of children in care

There is clearly a difference between both the actual numbers of children
in care and the overall child population of England and Wales. It is therefore much more useful and meaningful to express these figures in other
ways. Converting numbers of children and young people 'looked after'
into rates per 10,000 of the child population enables adjustment for these
differences. In order to do this it is necessary, first, to establish the child
populations for each country for the period being considered to calculate
population adjusted rates. What consideration of the mid-year population
estimates used for such calculations for the period covered by the administrative data highlights are child population changes that have an effect
on the comparative figures.

For example, during the period from 2003 to 2014, Wales had a
decreasing child population (under 18 years). During this period there
was a reduction of 23,900, a decrease in the child population of more

than 3.75 per cent. In England, during the same period, the child population increased by 380,951, an increase of 3.4 per cent. This would suggest that, in the case of Wales, there have been an increasing number of children becoming 'looked after' from a child population, which is reducing in size, whilst in England although numbers of children in care increased, this was against a background of an overall child population that was also increasing.

In order to identify the impact on rates per 10,000 of the changes in child population in both England and Wales an unadjusted rate was calculated. This allows some quantification of the effects of demographic changes on the rates in each country and on the gap in rates between them. This was done using the child populations for England and Wales in 2003 to calculate rates per 10,000 for the years 2003 to 2014. This is therefore based on the assumption of no variation in overall child population during the period being considered. In 2014 the difference in rates of children 'looked after' between England and Wales was 32 children per 10,000. Had the overall children's population remained at 2003 levels and not decreased in Wales and increased in England, as highlighted earlier, the gap in rates would reduce to 26 children per 10,000. This is based on the fact that three children per 10,000 of the rate in Wales is accounted for by more children coming into care from a reducing child population. In contrast, in England a further difference of three children per 10,000 is accounted for by more children entering care from a child population that was increasing at the same time. This suggests that in making comparisons of rates over time, some attention needs to be paid to what has happened not only to the numbers of children in care but also to changes in the overall child population from which these rates are calculated, which may contribute in part to the reported differences.

Local authority level comparison

Whilst analysis of country level data shows an increase in likelihood of children in Wales entering care than their peers in England, analysis of the administrative data relating to the twenty-two local authorities within Wales, allows consideration of whether that is the case for all children living in Wales; whether there is variation between authorities; and the extent of that variation. When rates of children 'looked after' on the census day in each local authority are calculated for each of the 12 years between 2003 and 2014, the most striking first impression from this data is the level of variability between local authorities in Wales. Children in Monmouthshire, for example, are on average less likely to enter the 'looked after' system than children in England based on a comparison of the authority's rates for 2003–14 and the overall English rates for that period. Conversely, based on their rate per 10,000, in 2013, for example, children in Neath Port Talbot were almost three times more likely to enter public care than children on average would in England during the same year.

Whilst there is a group of local authorities (Monmouthshire, Wrexham, Flintshire, Pembrokeshire, Ceredigion, Carmarthenshire) whose rates routinely fall below the all Wales average figure, equally there are authorities whose rates are consistently higher (Neath Port Talbot, Torfaen, Merthyr Tydfil, Bridgend, Rhondda Cynon Taf, Blaenau Gwent). Within this complex picture there are also authorities such as Caerphilly who appear to break with the prevailing trend in rates in England and Wales. Having had a rate (70 per 10,000) which was above the Wales national average in 2003 (64 per 10,000), the same authority by 2014 had a rate (71 per 10,000) below the average for Welsh local authorities (91 per 10,000).

Children 'looked after' and the wider population of vulnerable children

The children 'looked after' population is a subset of a much larger population of children and their families in Wales who are known to local authority social services departments. It is therefore important to consider the numbers of children who are 'looked after' within this wider context of vulnerable children within a local authority area. Each year on 31 March, alongside the SSDA903 data, each Welsh local authority also collects and submits data for the Children in Need Census [1] (Welsh Government, 2014; Welsh Government, 2014c). The data collected 'covers all children receiving support which is financed from children's social services budgets, including those supported in their families or independently

Figure 2.2: *Scatterplot of mean children 'looked after' rates (2010-14) against mean children in need rates (2010-14)*

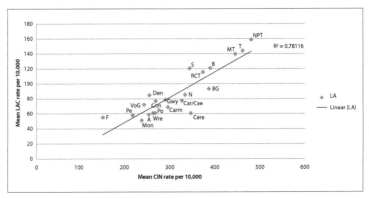

and children on the child protection register' (Welsh Government, 2014c, p. 5). It is therefore important to explore what relationship exists between the numbers of children 'looked after' and the wider population of children in need in each Welsh local authority.

Figure 2.2 is a scatterplot, produced using the average rate per 10,000 for both children 'looked after' and children 'in need' for each Welsh local authority. The mean averages were calculated using the rates per 10,000 for both groups of children for a five-year period (2010–2014). The graph shows that broadly there is a relationship between rates for 'looked after' children and children 'in need'. Specifically, those authorities with higher rates of children in need are usually those with higher rates of 'looked after' children and vice versa. The graph does, however, also identify some authorities where this is not the case.

For example, Ceredigion (Cere) and Swansea (S) have very similar mean rates of children in need over the period, 344 and 341 per 10,000 respectively. However, there is a significant difference in their mean rates of children 'looked after'. Swansea, with a mean rate of children 'looked after' of 121 per 10,000 population, has a rate which is almost double that of Ceredigion, with a rate of 61 per 10,000. Similarly, there are noticeable differences between Ceredigion and authorities such as Flintshire (F) and Pembrokeshire (Pe) and their rates of children in need. Whilst these authorities have a mean average of 'looked after' rates, which are within six children per 10,000 of each other, there are significantly larger gaps between their children 'in need' rates. With a rate of only 148 per 10,000, Flintshire has a children 'in need' rate which is less than half of Ceredigion's at 344 per 10,000. Similarly, Pembrokeshire has a mean average rate per 10,000 of 214, which is 130 children per 10,000 lower than that of Ceredigion. These differences between certain local authorities have provided a useful focus within the child-level analysis.

The relationship between deprivation and rates

One of the key aims of the research reported here is to consider the relationship between rates of children 'looked after' in Wales and deprivation. The intention in undertaking the initial analysis of aggregate level data, some of which is outlined here, was not only to provide a context for the child-level analysis that makes up the majority of the study, but also to inform decisions about how that child-level analysis is undertaken. To explore the relationship between deprivation and rates of children 'looked after' at the local authority level in Wales, an analysis was undertaken using two variables: the mean 'looked after' children rates per 10,000 (2008–14); and a measure of 'neighbourhood' level deprivation. In order to make comparisons between 'neighbourhoods', units of comparison called Lower Super Output Areas or LSOA were used. LSOA

Figure 2.3: *Mean rates per 10,000 children 'looked after' (2008-2014) relative to the proportion of LSOA in 10 per cent most deprived (WIMD, 2014)*

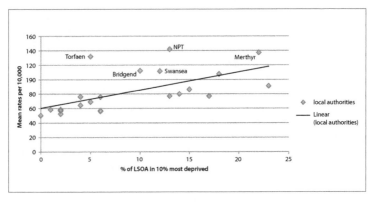

are constructed from geographies containing a population of between 1,000 and 3,000 people living in between 400 and 1,200 households and are used for the reporting of small area statistics in England and Wales in the Population Census; for ease we will refer to these in terms of 'neighbourhoods'.

To identify any relationship between deprivation and rates of children 'looked after' an analysis was undertaken using the percentage of 'neighbourhoods' within a local authority which are in the 10 per cent most deprived in Wales based on the overall Welsh Index of Multiple Deprivation (2014). The percentage of 'neighbourhoods' at a given level of deprivation within a local authority is the recognised method of undertaking such comparison at a local authority level in Wales (Welsh Government, 2014b). Therefore, the 10 per cent most deprived were selected.

Figure 2.3 shows the mean rates per 10,000 children 'looked after' for each Welsh local authority plotted against the percentage of 'neighbourhoods' in the 10 per cent most deprived based on the Welsh Index of Multiple Deprivation (2014). The scatterplot has been produced with a trend line, which illustrates the mean average rate for a given proportion of deprived 'neighbourhoods' based on the 'observed' mean rates in Wales.

The scatterplot appears to show a relationship between levels of neighbourhood level deprivation within a local authority and its 'looked after' children rates. As the proportion of neighbourhoods within the 10 per cent most deprived in Wales within local authorities increases it appears that broadly the rates of children in public care in those authorities also increases. The scatterplot does, however, highlight some authorities: for example, Torfaen and Neath Port Talbot, which have 'observed' rates per 10,000 that appear to be substantially higher than the rates that would be 'expected' based on the proportion of 'neighbourhoods' in those authorities in the 10 per cent most deprived in Wales.

To test whether the relationship between rates and levels of deprivation is statistically significant and the extent to which the proportion of deprived neighbourhoods within local authorities explains variations in rates between those authorities, a linear regression (Field, 2013) was undertaken. The regression analysis shows that there is a statistically significant relationship between rates of children 'looked after' and the proportion of neighbourhoods in each local authority that are in the 10 per cent most deprived in Wales. The linear regression indicates that variations in the percentage of neighbourhoods in the 10 per cent most deprived in Wales within a local authority explains 34.2 per cent of the variation in mean rates of children 'looked after'. This would appear to suggest that levels of neighbourhood level deprivation within a local authority play an important role in explaining variations between local authority rates of children 'looked after'. However, the flipside of this is that it also suggests that, whilst 34 per cent of the variation can be explained by the proportion of neighbourhoods in the 10 per cent most deprived in Wales, 66 per cent of the variation is explained by other, as yet unidentified, variables. Within the context of trying to develop understandings of the factors impacting on variations in rates between local authorities, this would suggest that deprivation is potentially a significant factor, but in conjunction with a range of other factors.

Final thoughts

The preliminary findings presented within this chapter suggest that in comparison to English local authorities there is potentially something different happening in the pattern of children becoming 'looked after' in Wales and that pattern has been different for many years. At a country level, both England and Wales appear to have had their overall rates affected by the so-called 'Baby P effect' (CAFCASS, 2009) and that is observable within the data; but, as noted earlier, rates have been higher in Wales for many years, were already rising before 2009, and the increase has been more pronounced since. Both here in Wales and in England there have been calls in recent years to reduce the numbers of children in care (Drakeford, 2015; Tickle, 2016). Given the paucity of research undertaken in Wales on the numbers of children 'looked after' and changes over time, the data outlined here provide much needed comparisons, which can inform these debates.

Equally, within Wales there are often substantial differences in rates between local authorities, even when differences in their child populations are taken into account. The data presented show a relationship between levels of relative deprivation within local authorities and the rates of children becoming 'looked after'. From a policy perspective, this engenders an argument for more joined-up thinking around poverty reduction and child welfare services, a point further made in the context of Wales by the report by Elliott and Scourfield (2017). However, deprivation is only one of a number of factors that influence rates of children in care. Factors that cannot be identified through these data, such as organisational culture and leadership, services and community resources and levels of risk aversion in social work practice (Hood et al., 2016), may all play a role in the variation between local authorities and the observed changes over time. Further understanding of the influence of these factors requires fine-grained qualitative research within organisations, and in and across local authorities.

Note

1. Children in Need has been replaced in Wales by Children in Need of Care and Support under the Social Services and Well-being (Wales) Act 2014.

References

British Academy, *Society Counts: A Position Statement* (2012). Available at http://www.britac.ac.uk/policy/Society_Counts.cfm (accessed 11/07/17).

Children and Family Court Advisory and Support Service (CAFCASS), *The Baby Peter Effect and the Increase in S31 Care Order Applications* (Cardiff: CAFCASS, 2009). Available at http://www.cafcass.gov.uk/media/2567/Baby%20Peter%20exec%20summary%20final.pdf (accessed 11/07/17).

Cordis Bright, *Research on Differences in the Looked After Children Population* (London: Cordis Bright, 2013).

Department for Education, *Haringey Local Safeguarding Children Board: Serious Case Review Child 'A'* (London: Department for Education, 2008). Available at https://www.gov.uk/government/uploads/system/uploads/attachment_data/file/182527/first_serious_case_review_overview_report_relating_to_peter_connelly_dated_november_2008.pdf (accessed 11/07/17).

Drakeford, M., *Speaking notes – Looked After Children's Summit 12/3/15* (2015).

———, *Number of Children in Care Increasing at a Greater Rate in Wales than England* (Cardiff: Institute of Welsh Affairs, 2012). Available at http://www.clickonwales.org/2012/11/far-more-welsh-than-english-children-in-care/ (accessed 11/07/17).

Elliott, M., 'Quantitative research and the secondary analysis of longitudinal data in social work research', in Hardwick, L., Smith, R. and Worsley, A. (eds),

Innovations in Social Work Research: Using Methods Creatively (London: Jessica Kingsley Publishers, 2015), pp. 259–71.

Elliott, M. and Scourfield, J., *Identifying and Understanding Inequalities in Child Welfare Intervention Rates: Comparative Studies in Four UK Countries. Single Country Quantitative Study Report: Wales. Child Welfare Inequalities Project* (2017). Available at *http://www.coventry.ac.uk/research/research-directories/current-projects/2014/child-welfare-inequality-uk/cwip-project-outputs/* (accessed 13/02/18).

Field, A., *Discovering Statistics Using IBM SPSS Statistics* (4th edn) (London: Sage, 2013).

Higher Education Funding Council for England (HEFCE), Overview Report on Social Work, Research Assessment Exercise 2001 (HEFCE, 2001). Available at http://www.rae.ac.uk/2001/results/byuoa/51.htm (accessed 13/03/18).

Hood, R., Goldacre, A., Grant, R. and Jones, R., 'Exploring Demand and Provision in English Child Protection Services', *British Journal of Social Work. Advanced Access*, 46/4 (2016), 923–41.

Maxwell, N., Scourfield, J., Gould, N. and Huxley, P., 'UK Panel Data on Social Work Service Users', British Journal of Social Work, 42 (2012), 165–84.

McGhee, J., Bunting, L., McCartan, C., Elliott, M., Bywaters, P. and Featherstone, B., 'Looking After Children in the UK – Convergence or Divergence?', *British Journal of Social Work* (2017) *https://doi.org/10.1093/bjsw/bcx103.*

National Assembly for Wales, *In Figures: Looked After Children* (Cardiff: Members Research Service, 2009).

Research Assessment Exercise, *UOA 40 Subject Overview Report* (2009). Available at *http://www.rae.ac.uk/pubs/2009/ov* (accessed 13/03/18).

Statham, J., Candappa, M., Simon, A. and Owen, C., *Trends in Care: Exploring Reasons for the Increase in Children Looked After by Local Authorities* (London: Institute of Education, 2002).

StatsWales, *Children Looked After in Wales: Numbers and Characteristics of Children Looked After by Local Authorities 2003–2014* (2014). Available at *https://statswales.wales.gov.uk/Catalogue/Health-and-Social-Care/Social-Services/Childrens-Services/Children-Looked-After* (accessed 13/03/18).

Tickle, L., *Dave Hill: 'You've got to look after fewer children'* (The Guardian, 11 May 2016). Available at *http://www.theguardian.com/society/2016/may/11/dave-hill-childrens-services-look-after-fewer-children-families?CMP=share_btn_tw* (accessed 13/02/18).

Welsh Government, *Guidance Notes for the Completion of the Children in Need Census 2014* (Cardiff: Welsh Government, 2014). Available at *http://gov.wales/statistics-and-research/wales-children-need-census-data-collection/?lang=en* (accessed 13/03/18).

———, *Guidance Notes for the Completion of SSDA903 Records 1 April 2013 to 31 March 2014* (Cardiff: Welsh Government, 2014a).

————, *Welsh Index of Multiple Deprivation 2014: Guidance on Use* (Cardiff: Welsh Government, 2014b). Available at *http://gov.wales/docs/statistics/2014/141112-wimd-2014-guidance-en.pdf* (accessed 13/03/18).

————, *Wales Children in Need Census 2010–2014* (Welsh Government, 2014c). Available at *http://gov.wales/statistics-and-research/wales-children-need-census/?tab=previous&lang=en* (accessed 13/03/18).

3 | Educational interventions for children and young people in care

A review of outcomes, implementation and acceptability

Gwyther Rees, Rachel Brown, Phil Smith and Rhiannon Evans

Introduction

CHILDREN AND YOUNG PEOPLE in care have poorer educational outcomes compared to the general population in the United Kingdom (UK) (Sebba et al., 2015; Rees and Stein, 2016) and in other countries (Vinnerljung and Hjern, 2011; Berger et al., 2015). National attainment data reports that 23 per cent of care-experienced young people in Wales obtain five GCSEs (Grade A*–C), compared to 60 per cent of the respective total student population (Welsh Government, 2016). Educational disadvantage continues into higher education, with lower rates of university access and completion. Of young people in care, it has been reported that only two per cent in Wales are estimated to enter higher education compared to approximately 50 per cent of the general population (Welsh Audit Office, 2012). It should be noted that there are some issues related to reporting of care leavers' engagement with higher education (see Allnatt, 2019 [Chapter 6 this volume]); however, overall there are pervasive gaps across all stages of education.

It is important to address these issues and this chapter reviews the best available evidence on educational interventions intended to improve educational outcomes for children and young people who have resided in care. It describes existing interventions and provides a summary of evaluation outcomes. The chapter then discusses the relevance of reported interventions and associated evaluation outcomes to the context of children and young people in care in Wales.

Methods

The interventions presented in this chapter were identified through systematic searching of academic journals, databases and websites to retrieve relevant materials. As part of a wider study relating to the aspirations, outcomes and experiences of children and young people looked after (Mannay et al., 2015), we searched for studies that reported evaluations of interventions intended to improve educational outcomes of children and young people, aged up to 18 years, who were currently or had previously been in care. Included evaluations were limited to randomised controlled trials (RCTs), which have been reported as the most scientifically robust approach to evaluating intervention effectiveness (McGovern, 2001). RCTs involve the random allocation of individuals to receive an intervention or to carry on with usual practice. Outcomes between the two groups are compared, and, if favourable in the group that received the intervention (when controlling for all other factors that may explain the difference), we can state that the intervention is effective (Bryman, 2012).

To be included in the review, evaluations had to be reported since the issuing of the UK Children Act (1989) and be published in the English language. We searched 12 databases for relevant studies, retrieving 2,514 results, with a further 16 identified through consultation with international experts. We removed duplicated references, leaving 1,620 studies, with titles and abstracts then independently assessed for relevance by two researchers. Disagreements about inclusion were resolved through discussion with a third researcher. Sixty studies were considered to be relevant and full texts were independently assessed by two researchers, leading to 45 exclusions. A total of 15 evaluations reporting on 12 interventions (including different versions of the same named intervention) were subsequently included in the review, representing the highest quality of available evidence. Full technical details of the systematic review are provided in Mannay et al. (2015) and Evans et al. (2017).

The design and outcomes of educational interventions for children and young people in care

The 12 interventions included in the systematic review were diverse in terms of delivery settings, who delivered them, and the characteristics of the children and young people included as participants. Seven of the interventions were evaluated within the USA, two were in Canada, and two were in the UK. The fact that most interventions were evaluated outside the

UK should be borne in mind when considering the relevance of evidence within the Welsh context. These interventions are discussed in the following sections.

Fostering Individualized Assistance Program (FIAP)

Fostering Individualized Assistance Program (FIAP) is a wrap-around service delivered by family specialists serving as family-centred, clinical case managers and home-based counsellors, working across all settings to tailor services for individual children (Clark et al., 1998). The target population is children and young people aged seven to 15 years old in foster care. The intervention addresses a range of outcomes, including school absence, suspension, student drop-out and number of changes in school placements. Evaluation was conducted in the USA and included 54 individuals in the intervention group and 77 receiving usual practice (control group). Positive impacts were reported on the number of days that intervention group were suspended from school compared to control group, with control group members also more likely to be suspended from school than those who received the intervention (OR = 2.5, p = < .05). There was no impact on the upper number of school absences (more than 40 per cent of school days missed), extreme number of school to school movements (more than three per year), or school drop-out.

Early Start to Emancipation Preparation (ESTEP)

The Early Start to Emancipation Preparation (ESTEP) intervention is a home-based tutoring programme delivered by undergraduate and graduate students to young people aged 14 and 15 years in foster care (Courtney et al., 2008; Zinn and Courtney, 2014). Tutors meet with the children and young people within the care setting twice a week, delivering up to 50 hours of tutoring in mathematics, spelling, reading and vocabulary curriculum. The aim is to improve participants' reading and mathematics skills, as well as empowering them to use other educational services and resources. Development of a mentoring relationship is also anticipated between tutor and student, helping young people acquire skills and experience in developing healthy relationships. Tutors receive one day of training on the intervention and further supervision and development twice a year. The intervention has been evaluated within the USA, and included 246 individuals in receipt of the ESTEP intervention and 219 individuals who received usual practice. Outcomes for both groups were assessed at 26.8 months following commencement. Measured outcomes were academic skills, grade completion, Grade Point Average (GPA), high school diploma completion, and school-related behaviour.

Results reported no impact on academic skills, including word letter identification, calculation, or passage comprehension, and no impacts on grade completion, GPA, high school diploma or school behaviour.

The authors attributed this to the high number of individuals in the study having mental health and/or behavioural problems, reporting that 6.5 per cent of participants in the study experienced post-traumatic stress, 26.1 per cent had a learning disability and 35.1 per cent were participating in other specialist educational programmes prior to the study. Those delivering the intervention did not have specialist training to meet these diverse, additional needs, leading the authors to suggest that outcomes may be improved with more highly trained tutors. The study also reported conflicting participant views of the intervention, with some young people expressing a preference for school-based over home-based approaches, potentially due to them being less stigmatising (Courtney et al., 2008).

Teach Your Children Well (individual and group)

Teach Your Children Well is a structured reading and mathematics tutoring programme for six to 13-year-old children in foster care (Flynn et al., 2011, 2012; Marquis, 2013; Harper, 2012; Harper and Schmidt, 2012), with two versions. One offers direct instruction by trained foster carers (Flynn et al., 2011, 2012; Marquis, 2013), consisting of three hours of tutoring per week (two hours' one-to-one reading practice, 30 minutes' reading aloud by the foster child, and 30 minutes' self-paced instruction in mathematics). A second version includes small, group-based curriculum delivery by trained university students, with groups comprising three to four children. One study of the group-based approach reported on a 25-week version (Harper and Schmidt, 2012), whilst a second study considered a 30-week version (Harper, 2012).

All intervention evaluations have been conducted in Canada (Flynn et al., 2011, 2012; Marquis, 2013; Harper, 2012; Harper and Schmidt, 2012). The evaluation of the individualised version by Flynn et al. (2011; 2012) included 42 individuals in the intervention group and 35 receiving usual practice. The study found that the intervention had positive effects on sentence comprehension (E.S. = 0.38, p = .035) and mathematical computation (E.S. = 0.46, p = .009), but no impacts on reading or spelling. Flynn et al. (2011) further report that mental health problems, attention deficit hyperactivity disorder (ADHD) and other pre-existing behavioural problems can reduce the effect of the intervention on academic skills. Foster carers' perceptions of the intervention were explored, with 79 per cent stating that they would recommend the tutoring programme (Flynn et al., 2011, 2012; Marquis, 2013). Evaluation of the group-based version of Teach Your Children Well included 33 children in the intervention group and 35 continuing with usual practice (Harper, 2012; Harper and Schmidt, 2012). Outcomes were mixed, with positive impacts on reading (E.S. = 0.42, p = .002) and spelling (E.S. = .038, p = .004), but not on sentence comprehension or mathematics.

Multidimensional Treatment Foster Care (MTFC)
Multidimensional Treatment Foster Care (MTFC) is targeted at females aged 13 to 17 years old who have been in the juvenile system (Leve and Chamberlain, 2007). Participants move into placements with trained specialist foster carers for an average of six months, for behaviour monitoring, weekly meetings with a therapist and a range of skills-based training. An evaluation of the intervention has been conducted in the USA, with intended outcomes of improved homework completion and school attendance. Evaluation comprised 37 young people receiving MTFC and 44 receiving usual practice. The intervention indicated a positive impact on homework completion at three to six months ($p = < .05$) and at 12 months ($p = < .05$), with individuals in the intervention group also spending approximately 150 per cent more days per week on homework at 12 months, while those receiving usual practice saw a decline in homework completion. The evaluation also reported improvements on school attendance ($p = < .05$) in the intervention group.

Multidimensional Treatment Foster Care for Adolescents (MTFC-A)
Multidimensional Treatment Foster Care for Adolescents (MTFC-A) is a UK intervention, based on the principles of MTFC, providing nine months of specialist training and brief aftercare to foster carers (Green et al., 2014). The intended group for the intervention is children and young people in foster care aged 10 to 17 years old. Intervention outcomes are academic skills and school attendance. Evaluation of the intervention compared outcomes for 20 individuals in the intervention and 14 individuals receiving usual practice. The evaluation was conducted in the UK and did not report effects for any outcomes.

Head Start
Head Start is an early education and care programme in the USA (Lipscomb et al., 2013), targeted at disadvantaged children aged three to four years. It provides community-based, wraparound services focusing on child development and parental support to improve the development of pre-academic skills and quality of child–teacher relationships. Several evaluations of Head Start have been conducted, but Lipscomb et al. (2013) are the first to report on the specific impact on children and young people in non-parental care. In this study, the sample comprised 76 per cent of individuals living with relatives, 13 per cent living in foster care, and 11 per cent living with non-relatives. As part of the evaluation, 154 children received the intervention and 99 individuals, also in non-parental care, received usual practice.

Head Start participants reported positive impacts on pre-academic skills six months following the start of the intervention ($ß = 0.16$, $p = .02$). At 18 months follow-up, Head Start continued to demonstrate some effect on pre-academic skills (ß = 0.12, p = .05), but only where there had been gains in pre-academic skills, positive teacher–child relationships, and behaviour at six months. Teacher–student relationships also improved at six months following intervention commencement (ß = 0.30, p < .01), with some of the effect retained where there had been other improvements in measurements at six months (ß = 0.17, p = .02).

The Letterbox Club

The Letterbox Club focuses on children aged seven to 11 years old in foster care (Mooney et al., 2016), and involves gifting personalised educational resources to children, including books, stationery items, and mathematical games. Parcels are delivered monthly over a six-month period and, while the intervention does not rely on or demand foster carer involvement, it is hoped that they will engage with the learning process.

There have been several evaluations of the Letterbox Club, but Mooney et al. (2016) provide the first RCT to date. The study was conducted in Northern Ireland, and involved 56 children receiving the intervention and 60 continuing with usual practice. Evaluation measured reading skills and attitudes to reading and school. Findings demonstrated no impact on reading accuracy, reading comprehension or reading rate. At approximately eight months following the intervention commencement there was no difference between the two groups for attitudes towards reading or for attitudes towards school. The study included a qualitative exploration of children's perceptions of the intervention, finding mixed views. Some individuals liked the books, while others felt that they were not pitched at the right level or were already familiar. The intervention is based on the hypothesis that children's ownership of books will increase their interest in reading; however, some participants felt 'book burdened' rather than 'book deprived', meaning increasing access did not necessarily increase opportunities to read.

Kids in Transition to School

Kids in Transition to School is a USA-based classroom intervention targeted at children aged six years or younger in a foster care placement (Pears et al., 2013). The intervention is delivered two months prior to a child starting kindergarten and for two months following commencement. Children attend 24 sessions, in groups of 12–15, with groups lasting approximately two hours and focused on a range of skills, including development in early literacy. Sessions are delivered by a graduate-level teacher and two assistant teachers. Foster carers attend eight parallel meetings intended to develop their capacity to support the child in practising newly acquired skills, routines and behaviour. Carer groups are delivered for two hours fortnightly by a facilitator and assistant. Evaluation was conducted with 102 children who received the intervention and

90 who continued with usual practice. The programme was noted for its high level of adherence to the provided materials, with 100 per cent of material being covered in the carer group and 98 per cent being covered in the child group. Results showed the intervention had a small effect on early literacy skills (E.S. = 0.26) and on self-regulatory skills (E.S. = 0.18), but no significant effect on pro-social skills.

On the Way Home

On the Way Home is targeted at young people aged 13 to 18 years old identified as having, or being at risk of having, a disability (Trout et al., 2013). The 12-month intervention is delivered when young people leave a period in residential care and return to live within the family home. Each family is assigned a trained consultant who delivers the majority of the intervention. Components include: Check & Connect, which involves the consultant working with a school mentor to monitor school engagement and working with the family to ensure their involvement in educational goals; Common Sense Parenting, involving one-to-one sessions for parents on the skills required to support academic and behavioural success; and homework support. Over the course of the intervention, family consultants can expect to spend approximately 138 hours with each family, with primary intended outcome of continued school enrolment. Evaluation of the intervention compared outcomes for 47 young people who participated in On the Way Home, and 41 individuals who received usual practice. The intervention provided no evidence of effect on maintenance of enrolment in a school placement.

Educational Specialist

Educational Specialists are certified special education teachers placed within child welfare agencies (Zetlin et al., 2004), with knowledge of the rules and regulations of the school system and available educational resources. Children and young people are referred to them by social workers when they are encountering unresolvable educational barriers. The specialist then advises the child welfare agency, provides advocacy for the young person, and investigates alternative school options where necessary.

Evaluation of the Educational Specialist service was conducted in the USA, and involved 60 children receiving the intervention and 60 assigned to usual practice. Measured outcomes were mathematics test achievement, reading test achievement, and grade point average (GPA) over a 24-month period, in addition to special education status, school attendance and number of school placements. The study reported differences in mathematics test achievement scores and reading test achievement scores between the intervention group and usual practice group before the intervention was delivered. However, following the intervention there was no difference between the two groups for mathematics (p = .082) or reading (p =.448) and no reported effect on GPA. For special educational status, there were 18 young people in the intervention group recorded as being in special education at the start of the study, which was reduced to nine at 24 months. In the usual practice group, the number decreased from 10 to seven. The significance level of this finding is not presented. There was no indicated impact on school attendance, and those receiving usual practice actually appeared to fare better at 24 months, with similar results found for number of school placements. Between the start of the study and 24-month follow-up, the number of schools attended dropped from an average of 1.30 to 1.18 in the intervention group, and from 1.28 to 1.12 in the usual practice group, meaning a more significant reduction in the number of school placements in the usual practice group (p < .05).

Discussion

Our systematic review demonstrates that the evidence base for interventions addressing the educational outcomes for children and young people who have been in care is limited. Five interventions reported an effect for academic skills: Kids in Transition (Pears et al., 2013); Headstart (Lipscomb et al., 2013); the individual-level Teach Your Children Well (Flynn et al., 2011, 2012; Marquis, 2013); and both the 25-week and 30-week group-based Teach Your Children Well (Harper, 2012; Harper and Schmidt, 2012). One intervention, the Multidimensional Treatment Foster Care for girls leaving the youth justice system (Leve and Chamberlain, 2007), reported an effect for homework completion. Three interventions indicated an effect on school attendance, suspension or drop-out: Multidimensional Treatment Foster Care (Leve and Chamberlain, 2007); On the Way Home (Trout et al., 2013); and the Fostering Individualized Assistance Programme (Clark et al., 1998). The latter of these reported impacts on extreme absences and suspension, although mainly for the older subset of participants. Only the Head Start intervention (Lipscomb et al., 2013) demonstrated a positive effect on teacher–student relationships. The impact of programmes on the number of school placements is unclear. No interventions demonstrated an improvement on academic achievement and grade completion, school behaviour, or academic attitudes. Green et al.'s (2014) Multidimensional Treatment Foster Care for Adolescents, the Letterbox Club (Mooney et al., 2016), and the ESTEP programme (Courtney et al., 2008; Zinn and Courtney, 2014) found no positive effect for any outcome measured.

The findings from the review should be treated with caution due to a number of limitations with both delivery of the interventions and the study design utilised. Studies did not consistently report on how much of the intervention was delivered as planned or on the quality of delivery. This means it is unclear whether cases of ineffectiveness may be due to the intervention being inherently problematic, or that it has not been implemented properly. For example, the ESTEP programme did not demonstrate effects, but only 61 per cent of the intervention group actually received it (Courtney et al., 2008; Zinn and Courtney, 2014). This was explained by the average wait of 15.3 weeks between assignment to the intervention and actual commencement, with 13 per cent waiting up to two years to start. Further barriers to receiving the interventions included the transience of care placements, which meant children sometimes moved on before the intervention started, conflict between carers and children, and carers being too busy to support learning processes (Flynn et al., 2012).

There was also variation in the methodological quality of studies, with a number of clear limitations ensuring that we are unable to make any certain claims about which interventions work. Studies had small sample sizes or did not report the sample size required to calculate a statistical effect. In order for a study to be able to ensure that statistical analysis is able to detect any changes in outcomes, they must include a minimum sample size. A power calculation should be undertaken to ascertain the requisite sample size. Only two of the identified interventions had evaluations with a sufficient sample size based on a power calculation (Flynn et al., 2012; Harper, 2012; Marquis, 2013). Two studies with power calculations were underpowered (Green et al., 2014; Mooney et al., 2016). The remaining studies did not report a power calculation. There was also a likely risk of contamination, whereby participants in the usual practice group ended up receiving the intervention. For example, in the ESTEP evaluation 12 per cent of the usual practice group received the intervention, whilst 19 per cent received other types of comparable school-based tutoring programmes during the evaluation period (Courtney et al., 2008; Zinn and Courtney, 2014). Contamination is important as it reduces the differences between the two study groups and can lead to the underestimation of intervention effects. Further details on studies' methodological limitations are reported in the full systematic review (Mannay et al., 2015; Evans et al., 2017).

The relevance of educational interventions within the Welsh context

The methodological limitations associated with the evaluations included in the review means that we are unable to unequivocally claim which, if any, interventions are effective. Yet even if evaluations demonstrated methodological robustness, it would still be difficult to argue that 'effective' interventions could directly improve the educational outcomes for children and young people in Wales. This is because despite the review including evaluations of international interventions, the majority were conducted in the USA or Canada. We do not know how contingent intervention processes and outcomes are on the specific cultural and social characteristics of these contexts. As such, it is unclear if interventions effects could be replicated in a Welsh context, and the degree of adaptation that may be required to ensure cultural sensitivity.

The wider research study that encompassed this systematic review has explored the relevance and acceptability of the interventions included in this review for children and young people in care within the Welsh context (see Mannay et al. 2015; Evans et al., 2016). Focus groups, facilitated by peer researchers from Voices from Care Cymru, were conducted with 26 care-experienced young people aged 16 to 27 years old in Wales. Young people identified positive features of interventions, including their focus on improving social and emotional competencies. However, for the large part, most young people felt that existing interventions would not address the structural determinants of their educational disadvantage. These barriers extended to include the lack of resources allocated to children and young people in care in Wales, placement instability, and the entrenched stigma and negative perceptions around their educational ability (Mannay et al., 2015, 2017). Participants also touched on the lack of minimum educational qualifications specified for foster and residential carers, and how this could lead to interventions and support being offered by individuals who themselves lack knowledge and skills (see Mannay et al., 2015).

As part of the qualitative element of the wider study, young people explored their preferences for different types of delivery agents and modes of intervention (Mannay et al., 2015; Evans et al., 2016). Generally, participants preferred interventions provided by carers, due to the excessive number of professionals already involved in their lives. Importantly, they also expressed a preference for interventions that are universally accessible, rather than those that are specifically targeted at children and young people in care, although some individuals indicated that they would like the opportunity to share their experiences with others who have been in care. Indeed one of the key recommendations from the wider research report was that universal programmes should be 'open to all children and young people . . . as they may be less stigmatising and more beneficial for a wider demographic' (Mannay et al. 2015, p. 121). Therefore, it is important to note that within the systematic review only one intervention was more universal in its approach, namely Head Start (Lipscomb et al., 2013). Although the methodological limitations outlined above should be considered, the intervention did report positive educational outcomes for individuals in non-parental care. Such findings might encourage us to think beyond interventions that are targeted at vulnerable subgroups, and to focus on more universal, structural interventions.

Young people's identification of limitations with existing interventions highlights the importance of engaging them in developing educational approaches (Evans et al., 2016). This resonates with a key action point included in the Welsh Government's (2016) strategy *Raising the ambitions and educational attainment of children who are looked after in Wales*. The strategy drew on the recommendations of the wider study (Mannay et al. 2015) and it emphasises the need to involve children and young people in action planning so that they have a say in the decisions that affect them. However, despite increasing calls for co-production of interventions with the populations that they are intended to engage (Wight et al., 2015), there remains limited practical guidance on how this process of co-production is best facilitated. There have been moves to articulate the steps required to move from tokenistic forms of participation towards effective co-produced research and practice (see, for example, Staples et al., 2019 [Chapter 15 this volume]). However, further research needs to be conducted to extend these examples of best practice, and further our understandings of how children and young people in care can have a voice in decision-making processes.

Conclusions

The present chapter has reported on a systematic review of educational interventions addressing outcomes for children and young people in care. It is apparent that the current evidence base is mixed, with existing evaluations being the subject of numerous methodological limitations. Future research needs to focus on developing theoretically sound interventions that maximise the likelihood of demonstrating effects, whilst evaluating these with methodologically robust study designs. Given the variability of international social care systems, and the children and young people that they care for, progression in intervention development and evaluation should also include a focus on the adaptability of effective programmes to different contexts and populations.

Acknowledgements

The research project from which this chapter is drawn was commissioned by the Welsh Government. The main study was based in the Children's Social Care Research and Development Centre (CASCADE), and the systematic review of educational interventions was undertaken with the Centre for the Development and Evaluation of Complex Interventions for Public Health Improvement (DECIPHer).

References

Allnatt, G., 'Transitions from care to higher education: A case study of a young person's journey', in D. Mannay, A. Rees and L. Roberts (eds), *Children and Young People 'Looked After'? Education, Intervention and the Everyday Culture of Care in Wales* (Cardiff: University of Wales Press, 2019), pp. 69–82.

Berger, L. M., Cancian, M., Han, E., Noyes, J. and Rios-Salas, V., 'Children's Academic Attainment and Foster Care', *Pediatrics*, 135/1 (2015), 109–16.

Bryman, A., *Social Research Methods* (4th edn) (Oxford: Oxford University Press, 2012).

Clark, H. B., Prange, M. E., Lee, B., Steinhardt Stewart, E., Barrett McDonald, B. and Adlai Boyd, L., 'An individualised wraparound process for children in foster care with emotional/behavioural disturbances: Follow-up findings and implications from a controlled study', in M. E. Epstein, K. Kutash and A. Duchnowski (eds), *Outcomes for Children and Youth with Emotional and Behavioural Disorders and their Families: Programs and Evaluation Best Practices* (Austin, TX: Pro-ed, 1998), pp. 513–42.

Courtney, M., Zinn, A., Zielewski, E., Bess, R., Malm, K., Stagner, M. and Pergamit, M., *Evaluation of the Early Start to Emancipation Preparation – Tutoring Program Los Angeles County, California: Final Report* (Chicago: The Urban Institute, Chaplin Hall Center for Children and National Opinion Research Center, 2008).

Evans, R., Brown, R., Rees, G. and Smith, P., 'Systematic Review of Educational Interventions for Looked-After Children and Young People: Recommendations for Intervention Development and Evaluation', *British Educational Research Journal*, 43/1 (2017), 68–94.

———, Hallett, S., Rees, A. and Roberts, L. 'The Acceptability of Educational Interventions: Qualitative Evidence from Children and Young People in Care', *Children and Youth Services Review*, 71 (2016), 68-76.

Flynn, R. J., Marquis, R. A., Paquet, M. and Peeke, L. M., *Effects of Tutoring by Foster Parents on Foster Children's Academic Skills in Reading and Math: A Randomised Effectiveness Trial. Final Report of the RESPs for Kids in Care Project* (Ottawa: Centre for Research on Educational and Community Services, 2011).

———, Marquis, R. A., Paquet, M., Peeke, L. M. and Aubry, T. D., 'Effects of Individual Direct-instruction Tutoring on Foster Children's Academic Skills: A Randomised Trial', *Children and Youth Services Review*, 34/6 (2012), 1183-9.

Green, J. M., Biehal, N., Roberts, C., Dixon, J., Kay, C., Parry, E., Rothwell, J., Roby, A., Kapadia, D., Scott, S. and Chamberlain, P., 'Multidimensional Treatment Foster Care for Adolescents in English Care: Randomised Trial and Observational Cohort Evaluation', *British Journal of Psychiatry*, 204/3 (2014), 214–21.

Harper, J., *The Effectiveness of a Group-based Tutorial Direct Instruction Program for Long-term Foster Care Children: A Randomised Controlled Trial* (Doctoral dissertation, Lakehead University, Orillia, ON, 2012). Available at *http://thesis.lakeheadu.ca:8080/handle/2453/385* (accessed 14/03/18).

———— and Schmidt, F., 'Preliminary Effects of a Group-based Tutoring Program for Children in Long-term Foster Care', *Children and Youth Services Review*, 34/6 (2012), 1176–82.

Leve, L. D. and Chamberlain, P., 'A Randomised Evaluation of Multidimensional Treatment Foster Care: Effects on School Attendance and Homework Completion in Juvenile Justice Girls', *Research on Social Work Practice*, 17/6 (2007), 657–63.

Lipscomb, S., Pratt, M., Schmitt, S. A., Pears, K. and Kim, H., 'School Readiness in Children Living in Non-parental Care: Impacts of Head Start', *Journal of Applied Developmental Psychology*, 34/1 (2013), 28–37.

Mannay, D., Staples, E., Hallett, S., Roberts, L., Rees, A., Evans, R. and Andrews, D., *Understanding the Educational Experiences and Opinions, Attainment, Achievement and Aspirations of Looked After Children in Wales* (Cardiff: Welsh Government, 2015).

————, Evans, R., Staples, E., Hallett, S., Roberts, L., Rees, A. and Andrews, D., 'The Consequences of Being Labelled "Looked-After": Exploring the Educational Experiences of Looked-after Children and Young People in Wales', *British Journal of Educational Research*, 43/4 (2017), 683–99.

Marquis, R., *The Gender Effects of a Foster Parent-Delivered Tutoring Program on Foster Children's Academic Skills and Mental Health: A Randomised Field Trial* (Doctoral dissertation, University of Ottawa, Ottawa, ON, 2013). Available at *http://www.ruor.uottawa.ca/handle/10393/24324* (accessed 14/03/18).

McGovern, D. P. B., 'Randomized controlled trials', in D. P. B. McGovern, R. M. Valori, W. S. M. Summerskill (eds), *Key Topics in Evidence Based Medicine* (Oxford: BIOS Scientific Publishers, 2001), pp. 26–9.

Mooney, J., Winter, K. and Connolly, P., 'Effects of a Book Gifting Programme on Literacy Outcomes for Foster Children: A Randomised Controlled Trial Evaluation of the Letterbox Club in Northern Ireland', *Children and Youth Services Review*, 65 (2016), 1–8.

Pears, K. C., Fisher, P. A., Kim, H. K., Bruce, J., Healey, C. V. and Yoerger, K., 'Immediate Effects of a School Readiness Intervention for Children in Foster Care', *Early Education and Development*, 24/6 (2013), 771–91.

Rees, G. and Stein, M., 'Children and young people in care and leaving care', in J. Bradshaw (ed.), *The Well-being of Children in the UK* (Bristol: Policy Press, 2016), pp. 231–62.

Sebba, J, Berridge, D., Luke, N., Fletcher, J., Bell, K., Strand, S., Thomas, S., Sinclair, I. and O'Higgins, A., *The Educational Progress of Looked-after Children in England: Linking Care and Educational Data* (Oxford: Rees Centre for Research in Fostering and Education and University of Bristol, 2015).

Staples, E., Roberts, L., Lyttleton-Smith, J., Hallett, S. and CASCADE Voices, 'Enabling care-experienced young people's participation in research: CASCADE Voices', in D. Mannay, A. Rees and L. Roberts (eds), *Children and Young People 'Looked After'? Education, Intervention and the Everyday Culture of Care in Wales* (Cardiff: University of Wales Press, 2019), pp. 169–209.

Trout, A. L., Lambert, M. C., Epstein, M. H., Tyler, P., Thompson, R. W., Stewart, M. and Daly, D. L., 'Comparison of On the Way Home Aftercare Support to Traditional Care Following Discharge from a Residential Setting: A Pilot Randomised Controlled Trial', *Child Welfare*, 92/3 (2013), 27–45.

Vinnerljung, B. and Hjern, A., 'Cognitive, Educational and Self-support Outcomes of Long-term Foster Care versus Adoption. A Swedish National Cohort Study', *Children and Youth Services Review*, 33/10 (2011), 1902–10.

Welsh Audit Office, *The Educational Attainment of Looked After Children and Young People* (2012). Available at *https://www.wao.gov.uk/publication/educational-attainment-looked-after-children-and-young-people* (accessed 14/03/18).

Welsh Government, *Raising the Ambitions and Educational Attainment of Children Who Are Looked After in Wales* (2016). Available at *http://gov.wales/topics/educationandskills/schoolshome/deprivation/educational-attainment-of-looked-after-children/?lang=en* (accessed 14/03/18).

Wight, D., Wibush, E., Jepson, R. and Doi, L., 'Six Steps in Quality Intervention Development (6SQuID)', *Journal of Epidemiology and Community Health*, 70 (2016), 520–5.

Zetlin, A., Weinberg, L. and Kimm, C., 'Improving Education Outcomes for Children in Foster Care: Intervention by an Education Liaison', *Journal of Education for Students Placed at Risk*, 9/4 (2004), 421–9.

Zinn, A. and Courtney, M., 'Context Matters: Experimental Evaluation of Home-based Tutoring for Youth in Foster Care', *Children and Youth Services Review*, 47/3 (2014), 198–204.

4 | Exploring the educational attainment and achievement of children who are 'looked after' in formal kinship care

Rebecca C. Pratchett and Paul Rees

Introduction

PRACTITIONERS ARE ROUTINELY faced with the challenge of having to consider which type of care placement is best for a child who is not able to live with their birth parents. Consideration is typically given to the probable outcomes of each option in key areas such as well-being and education. For a sizeable proportion of the care population, formal kinship care (where the child is placed with family or friends by the state) is the choice that is made. Practitioners are increasingly encouraged to evidence their decision making. While there is a growing body of literature to suggest that outcomes for children who are in kinship care placements are relatively favourable in respect of, for example, placement stability (Koh, 2010) and positive birth-parent relationships (Berrick, 1997), the evidence base on educational outcomes remains limited (Leslie et al., 2005).

In this chapter we report on a study involving a group of children in formal kinship care aged eight to 18 (n = 21) from two local authorities in south Wales. We report on their level of attainment and achievement in literacy and numeracy. Although we found that the children's average performance was much lower than that of their peers in the general population, many were performing within the average range. Similarly, more than half had reading skills in keeping with their cognitive ability. Throwing useful light on the relative efficacy of formal kinship care placements, we also note that as a group they performed as well in literacy, in fact marginally better, than children in other types of care placement. We do stress, however, that their literacy and numeracy skills remain a cause for concern and call for all involved to maintain higher expectations. We also call for greater consideration of how care-related experiences may impact individual curriculum subject areas differently.

Background

Precise information on the total number of children in the United Kingdom (UK) who are not living with a birth parent, but cared for by a relative, is difficult to obtain. There is no legal obligation on families to inform the state when a child is being cared for by a close relative. Selwyn and Nandy (2014) have estimated from census data that around 1.4 per cent (9,200) of children in Wales are living in kinship care. The term kinship care is an eclectic term, used in many different ways, depending on the legal and operational criteria that is applied (see DfE, 2011). For the purpose of this chapter it is helpful to have an understanding of the two most commonly used categories of kinship care. 'Informal kinship care' typically refers to full-time care provided by a relative (other than parent) or friends who have a prior connection with the child, where the child has not been placed by the state. In contrast, 'formal kinship care' refers to care provided by a relative or family friend where the child has been placed by the state. Children in 'formal kinship care' are typically 'looked after' and their carers approved as foster carers following assessment. Previous research has shown that formal kinship carers tend to experience greater financial hardship and household overcrowding than unrelated foster carers (Farmer et al., 2013). They also tend to be less well educated, trained and remunerated than non-related foster carers (Wade et al., 2014).

In Wales, the proportion of the 'looked after' population who are in 'formal kinship care' has risen to 16 per cent and as many as one in five (21 per cent) of all foster carers are 'formal kinship' foster carers (see StatsWales, 2016). Even though the use of 'formal kinship care' has increased, research on the outcomes of these children has been limited. Much of the research has been undertaken overseas and focuses mainly on issues such as reunification rates, placement stability, mental health and behaviour (see Fechter-Leggett and O'Brien, 2010; Testa, 2001; Winokur et al., 2014, 2015; Wu et al., 2015). The findings of these studies have also provided mixed results (Bell and Romano, 2015). While evidence suggests that the needs of children in 'formal kinship care' are similar to those in mainstream placements, it is unclear whether those needs are sufficiently met (Farmer and Moyers, 2008; Selwyn and Nandy, 2014).

Children in care have long been recognised as especially vulnerable to low educational attainment (Colton and Williams, 2006; Mannay et al., 2015). In Wales, for example, the attainment of five A*–C General Certificate of Education (GCSEs), a key national benchmark, is achieved by around 80 per cent of the general population, whereas around 11 per cent of care leavers attain at this level (DfE, 2016; Statistics for Wales, 2016). Furthermore, 43 per cent of care leavers are not in education, training or employment by their 19th birthday (Statistics for Wales, 2016). Yet research on the education of children in 'formal kinship care', who now form a sizeable proportion of the care population, is limited. Winokur et al. (2014) conclude from the few studies that do exist that there is no detectable difference in educational outcomes for children in 'formal kinship care' than for the wider care population, but they call for more research. It is vital that research establishes not only the relative level of attainment, but the effectiveness of 'formal kinship care' in promoting individual educational achievement.

Studies have suggested that factors which impede the educational progress of the wider care population, such as the latent effects of early abuse also affect those in 'formal kinship care' (Sawyer and Dubowitz, 1994). The impact of early abuse and trauma on a child's ability to connect with educational systems is often apparent irrespective of where they are placed (Bombèr, 2007). However, for those in 'formal kinship care' some of the impact may be lessened. It is more common, for example, for these placements to be in close proximity to the child's birth address and catchment area school, reducing discontinuity in schooling (Testa, 2001). Local schools often have knowledge of several generations of the child's family, and an established relationship with them which cannot be easily replicated elsewhere. Consistency of school placement may also allow for the embedding of behavioural programmes where needed (Dubowitz and Sawyer, 1994; Leslie et al., 2005). Others have suggested that the open demonstration of socially appropriate familial affection that is permissible in 'formal kinship care' can assist the child to form relationships with others (Berrick et al., 1994; Johnson-Garner and Meyers, 2003; see also Rees, 2019 [Chapter 7 this volume]).

Research examining the educational performance of children in care is complicated by challenges in assessing educational achievement: the extent to which the child is reaching their perceived potential. Instead, the majority of studies have focused on attainment: mastery of a skill or acquisition of specific knowledge. Routine publication of examination data by government agencies, for example, offers a readily accessible means of evaluating attainment, but the value of the data for estimating educational achievement is questionable. Deciding on who to compare the children's performance with is also complicated and contentious: should performance be compared with, for example, the general population of children, the wider care population, children from the same socio-economic backgrounds or children with a similar level of cognitive functioning?

A core aim of the present study was to offer some insight into the relative performance of children in 'formal kinship care'. In seeking to fulfil this aim we first provide an overview of the level of attainment in literacy and numeracy of a sample of children in 'formal kinship care'. Secondly, we compare their level of attainment to that of the general population and their literacy with a large sample of children in care. Thirdly, we examine their level of achievement in literacy and numeracy, based on any difference observed between their predicted scores (based on their cognitive functioning) and their actual scores.

Methods

Sample and participants
The participants were drawn from two local authorities (LAs) in south Wales: one rural, the other urban. On the Welsh Index of Multiple Deprivation approximately 22 and 28 per cent of wards in the two LAs fell within the bottom quartile (most deprived) of all wards within Wales.

Participant inclusion criteria
To be defined as being in 'formal kinship care' and invited to participate in this study, children had to be living full-time with a close relative other than their birth parents (for example, grandparent, aunt, uncle, sibling or step-parent) to whom they were related by blood or marriage, or, a carer with whom they had a pre-existing relationship (kith). They also needed to be legally 'looked after', eight to 18 years of age and living within the boundaries of the 'home' local authority (LA).

In total 54 children and young people met the inclusion criteria. Social workers were contacted regarding the appropriateness of proceeding in each case. The carers of the children were contacted and full explanations of the aims of the study provided. Finally, the remaining children were contacted and, following an explanation of the study, asked whether they wished to participate. Overall, 21 children agreed to participate (nine males; 12 females). The mean age was 13 years one month, with a range from nine years five months to 17 years one month. All of the children attended mainstream schools. Two of the children were in receipt of a Statement of Special Educational Needs.

Reasons for non-participation are provided in Table 4.1. Approval for the study was given by the Director of Children's Services of each participating LA and Human and Health Sciences, Swansea University.

Carer qualifications
Eighteen of the carers shared information on their qualifications, around half of whom had no formal qualifications. The remaining carers held

Table 4.1: *Reasons for non-participation*

	LA 1	LA 2	Total
LA considered placement too unsettled	6	1	7
Carer considered placement too unsettled	4	0	4
Carer keen to avoid child appearing different	0	1	1
Carer unable to afford the time	1	1	2
Carer keen to maintain distance from LA	0	1	1
Carer declined: no reason given	3	4	7
Child felt they were too unsettled	1	1	2
Child declined: no reason given	2	5	7
Child did not respond	1	1	2
Total			**33**

qualifications ranging from Level 3 (GCE A' Level) through to Level 8 (Doctoral level).

Measures/instruments
We chose to use the following standardised measures that could be administered at any point in the child's education and still yield comparative data.

Wechsler Abbreviated Scale of Intelligence (WASI-II): The WASI-II is an established standardised measure of cognitive functioning for children and adults aged six years to 90 years (Wechsler, 2005). Four subtests comprise a Full Scale Intelligence Quotient (FSIQ): Block Design, Vocabulary, Matrix Reasoning and Similarities. The FSIQ is considered to be a good predictor of educational performance (Hrabok et al., 2014). Reported reliability coefficients are high.

Wechsler Individual Achievement Test, Abbreviated (WIAT-II-UK): The WIAT-II-UK is a standardised test of academic attainment for children and adults (Wechsler, 2005). UK norms are available. It is comprised of a number of subtests including, for example, Word Reading, Spelling and Numerical Operations. Reliability coefficients are high.

Bespoke measures: We also used bespoke interview measures relating to a wide range of well-being issues such as sense-of-self and relationships with others, which will be reported on in more detail elsewhere. Aspects of measures allowed for the children and their carers to comment on education.

Design

It is possible to directly compare attainment on the WIAT-II and cognitive performance (FSIQ) standardised scores to gain a basic insight into the extent to which a child is achieving. Generally speaking a child who obtains the same score or higher on the attainment measure can be said to be achieving. We also used a more complex model that takes into account norm sample discrepancy distributions. This allowed us also to check the magnitude of the discrepancies we observed against the frequency they occurred in the norm sample. One sample z tests were used to compare differences in the mean scores of the study sample and general population (norm sample) data as well as the wider care population (Rees, 2010, 2013).

Key findings

Literacy and numeracy standardised scores

Table 4.2: *Literacy and numeracy standardised test scores*

Domain	Mean (standard deviation)	Qualitative descriptor
Reading*	87.86 (17.07)	Low average range
Spelling*	87.62 (15.86)	Low average range
Numeracy*	83.14 (12.38)	Below average range

*Scores on these tests are standardised to a $\bar{x}$ of 100 and SD of 15. The average range is 85 to 115.

Comparison with general population (norm sample)
When compared with general population norms, the children's mean score was significantly lower in Reading, Spelling and Numeracy (z = –3.71, –3.78 and –5.15 respectively, *p* < .0001 in each analysis).

Comparison with the wider population of children in care
Reading and Spelling scores were compared with the performance of a looked after sample on the British Ability Scales, Achievement Scales (BAS, II). For context on the wider larger sample see Rees (2013). As the numeracy of the wider looked after population was not assessed in the Rees (2013) study, comparison was not possible. The Reading and Spelling tests used in the Rees (2013) study correlate well with those used in this study.

Children in kinship care in the wider sample (Rees, 2013) were not included in this analysis to avoid like-with-like comparison. The data suggest that the average level of literacy of children in 'formal kinship care' is very similar to that of the wider population of children in care. The differences are not statistically significant.

Table 4.3: *Comparison of literacy of children in 'formal kinship care' and wider care population*

	Group	N	Mean (SD)
Reading	Wider care population	160	86.43 (17.93)
	'formal kinship care'	21	87.86 (17.07)
Spelling	Wider care population	159	86.16 (17.06)
	'formal kinship care'	21	87.62 (15.86)

Achievement in literacy and numeracy

The average level of cognitive performance (WASI-II, FSIQ) was recorded as $\bar{x}$ = 84.29 (standard deviation = 10.67).

Direct comparison between literacy and numeracy scores and cognitive performance:
63 per cent (n = 13) of the children obtained Reading and Spelling scores the same or higher than their cognitive test score; 48 per cent (n = 10) of the children obtained a Numeracy score the same or higher than their cognitive test score.

Comparisons based on norm group distribution of differences:
52 per cent (n = 11) of the children obtained Reading scores as high, or higher than the score predicted by cognitive ability and age.

48 per cent (n = 10) of the children obtained Spelling scores as high, or higher than the score predicted by cognitive ability and age.

23 per cent (n = 5) of the children obtained Numeracy scores as high, or higher than the score predicted by cognitive ability and age.

Discussion

Performance relative to general age-matched population

When compared with the general population of children of their own age, the average level of educational attainment of the children in this study was found to be low, at a statistically significant level. More positively, a large proportion of the children were attaining in the average range or above in Reading and Spelling. This finding is a helpful reminder that average (mean) attainment should be interpreted with caution. Expectations at the individual level should not be based on the average group level performance. The findings demonstrate that low attainment in literacy is certainly not an inevitability; in fact, 'below average' attainment was the exception. In contrast, only one-quarter obtained numeracy scores in the average range for their respective age group and none were attaining above the average. The disparity in the relative level of attainment between literacy and numeracy will be discussed further.

The data indicate that low attainment, when it does occur, can be seen long before the end of statutory schooling: all but one had not reached the end of school examinations. It is vital that educational intervention, when needed, is offered before the approach to end of school examinations. The move within Wales to record and report end of Key Stage test data for all children in care may help in the early detection of low performance. The use of more sophisticated tests with acceptable psychometric properties, would also be a good way forward with children in 'formal kinship care'.

Performance relative to the wider population of children in care

No statistically significant differences were observed in the average literacy attainment of a larger sample of children in care and this group of children in 'formal kinship care'. It would be difficult to argue from this data that children in 'formal kinship care' are either advantaged or disadvantaged compared to other placement types.

Robust data on the numeracy of the wider population of children in care was not found in a search of existing literature. There are a small number of small-scale studies that report some data. Jackson et al. (2010), for example, assessed four children in care with the WIAT-II and reported a mean standardised score of 75 on the numeracy subscale. As these four children were all attending a special school for children with emotional and behavioural difficulties it would be questionable to use this mean as an estimate of the average level of numeracy of the wider care population. Further research and data on the numeracy of children in care is needed. All of the children in this group were attending mainstream school in contrast to 81 per cent of children in care (comparative data drawn from Rees, 2013 and adjusted, to exclude those in kinship care). This supports, to some degree, the argument that 'formal kinship care' promotes engagement in mainstream schools and associated benefits.

Performance relative to cognitive functioning

Direct and distribution informed comparisons of predicted and actual performance suggest that the children are generally performing at a level in literacy that is commensurate with their current cognitive functioning. That is to say, at the individual level, their literacy was as might reasonably be expected given their cognitive reasoning.

Although direct comparison of predicted and actual scores in numeracy suggests a similar pattern, when norm group differences are used for comparison, a large proportion (77 per cent) of the sample was found to be underachieving to some extent. For the majority of these children the degree of their underachievement in numeracy would still be insufficient to trigger additional support in many schools although the threshold varies widely across schools. The threshold can be influenced by a school's philosophy of education, methods of assessment and resources. Schools typically recognise, however, that if support is not given to a child experiencing extensive underachievement frustration occurs, which manifests itself in many different ways.

It might reasonably be expected that where the level of underachievement is so great that it occurs in less than 10 per cent of children, support might be given. If this somewhat arbitrary threshold is applied to the dataset 18 per cent (n = 4) of the children in this sample would warrant support in numeracy. This is similar to that observed with reading and spelling: 23 per cent (n = 5), 14 per cent (n = 3) respectively.

Differences between literacy and numeracy

There are clearly subtle differences in the performance of the children in literacy and numeracy. More children appear to struggle to perform well in numeracy even if their underachievement is not extreme enough to receive support. It is possible, of course that as knowledge, skills and concepts in number are acquired in a more sequential way than in literacy, disruption to learning has, therefore, a greater impact on numeracy development. Even if the number of school changes is low, the impact of emotional disturbance due to care-related issues may be far higher than for their peers. It is important that educationalists are alert to the disparate impact across the curriculum. Careful curriculum-based assessment may help to identify these differences and inform interventions.

Limitations

This study, although providing novel data on 'formal kinship care', does have a number of limitations that must be highlighted. The number of children involved in this study was relatively small. Similarly, the entirely appropriate gatekeeping of access to children in 'formal kinship care' and the declined invitations to participate may have led to some sample bias. There is also a long history of debate around the predictive validity of cognitive tests (see Rowe, 1991). Most would agree that no cognitive measure is a pure measure of cognitive ability and accept that cognitive tests may contain unintentional social and cultural bias (see Miller, 1996). In the same vein, children who have experienced early trauma and much disruption in early childhood may be especially disadvantaged on formal tests. For this reason the cognitive test scores may be an underestimate of the children's true abilities. Care does need to be taken, therefore, when using cognitive tests as a means by which to assess achievement. Conversely, as has been pointed out, without any indication of how a child is functioning cognitively, the extent of achievement will remain largely unknown.

Conclusion

This chapter has focused primarily on the performance of a group of children in 'formal kinship care' in literacy and numeracy. Functional skills in literacy and numeracy are the key to the wider curriculum and vital for educational success. Success in acquiring these skills is dependent upon many factors, but it has long been recognised that parental support is one of the most important ingredients. For these children in 'formal kinship care', the scope for parental support is severely restricted and yet many are still managing to perform within the average range or above. It would appear that the alternative care that the carers are providing is beneficial. As Broad (2007) has noted, there has been some unsubstantiated concern that the growth of kinship care placements may lead to children being placed in inappropriate placements with poor outcomes. In the educational context we found no evidence to suggest that 'formal kinship care' is less beneficial than other placements including non-kinship foster care. Further, many of the children in this study were attaining at a rate in literacy, and to a lesser degree numeracy, that is commensurate with their perceived cognitive ability and age. It is reasonable to anticipate that the majority of the group will have sufficient functional literacy and numeracy to allow them to demonstrate their knowledge of the academic curriculum in public examinations.

As Broad (2007) notes, kinship care is not a panacea for children separated from their birth parents. As is the case with all other placement types, kinship care does not suit every child and risks can arise in these families as with all others. While this is a small-scale study it does suggest, however, that the academic performance of children in formal kinship care is no weaker, at the group level, than that of children in better-resourced non-relative foster care placements. The kinship carers' access to birth parents and the continuity of care afforded by kinship care (see Andersen and Fallesen, 2015) may help to compensate for other disadvantages that are sometimes observed in kinship care placements (Farmer et al., 2013; Wade et al., 2014).

However, these findings suggest that the literacy and numeracy skills of children in 'formal kinship care' remain a cause for concern when compared to their non-care-experienced peers. Therefore, future research should explore how children's and young people's experiences may impact individual curriculum subject areas differently, and what strategies can be put in place to best support the educational trajectories of children in 'formal kinship care'.

Acknowledgements

We would like to thank all of the children and carers who took part. We would also like to thank the Economic and Social Research Council and the local authorities who took part and jointly funded this study.

References

Andersen, S. H. and Fallesen, P., 'Family Matters? The Effect of Kinship Care on Foster Care Disruption Rates', *Child Abuse & Neglect*, 48 (2015), 68-79.

Bell, T. and Romano, E., 'Permanency and Safety Among Children in Foster Family and Kinship Care: A Scoping Review', *Trauma, Violence, & Abuse*, 11 (2015), 268-86.

Berrick, J. D., 'Assessing Quality of Care in Kinship and Foster Family Care', *Family Relations*, 46/3 (1997), 273-80.

————, Barth, R. P. and Needell, B., 'A Comparison of Kinship Foster Homes and Foster Family Homes: Implications for Kinship Foster Care as Family Preservation', *Children and Youth Services Review*, 16/1 (1994), 33-63.

Bombèr, L. M., *Inside I'm Hurting: Practical Strategies for Supporting Children with Attachment Difficulties in Schools* (London: Worth, 2007).

Broad, B., 'Kinship Care: What Works? Who Cares?', *Social Work and Social Sciences Review*, 13/1 (2007), 59-74.

Colton, M. and Williams, M., *Global Perspectives on Foster Family Care* (Lyme Regis: Russell House, 2006).

Department for Education, *Family and Friends Care: Statutory Guidance for Local Authorities* (London: Department for Education, 2011).

————, *Children Looked After in England Including Adoption: 2015 to 2016* (London: Department for Education, 2016).

Dubowitz, H. and Sawyer, R. J., 'School Behavior of Children in Kinship Care', *Child Abuse & Neglect*, 18/11 (1994), 899-911.

Farmer, E. and Moyers, S., *Kinship Care: Fostering Effective Family and Friends Placements* (London: Jessica Kingsley Publishers, 2008).

————, Selwyn, J. and Meakings, S., '"Other children say you're not normal because you don't live with Your Parents." Children's Views of Living with Informal Kinship Carers: Social Networks, Stigma and Attachment to Carers', *Child & Family Social Work*, 18/1 (2013), 25-34.

Fechter-Leggett, M. O. and O'Brien, K., 'The Effects of Kinship Care on Adult Mental Health Outcomes of Alumni of Foster Care', *Children and Youth Services Review*, 32/2 (2010), 206-13.

Hrabok, M., Brooks, B. L., Fay-McClymont, T. B. and Sherman, E. M., 'Wechsler Intelligence Scale for Children–(WISC-IV) Short-form Validity: A Comparison Study in Pediatric Epilepsy', *Child Neuropsychology*, 20/1 (2014), 49-59.

Jackson, E., Whitehead, J. and Wigford, A., 'In an EBD Population do Looked After Children Have Specific Needs Relating to Resilience, Self-perception and Attainment?', *Educational Psychology in Practice*, 26/1 (2010), 69–77.

Johnson-Garner, M. Y. and Meyers, S. A., 'What Factors Contribute to the Resilience of African-American Children Within Kinship Care?', Child & Youth Care Forum, 32/5 (2003), 255–69.

Koh, E., 'Permanency Outcomes of Children in Kinship and Non-Kinship Foster Care: Testing the External Validity of Kinship Effects', *Children and Youth Services Review*, 32/3 (2010), 389–98.

Leslie, L. K., Gordon, J. N., Meneken, L., Premji, K., Michelmore, K. L. and Ganger, W., 'The Physical, Developmental, and Mental Health Needs of Young Children in Child Welfare by Initial Placement Type', *Journal of Developmental and Behavioral Pediatrics*, 26/3 (2005), 177–85.

Mannay, D., Staples, E., Hallett, S., Roberts, L., Rees, A., Evans, R. E. and Andrews, D., *Understanding the Educational Experiences and Opinions, Attainment, Achievement and Aspirations of Looked After Children in Wales* (Cardiff: Welsh Government, 2015).

Miller, J. G., 'A cultural-psychological perspective on intelligence', in R. J. Sternberg and E. L. Grigorenko (eds), *Intelligence, Heredity, and Environment* (New York: Cambridge University Press, 1996), pp. 269–302.

Rees, A., 'The daily lived experiences of foster care: The centrality of food and touch in family life', in D. Mannay, A. Rees and L. Roberts (eds), *Children and Young People 'Looked After'? Education, Intervention and the Everyday Culture of Care in Wales* (Cardiff: University of Wales Press, 2019), pp. 85–98.

Rees, P., 'The Mental Health, Emotional Literacy, Cognitive Ability, Literacy Attainment and "Resilience" of "Looked After Children": A Multidimensional, Multiple-Rater Population Based Study', *British Journal of Clinical Psychology*, 52/2 (2013), 183–98.

———, 'State Dilemmas in the Provision of Alternative Care for Children: Relative Efficacy of Public Sector and Independent Sector Foster Placements', *International Journal of Public Administration*, 33/6 (2010), 325–34.

Rowe, H. A. H., *Intelligence: Reconceptualization and Measurement* (Mahwah: Lawrence Erlbaum Associates, 1991).

Sawyer, R. J. and Dubowitz, H., 'School Performance of Children in Kinship Care', *Child Abuse & Neglect*, 18/7 (1994), 587–97.

Selwyn, J. and Nandy, S., 'Kinship Care in the UK: Using Census Data to Estimate the Extent of Formal and Informal Care by Relatives', *Child & Family Social Work*, 19/1 (2014), 44–54.

StatsWales, Children Looked After by Local Authorities in Foster Placements, at 31 March 2016 (Cardiff: Welsh Government, 2016). Available at: *https://statswales. gov.wales/Catalogue/Health-and-Social-Care/Social-Services/Childrens-Services/Children-Looked-After/childrens-services-children-looked-after-childrenlookedafterinfosterplacementsat31march-by-localauthority-placement type* (accessed 03/02/18).

Testa, M. F., 'Kinship Care and Permanency', *Journal of Social Service Research*, 28/1 (2001), 25–43.

Wade, J., Sinclair, I. A. C., Stuttard, L. and Simmonds, J., *Investigating Special Guardianship: Experiences, Challenges and Outcomes* (London: Department for Education, 2014).

Wechsler, D., *Wechsler Individual Achievement Test (WIAT-II UK)* (New York: Harcourt Assessment, 2005).

Winokur, M., Holtan, A. and Valentine, D., *Kinship Care for the Safety, Permanency, and Well-Being of Children Removed from the Home for Maltreatment* (Oslo: Campbell Collaboration, 2014).

———, Holtan, A. and Batchelder, K. E., 'Systematic Review of Kinship Care Effects on Safety, Permanency, and Well-Being Outcomes', *Research on Social Work Practice*, 28/1 (2015), 19–32.

Wu, Q., White, K. R. and Coleman, K. L., 'Effects of Kinship Care on Behavioral Problems By Child Age: A Propensity Score Analysis', *Children and Youth Services Review*, 57 (2015), 1–8.

5 | Promoting the education of children in care

Reflections of children and carers who have experienced 'success'

Paul Rees and Amy Munro

Introduction

THE EDUCATIONAL PERFORMANCE of children in care has been a cause of concern for decades (see Mannay et al., 2015). Much energy has gone into highlighting this concern and in calling for improvement (Welsh Government, 2016). However, there has been far less focus on the identification of educational 'success' and how it can be secured. Drawing on a large study of the characteristics, experience and views of children in care in Wales (see Rees, 2013), this chapter considers how 'success' can be defined and promoted. Encouragingly, our research demonstrates that educational achievement can be secured for children in care. We argue, however, that educational 'success' is inextricably linked to all other aspects of a child's life and experience including contact with birth relatives, relationship with carers, peer group friendships and the extent to which they genuinely understand why they are in care. For success to be achieved there needs to be an understanding of the whole child and a holistic approach to meeting their needs. Consequently, it is unlikely that any single agency will be able to offer independently all that a child in care needs and, therefore, effective interagency collaboration is essential.

Defining 'success'

The answer to the question *'What constitutes success for children?'* varies depending on who is asked. Within literature the views of children, parents/carers, educators, social workers and policy makers differ. Statements such as 'they are happy' or 'fulfil their potential' are common, but generally nebulous. In the absence of an agreed definition, evaluating whether 'success' is being secured is fraught with difficulty. The United Kingdom (UK) articulated its aims for children, as demonstrated in the five *Every Child Matters* 'outcomes'. Similarly, underpinned by the United Nations Convention on the Rights of the Child, the Welsh Government (2004) has penned seven core 'aims' which form the heart of its *Rights to Action* agenda. These aims now inform all new legislation and provide the framework for the State's inspection regime. The Welsh Government's education and training inspectorate, for example, now routinely reports on how well individual schools promote children's well-being.

Defining 'success' for children in care is especially complex and can appear as an 'elusive notion' (Pithouse and Rees, 2014, p. 19). From the State's perspective, setting aspirational targets for educational attainment is logical, but may lead to other meaningful performance at the individual level being overlooked and undervalued. However, for children in care and those around them, some of the more subtle measures of performance are what matter most. For example, Coulling (2000) explored 'success in education' with children in care and a range of practitioners, concluding that 'engagement in education', 'positive socialisation' and the 'reaching of potential' (the child's ability to do his or her best) were viewed as 'success' rather than examination performance.

Data on the educational performance of children in care has many shortcomings with 'weaknesses ... and ... gaps in data' reported (Thomas, 2012, p. 4; see also Allnatt, 2019 [Chapter 6 this volume]). Similarly, a review of interventions aimed at improving educational outcomes for children in care in Wales concluded 'the existing evidence-base for educational interventions is generally weak' (Mannay et al., 2015, p. 113; see also Rees et al., 2019 [Chapter 3 this volume]). The most commonly cited data on the education of the care population are General Certificate of Secondary Education (GCSE) examination grades, but this provides an incomplete picture as many children leave care before they take the examinations. The ability of GCSE data to provide insight into educational 'success' is also questionable as they reflect 'attainment' (mastery at a given level) rather than 'achievement' (the extent to which performance matches capability). The generally low attainment of children in care has been associated with pre-care experiences, disrupted schooling and the low socio-economic status of birth families (Forrester et al., 2009; Berridge, 2007; Rees and Holding, 2014). To gain an understanding of achievement, not just attainment, robust data is required on children's biological, social and educational history.

The phenomenon of 'resilience' in the face of adversity (Luthar et al., 2000; Rees and Bailey, 2003) has given rise to hope that it may have an impact on the educational context for children in care. Lambert (2001), for example, advocates that attention be paid to relationships with family members, social networks, leisure activities, and secure attachments. Some have argued for the primacy of certain factors in developing resilience, such as the child's attachment to the caregiver, but few empirical studies on the educational resilience of children in care have been undertaken (Flynn et al., 2004).

In the context of differing perspectives on what constitutes 'success' for children in care, the limited utility of group level attainment data and the absence of an agreed framework for softer outcome measures, exploration of the views of children and their carers on 'success' is warranted. Accordingly, this chapter describes the findings of a qualitative follow-up to a quantitative study that had identified 'success' in a group of children and their carers. These children considered themselves to be doing well educationally, socially, emotionally and behaviourally. Their carers and teachers shared their views. The children were attending school regularly and achieving at the expected level, relative to cognitive ability. Our aims were to ascertain the children's and carers' views on:

- What (in general) constitutes 'success' for children in care?
- What (in general) promotes 'success' in the lives of children in care?
- What led to 'success' for them?
- What advice they might offer teachers?

Additionally, we were keen to consider the characteristics and practices of the children and carers, with a view to identifying commonalities.

Methods

This study followed on from research involving all children in care aged seven to 15 years of age in one local authority in Wales (n = 193). Children were all assessed on measures of mental health, cognitive ability, emotional literacy, socialisation and educational functioning (see Rees, 2013). Their carers and teachers also completed relevant versions of the measures on the functioning of the children. A range of other data was also collated: for example, legal status and school attendance rate. Children were considered to have met the 'success' criteria if all of their ratings on the measures fell within the average range (or above), their literacy scores were close to their predicted scores (reflecting achievement rather than attainment) and their school attendance was ≥85 per cent. In short, all available data indicated that the children were doing well. A check was also made with social workers and the current status of the care placement considered.

All of the 'success' criteria were met by 30 children. It was not possible to proceed to interview in all cases as, for example, some children had left care or were experiencing ill health. A total of 17 children and 14 carers (three carers had sibling pairs) agreed to participate and were interviewed separately. The average length of time from assessment to interview was 13 months.

The mean age of the interviewed children was 11 years (range eight to 15). Nine were male. The average length of time in their current placement was three years two months (n = $16 \geq 12$ months); and all of the children were in foster care, two in formal kinship foster care. All children attended mainstream school and two were the subject of a statement of special educational needs. Sixteen had regular contact with a birth parent(s), one had voluntarily withdrawn. The average length of time the carers had acted as foster carers was nine years and the average number of children cared for over that time was 11. The highest educational qualification held by any carer was Level 3 (A Level). Six had no academic qualifications.

Semi-structured interview inventories were constructed for use with the children and carers. A pilot study revealed that when children are asked '*What do you think success for a child is?*' a common response is '*they are happy*'. A projective technique was therefore designed and piloted with a view to exploring what '*happy*' means from the child's perspective. An artist was commissioned to draw a gender neutral image of the face of an imaginary child in a 'happy' state and a second picture of same child with a 'sad' expression. The images enabled scope for gender specific projection while optimising consistency of stimuli. At the appropriate point, each child was presented with the first image, informed that the picture represented an imaginary child and asked to confirm the emotion. They were then asked to imagine that the child was 'in care' and to suggest reasons why they might be 'happy'. The same process was then followed with the second image. Responses were recorded by hand, collated and thematic analysis undertaken (Braun and Clarke, 2006).

Summary of responses

The themes are referred to in order of frequency of occurrence, the most common first. When asked the question '*What is "success" for a child in care?*' children often discussed positive personal affect; happiness; positive caring relationships with carers and carers' family; achievement in school; ambitions; friendships with peers; and having a secure/stable/caring home. Other responses, although less frequent, included successfully managing behaviour; developing character; acceptance (of the past and reasons for being in care); open relationships; ability to concentrate; and hobbies/interests.

As anticipated, most of the children used a form of the word 'happy' in their initial response and the projective technique was administered. Resonating with constructions of 'success', the image of the happy child was associated with ongoing birth-family contact; open, warm and respectful relationships with carers and the carers' family; and positive friendships with peers. Children also suggested that the happiness of the pictured child could be due to them having someone to talk to, a pleasant care environment, an understanding why he or she is in care, needs met (clothing and food), hobbies and interests, and a willingness to share problems.

The image of the sad child was linked to limited or no contact with birth family; having no friends; not getting on with their foster family; being bullied; and not understanding why they are in care. Other responses were related to issues of safety; wanting to live with their 'real' family; a lack of basic resources; having a sibling still at home or adopted by another family; nobody listening to their concerns; not doing well in school; feeling that being in care is no better than being at home; birth-family bereavement; and adverse ('bad') early experiences.

Carers defined 'success' for children in care in relation to happiness and emotional stability; positive well-being; feeling loved; good social awareness and social skills; friendships and social acceptance; positive behaviour, acceptance of rules, trustworthiness; engagement in/doing well in school; good communication skills (especially around emotions); a sense of belonging; independent thinking; responsibility; and confidence. Carers also saw the child's acceptance by the foster family, ongoing contact and the child engaging in hobbies as indicators of success.

Factors both the children and their carers thought had promoted 'success' in their case included foster carers; school/teachers; personal motivation; peer group friendships; birth family; hobbies and interests; willingness to share problems; and support from a project worker. Foster carers placed particular value on the provision of love and care; moral guidance; praise; behaviour management; advocacy; household routines and holidays. They felt that it was important that carers were empathic, good listeners, patient, encouraging, persevering, protective and understanding; and encouraged open communication as well as trust. Factors including joint placement of siblings; educational/teacher support; good 'matching' by social worker; carer and child spending leisure time together; children finding something they are good at; and intense carer input during first three months of placement, were also positioned as advantageous.

Teachers were also cited as a source of support by children if they could: listen; assist in the communication between the child and their carer; protect them from bullying; help with their learning, explain schoolwork in a meaningful way; provide a fun, interesting and rewarding learning environment; help them to focus, concentrate and achieve; provide ideas on possible careers; and give advice on healthy living.

Discussion

As all the children were in foster care it may be tempting to cite this in support of foster care rather than other placement types, but caution is necessary as the majority (74 per cent) of the original sample were also in foster care. Nevertheless, it is reasonable to argue that foster care can provide fertile ground for 'success'. In keeping with previous research findings, the carers' educational qualifications were limited (see Department for Business, Innovation and Skills, 2012). However, this had not prevented the children from achieving in school, but it is possible that as the children draw close to end of school examinations and the academic demands of the curriculum intensify, further challenges may arise. In contrast to academic qualifications, the foster carers had considerable fostering experience, supporting the view that carer experience is an important ingredient for 'success'.

Children positioned positive affect as an authentic hallmark of 'success'. As difficult as it may be to evaluate 'happiness', it is what the children value. Accordingly, evaluative frameworks that pay little attention to children's happiness have limited validity. The projective technique proved helpful in unravelling how 'happiness' is defined by the children and generated many more comments regarding birth-family contact than the more general question, *'What is "success" for a child in care?'* It is also significant that when asked, *'Who are the most important people in your life at this moment?'* the first response of most of the children (n = 13) was a birth parent or close birth relative. Although birth-family contact is controversial, the potential benefits of 'contact' are widely accepted (Biehal, 2007; Winter and Cohen, 2005).

The finding that 26 of the 30 children met the 'success' criteria and all but one who took part in the interviews were having regular contact supports this view. The children's views will resonate with practitioners who know how extensively contact can impact on all aspects of the child's life including education (Moyers et al., 2006). The children gave examples of how contact influences their emotions even in the school setting, but suggested this is not an insurmountable problem as they can successfully manage the impact. It is also important to note, however, that contact is not always a prerequisite to 'success'. A small minority of children declined contact. The children's responses do suggest, though, that consideration of the frequency and quality of contact is critical.

The children also see a positive, caring and stable relationship with their carer as vital for their 'happiness'. This critical relationship will be discussed more fully as the children's comments on the role that carers have played in promoting their 'success' are considered. A salient point at this juncture, however, is that the children view the quality of the relationships they have with others, especially their carers and their carers' family as major determinants of happiness. For these children, happiness is not the product of one relationship within the home or school, but appears to be the composite of them all. This is mirrored in the findings of Pithouse and Rees (2014).

Some children felt that having a true understanding of why care is necessary is vital for emotional well-being, and limited understanding deleterious. They saw a profound difference between head knowledge, acquired by having been told why alternative care is necessary, and a genuine understanding. We came to see that what characterised these children was the latter. Moreover, they were no longer striving for reunification in the short term. Most appeared to harbour this hope for the longer term, but had reached psychological equilibrium regarding their current care plan. For many, regular birth-family contact, strong relationships with carers, peer group friendships, school life and an understanding of why they were in care was maintaining this equilibrium.

The responses offered by carers largely mirror what might be expected from loving parents. They spoke passionately and at length, which we read as highly significant: they had spent much time reflecting on the issue. They view 'success' as emotional stability in all relationships and settings. The fact that education did not always feature explicitly in the carers' responses does not imply, therefore, that it is unimportant in their eyes. Instead, the carers spoke more often about successfully equipping children for the future and the importance of transferable life-skills. It may be that they see emotional security as a prerequisite for educational achievement.

While the children had associated birth-family contact with 'happiness', the majority attributed their own 'success' to their carers. This may be partially explained by the way these carers, without exception, viewed their role in relation to the birth family. They expressed an acceptance of the importance of the birth family in the eyes of the child, even when they felt frustrated by the birth family's actions. Many of the carers spoke of a conscious decision to "never speak ill" of the child's birth family. By respecting the importance of the birth family, the carers seemed to have gained the trust of the children. Alongside a non-judgemental attitude, these carers had a well-formed view of what the children wanted from them: a place of happiness, love, care, sense of belonging, empathy, understanding, patience, perseverance, advocacy, protection, clear routines and boundaries. The fact that all but one of the children reported being 'happy' or 'very happy' in their care placement (and the remaining child 'okay') strongly suggests that these carers not only understood but delivered what the children wanted from them.

Many of the children identified school as having played a major part in their 'success'. Thirteen described themselves as happy or very happy in school, while the rest said they felt okay. They appeared to particularly value school staff who are *'there for me to talk to'* and *'patient'*, a point that has been observed in other research (see Mannay et al., 2017). Several spoke of how certain curriculum subjects had inspired them. School life was seen by many as highly important as it allowed them to socialise without having to share all of the details of their care situation. School friends with whom they could *'laugh'*, *'have fun'* and *'have a hug from'* helped them cope with stress.

Education did not feature extensively in the first response of carers. Similarly, when asked to indicate the frequency with which they spoke with school staff, more than half said 'once a month or less' and four 'rarely'. Less than half knew the name of the designated teacher [1] for children in care. Despite these potentially concerning findings, exploration of their practices revealed that they had considerable involvement in the children's schooling. While, for example, few could name the designated teacher all could name at least one member of school staff they could speak to if an issue arose. Most stressed that effective dialogue happened when needed, rather than at reviews.

All the children were over seven years of age, but several carers still read with them regularly. Most carers actively helped the children with homework and drew on their own family network if they lacked knowledge or confidence. The majority also diligently attended parents' evenings and all other school events. Only one carer never attended, but explained that there was an understanding that, as a way of optimising their involvement, a birth-family member would attend instead. Most carers had expended much thought, effort and money on arranging their home to ensure that the child had a quiet place to work. All but two children had a desk of their own and ready access to at least one room designated for quiet study. The remaining two children made use of the kitchen and living room at agreed times. Despite the additional time commitments and cost all carers encouraged extra-curricular activities.

Comments made by carers in response to *'What promotes success for children in care?'* revealed a common belief in the importance of education as reflected in statements such as *'encourage them to do well in school'*. The carers were not only encouraging the children to recognise the value of education, but supporting them in practical ways: they were investing heavily in the children's education. Interestingly, The Fostering Network (2014) has presented research evidence on the intrinsic motivation and values of foster carers, and have called for greater emphasis on the recruitment of what they refer to as 'pioneering carers' whose principal motivation appears to match the carers interviewed in this study: 'doing the right thing' and contributing to the improvement of society.

Carers are often the people children in care turn to when they want to be heard, but there may be occasions when a child feels unable to speak with their carer. The children said they want teachers to listen to them on a wide range of issues and, at times, act as confidants. While teachers are well aware of their obligations to promote the well-being of children, some might still be hesitant in involving themselves in discussion on care-related matters. Yet, the message from these children is that they want teachers to work with them on their relationships with carers outside school. Given that each school year, children spend around 25 per cent of their waking hours in school it is understandable that they see teachers as more than academic tutors. It is also possible that the turnover of social workers encourages children to look elsewhere for continuity of support: an audit by the Care Council for Wales in 2014 revealed that only 57 per cent of social workers in Wales had been in their current post for at least three years (CCW, 2014). Children also see teachers as protectors, primarily from bullying. The frequency with which children mentioned bullying suggests that it is a genuine concern for them. Whether they feel more susceptible to bullying than children who are not in care is unclear, but the fear is real and teachers need to be cognisant of this.

The breadth of roles that the children feel teachers can fulfil is broad and highlights the need for schools to tailor their support to the needs of each child. It is also important not to lose sight of the fact that the children also want teachers to focus on helping them to learn (Mannay et al., 2015). Listening to children talk about their care placements and relationships outside school should not be at the expense of learning. Interestingly, a number of the children spoke about the nature of the learning environment that children in care benefit from. This was typically described as an ordered, safe, studious, fun and friendly place. Such observations are likely to resonate with the views of their peers, but it must be remembered that these children may also be using the school environment as a setting in which they can temporarily detach, psychologically as well as physically, from reminders of previous abuse and/or neglect. School may for some children be one of the few places they can experience a degree of normality (Davey and Pithouse, 2008). Providing a place in which children can learn in an enjoyable and psychologically relaxed way is all the more important for children who have experienced trauma and abuse (Bombèr, 2007).

Resilience research has shown that having aspirations for the future is associated with positive outcomes (Rees and Bailey, 2003). It is significant, therefore, that the children had remarkably well-formed ideas on future careers (see also Mannay et al., 2015). Many identified aspiring to work in the helping professions such as social work, psychology, teaching and the police. Whether the seeds of interest in these goals were planted by their experience or carers and/or teachers is uncertain. The finding is a reminder, though, that all those working alongside children, especially teachers, need to actively promote longer term aspirations (see also Taussig et al., 2007).

Conclusion

The interviews confirmed how difficult it is to define 'success' for children in care, but, paradoxically, many of the messages converge: 'success' for children can and must be viewed holistically. The child's emotional state lies at the heart of what they and their carers consider 'success' to be and that is dependent on what is happening in all spheres of their life. From the child's perspective, therefore, a discrete term such as 'educational success' is something of a misnomer.

While the study design did not allow for robust quantitative analysis, the frequency with which some themes arose emphasises their importance. These include birth-family contact, the quality of the relationship with the carer and peer group friendships. Any attempt to improve the educational outcomes of children in care without also attending to these issues is unlikely to succeed. Conversely, to disregard the central importance of education may have a damaging effect on other domains: for example, frustration in the learning environment and disengagement from school can be the catalyst for placement breakdown. Therefore, it is important to stress that by identifying these factors we are not implying that other factors are unimportant.

An acceptance that 'success' for children in care can only be achieved through a holistic understanding of their needs leads to the conclusion that those who live and work alongside them must share a common language and understanding. No individual will possess all of the knowledge, skills and resources that are necessary to meet a child's needs. Many steps have been taken to break down professional boundaries that exist which have previously inhibited joint working, but more work is needed. Additionally, the high level of insight that these carers had of the children's emotions, especially around birth family, was significant. It is through experience that the carers had developed a respectful approach and thoughtful scripts to assist in their conversations about birth families.

Despite possessing few academic qualifications the carers had sought to convey to the children how important they viewed education to be. They were actively supporting the children's education, often sacrificially. When they lacked the requisite knowledge or resource they problem-solved, creatively marshalling the necessary support. In many ways, this models the way forward for all those who are charged with meeting the multifaceted needs of children in care.

Acknowledgements

We wish to thank all of the children and carers who took part. Our thanks are also due to the Local Health Board for funding this work.

Note

1. Section 20 of the Children and Young Persons Act 2008 requires all maintained schools to designate a lead person (DLP) as having responsibility for promoting the educational achievement of all looked after pupils who are registered at the school. The title used by DLPs varies from school to school, but they are often referred to as the 'designated teacher for looked after children'. The Welsh Government has recently issued guidance on the role of the DLP (see Welsh Government, 2017).

References

Allnatt, G., 'Transitions from care to higher education: A case study of a young person's journey', in D. Mannay, A. Rees and L. Roberts (eds), *Children and Young People 'Looked After'? Education, Intervention and the Everyday Culture of Care in Wales* (Cardiff: University of Wales Press, 2019), pp. 69–82.

Berridge, D., 'Theory and Explanation in Education: Education and Looked After Children', *Child and Family Social Work*, 12 (2007), 1–10.

Biehal, N., 'Reuniting Children with their Families: Reconsidering the Evidence on Timing, Contact and Outcomes', *British Journal of Social Work*, 37 (2007), 807–23.

Bombèr, L. M., *Inside I'm Hurting: Practical Strategies for Supporting Children with Attachment Difficulties in Schools* (London: Worth Publishing, 2007).

Braun, V. and Clarke, V., 'Using Thematic Analysis in Psychology', *Qualitative Research in Psychology*, 3 (2006), 77–101.

Care Council for Wales, *The Profile of Social Workers in Wales: Report from the Care Council for Wales Register of Social Care Workers June 2014* (Cardiff: Care Council for Wales, 2014). Available at *https://socialcare.wales/cms_assets/file-uploads/The-Profile-of-Social-Workers-in-Wales-2014.pdf* (accessed 14/03/18).

Coulling, N., 'Definitions of Successful Education for the "Looked After" Child: A Multi-agency Perspective', *Support for Learning*, 15 (2000), 30–5.

Davey, D. and Pithouse, A., 'Schooling and looked after children. Exploring Contexts and Outcomes in Standard Attainment Tests (SATS)', *Adoption and Fostering*, 32 (2008), 60–72.

Department for Business, Innovation and Skills, *Post-16 education & skills: Learner participation, outcomes and level of highest qualification held. Quarterly First Statistical Release* (2012). Available at: *www.thedataservice.org.uk/NR/rdonlyres/BF0E331FAF8F-437F-838F-5A0313CC81F7/0/SFR_Commentary_March2012.pdf* (accessed 02/02/18).

Flynn, R. J., Ghazal, H., Legault, L., Vandermeulen, G. and Petrick, S., 'Use of Population Measures and Norms to Identify Resilient Outcomes in Young People in Care: An Exploratory Study', *Child and Family Social Work*, 9 (2004), 65–79.

Forrester, D., Goodman, K., Cocker, C., Binnie, C. and Jensch, G., 'What is the Impact of Public Care on Children's Welfare? A Review of Research Findings from England and Wales and their Policy Implications', *Journal of Social Policy*, 38 (2009), 439–56.

Fostering Network, The, *Fostering in Wales: Who Cares and Why?* (Cardiff: The Fostering Network, 2014).

Lambert, C., *Promoting Resilience in 'Looked After' Children* (Norwich: University of East Anglia, Social Work Monographs, 2001).

Luthar, S. S., Cicchetti, D. and Becker, B., 'The Construct of Resilience: A Critical Evaluation and Guidelines for Future Work', *Child Development*, 71 (2000), 543–62.

Mannay, D., Staples, E., Hallett, S., Roberts, L., Rees, A., Evans, R. E. and Andrews, D., *Understanding the Educational Experiences and Opinions, Attainment, Achievement and Aspirations of Looked After Children in Wales* (Cardiff: Welsh Government, 2015).

———, Evans, R., Staples, E., Hallett, S., Roberts, L., Rees, A. and Andrews, D., 'The Consequences of Being Labelled "Looked-After": Exploring the Educational Experiences of Looked-After Children and Young People in Wales', *British Educational Research Journal*, 43 (2017), 683–99.

Moyers, S., Farmer, E. and Lipscombe, J., 'Contact with Family Members and its Impact on Adolescents and Their Foster Placements', *British Journal of Social Work*, 36 (2006), 541–59.

Pithouse, A. and Rees, A., *Creating Stable Foster Placements: Learning from Foster Children and the Families Who Care for Them* (London: Jessica Kingsley Publishers, 2014).

Rees, G., Brown, R., Smith, P. and Evans, R., 'Educational interventions for children and young people in care: A review of outcomes, implementation and acceptability', in D. Mannay, A. Rees and L. Roberts (eds), *Children and Young People 'Looked After'? Education, Intervention and the Everyday Culture of Care in Wales* (Cardiff: University of Wales Press, 2019), pp. 29–42.

Rees, P., 'The Mental Health, Emotional Literacy, Cognitive Ability, Academic Attainment and "Resilience" of "Looked After Children": A Multidimensional, Multiple-rater Population Based Study', *British Journal of Clinical Psychology*, 52 (2013), 183–98.

——— and Bailey, K., 'Positive Exceptions: Learning from Students Who Beat the Odds', *Educational and Child Psychology*, 20, (2003), 41–59.

——— and Holding, M., 'The health literacy of children who are "looked after" by the state', in R. Moore and D. Perry (eds), *Health Literacy: Developments, Issues and Outcomes* (New York: Nova Science Publishers, 2014), pp.189–200.

Taussig, H. N., Culhane, S. E. and Hettleman, D., 'Fostering Healthy Futures: An Innovative Preventive Intervention for Preadolescent Youth in Out-of-home Care', *Child Welfare*, 86 (2007), 113.

Thomas, H. V., *The Educational Attainment of Looked After Children and Young People* (Cardiff: Wales Audit Office, 2012).

Welsh Government, *Raising the Ambitions and Educational Attainment of Children Who Are Looked After in Wales* (Cardiff: Welsh Government, 2016).

———, *Making a Difference: A Guide for the Designated Person for Looked After Children in Schools. Guidance Document no: 255/2017* (Cardiff: Welsh Government, 2017).

Winter, K. and Cohen, O., 'Identity Issues for Looked After Children With No Knowledge of their Origins: Implications for Research and Practice', *Adoption and Fostering*, 29 (2005) 44–52.

6 | Transitions from care to higher education

A case study of a young person's journey

Gemma Allnatt

Introduction

INDIVIDUALS WHO HAVE been brought up in care often have greater health and housing needs and are more likely to come into contact with the criminal justice system in adulthood (Schofield et al., 2012); and it is argued that a substantial proportion of care leavers do not achieve the necessary levels of educational attainment to secure stability, safety, and independence (Welsh Government, 2016). There is significant research exploring the challenges associated with the educational achievements of children and young people in care (Berridge, 2012; O'Higgins et al., 2015); and attendance at university can be one way of protecting against the effects of social exclusion and enabling upward social mobility (Jackson and Cameron, 2014).

As Cameron et al. (2012, p. 387) contend, 'educational participation is positioned by policy makers across Europe as a key route to social inclusion through the acquisition of knowledge and skills that enable employment'. Yet, going to university from care is relatively rare compared to the general uptake in young adults (Jackson and Cameron, 2012). Consequently, there is an emerging interest from researchers and policy makers nationally and internationally to identify the factors that help or hinder higher education success for care-experienced young people (Jackson and Cameron, 2014; Mendes et al., 2014).

Research carried out by Mannay et al. (2015) demonstrated that despite entrenched negative stereotypes associated with the academic abilities of young people in care, most aspired to succeed in education, articulating career ambitions where degrees were a requirement. A disparity between care leavers and their peers in the UK has been noted in earlier publications. For example, the Office for Fair Access (OFFA, 2017) suggested in 2012 only six per cent of care leavers entered university compared to 60 per cent of the general population. However, despite high aspirations in Wales it is estimated that only 220[1] Welsh domiciled students defined as care leavers enrolled on a higher education course in 2015/16 (Higher Education Funding Council for Wales, 2017). This figure represents just 0.7 per cent of the total Welsh domiciled new entrants in 2015/16. In an increasingly competitive job market, where more roles require degree level qualifications (Jackson and Cameron, 2012), it remains a concern that so few care leavers enter university.

It is worth noting here that caution should be applied to the reliability of these statistics, as the Welsh Government does not routinely collect the numbers of young people leaving care and in higher education. Similarly, approximately seven per cent of young people do not keep in touch with local authorities once they have left care and may not be included in official figures (Welsh Government, 2016a). Furthermore, young people in the care of a local authority in Wales sometimes choose to attend a university outside Wales. Official figures will also not capture those who leave care and return to higher education in adulthood. Nonetheless, the pervasive gaps in higher educational attainment between looked after populations and their peers warrants further attention and this chapter will be concerned with exploring the challenges that young people face when moving from the care system to university study in Wales.

Research context

Focusing on the UK, Jackson (1987) argued that care-experienced children and young people are being failed by both the care and the education system. Her research demonstrated how those in care were over represented in school exclusions and very few were obtaining the General Certificate of Secondary Education (GCSE) qualifications necessary to continue in education. At this time, the educational achievement of those in care was not a priority for either social services or education authorities. As Cameron et al. (2015, p. 26) note, when:

the Children Act 1989 came into force there was little interest in the education of children in care. Britain was still a very class-based society and concern for education was mainly a characteristic of middle class parents.

Since then a number of changes have been implemented to support and encourage academic success, with the introduction of Looked After Children Education (LACE) teams, school based social workers and dedicated safeguarding staff in schools (Cameron et al., 2015). Additionally, the higher education application process now allows applicants to identify themselves as a care leaver, which triggers student support services to provide advice and assistance before and during the application and transitioning process (Jackson et al., 2005).

Accordingly, it is now accepted that those in care are an extremely vulnerable group, requiring a significant amount of support to ensure they have healthy and prosperous futures (Jackson and Höjer, 2013). Furthermore, failures to address the needs of young people in care are costly for both the individual and the state (Johnson and Mendes, 2014). Consequently, policy makers have recognised that education, and in particular involvement in further and higher education, plays an important role in facilitating young people's well-being. This includes improving career prospects, earnings, physical and mental health, access to and participation in broader social and community relationships (Mendes et al., 2014).

However, an interest in exploring the success stories of those leaving care and achieving high levels of academic achievement, has been juxtaposed with mainly negative attitudes and perceptions that young people in care cannot, and will not, succeed academically (Harker et al., 2003). For example, Berridge (2007), recognised that the conceptualisation of the educational underachievement of children looked after was unhelpful, confusing and simplistic. The notion of underachievement failed to take into account the unique characteristics of being looked after because comparisons were made with general school populations. Similarly, blame for low attainment in care is often directed at the care system; however, there are a number of factors such as socio-economic status, family background and early childhood adversities that can impact on educational attainment (Forrester, 2008). Indeed, recent research has suggested that the care system is not inherently bad and actually those who enter care can do better than those brought up at home but in difficult circumstances (O'Higgens et al., 2015).

Two key studies have explicitly focused on higher education and the experiences of care leavers, By Degree's (2005) and the Young People from a care background: pathways to education in Europe (YIPPEE) project (2014). By Degree's followed three successive cohorts of 50 young people with offers of places at UK universities. They found that young people from care who go to university and complete their studies had post care trajectories which 'were much more favourable than those recorded for the vast majority of care leavers' (Jackson and Cameron, 2014, p. 12).

The major cross-national project YIPPEE explored the education of young people in care beyond the legal age of school attendance. The collaboration between the UK, Denmark, Hungary, Spain and Sweden explored the differences and commonalities in the welfare regimes and their response to ensuring those in care in all European states are included in further and higher education to a much greater extent. They concluded that:

> Childhood adversity need not rule out educational success. Far more young people in care than previously thought have the ability to develop a strong learning identity and access tertiary education if we can give them the opportunity to do so and remove some of the many barriers that present and stand in their way (Jackson and Cameron, 2014, p. 263.)

As discussed in the following section, policy and legislation are key mechanisms to remove barriers and create opportunities for care-experienced young people.

Policy and legislation

The Children Act 1989 was a landmark piece of legislation covering all aspects of social care for children, demonstrating a commitment on the part of the state to improving the outcomes for young people. The Act led to significant improvements in social work and educational practice aiming to address and improve the educational attainment of children and young people in care (Cameron et al., 2015). Subsequent legislation, including the Children (Leaving Care) Act 2000, Adoption and Children Act 2002, Children Act 2004, Children and Young Persons Act 2008, Children and Families Act (2014), have placed a myriad of duties and requirements on local authorities to address the significant attainment gap (Mannay et al., 2017). One of the main principles underpinning all these statutes is that the educational experience and attainment of children in care should be 'as close as possible to that of children growing up in their own families' (Cameron et al., 2015, p. 26).

Legislation such as the Children Leaving Care Act 2000 (CLCA) acknowledges the unique difficulties those leaving care experience, which limit their opportunities to continue in education past the age of 16. For example, Stein (2006a) maintains that care leavers are negotiating transitions to adulthood and the responsibilities associated with adulthood at a younger age than most, often with little support. The CLCA aimed to address this accelerated independence by placing a duty on local authorities to provide financial, housing and emotional support to those leaving care, as well as a duty to provide financial security and vacation accommodation for those wishing to progress to university up until their 25th birthday. This was a significant development for those wishing to pursue an academic journey (Jackson, 2010).

To further embed the notion of education as a priority for social services, the Children Act 2004 placed a duty on local authorities to promote the educational achievement of those in care. This addressed some of the concerns outlined in earlier research (Jackson, 1987), suggesting that authorities worked in isolation of each other preventing 'joined up working'. The role of the Director of Children's Services was created to oversee the education and social service function of local authorities to bridge this divide; and attend to emotional and physical well-being, and educational achievement, simultaneously (Harris, 2004).

In the Welsh landscape, there has been a policy and legislative commitment to promote and support the educational achievement of those in care in Wales (Welsh Government, 2016b). The Welsh Government has used the powers devolved to Wales to implement policy that promotes the interests of those in care in Wales. For example, 'Towards a Stable Life and Brighter Future' (2007) set out guidance on strengthening educational arrangements, which include the designation of LACE coordinators to oversee education plans and most importantly bridge the gap between education and social services.

The Social Services and Well-being (Wales) Act 2014 underpins the delivery of improved outcomes for children and their families. This required local authorities to have special regard to the education and training needs of children in care, particularly when making decisions about placements. More recently, the strategy document *Raising the Ambitions and Educational Attainment of Children Who Are Looked After in Wales* (2016b) has demonstrated a further commitment to improving educational attainment of care-experienced children and young people.

Another important step towards addressing some of the issues facing those leaving care and improving the numbers of young people remaining in education post-16 is the introduction of 'When I'm Ready' (Welsh Government, 2016a). The scheme was set up by Welsh Government in 2015 and made legal by the Social Services and Well-being (Wales) Act under post 18 living arrangements. 'When I'm Ready' allows for young people to stay in their foster placements beyond the age of 18 and up until the age of 25 if they are involved in a programme of education or training [2]. Arrangements are organised and planned from the age of 16 in accordance with the Pathway Plan, which sets out the details of support required to ensure smooth transitions from care to adulthood including the support required to choose, apply and enter university. However, despite these positive developments in policy and legislation, it remains important to explore the factors that help or hinder the transition to university from care; to not only shed light on the topic but give a voice to those who have been in state care and are often overlooked in educational contexts. The following section discusses the individual experience of a care leaver in higher education.

Alice – the journey

The findings discussed here were drawn from a doctoral study, which considered how support from social services and universities helps those in care to complete their university studies. The study worked with young people (n = 21), exploring their views, experiences and opinions of their journey through the care system and to university. While all of the participants presented unique narratives, there were commonalities that are typically found in the care population; all had suffered traumatic events in their childhood necessitating care of the local authority and they had all overcome significant hurdles to get to university and succeed, often against a backdrop of continuing chaos and turmoil in personal circumstances.

This section will discuss one participant's account, and focus on the themes of placement stability, determination, motivation and stigma, as a framework to understand how care leavers negotiate their care status within transitions to higher education. A 19-year-old young woman, referred to by the pseudonym Alice, was at the beginning of her first year of university at the time of the research. Alice was studying at a Welsh university that had received the Buttle Trust Quality mark because of its excellent work in supporting care leavers (Buttle UK, 2015). Alice had lived with her foster carers for four years, in a rural part of Wales. Before this placement, Alice and her sister had lived in four other settings, as well as having experienced an unsuccessful return to her birth father. Alice and her sister were then placed successfully with long-term foster carers Mary and Jim. Alice spoke of many happy occasions with Mary and Jim, including family holidays. However, before leaving for university the relationship between Alice and Mary had become strained, which impacted on her transition and her ability to plan for the future.

Placement stability: The role of foster care and support services

It is widely acknowledged that fostering can be a preferable option, for replicating a stable family environment (Schofield and Beek, 2005). However, children and young people can be moved a significant number of times during their care career, often to the detriment of overall well-being including the negative impact on educational welfare (Ward et al., 2005). Most young people in the UK will move three times on average during their childhood and adolescence; but, those in care can experience this number of moves in just one year (Ward, 2009). Alice had five placement moves through her care career, and although the most frequent placement moves were in her early years of primary school age, she reflected on these moves during the interview, explaining how each of these moves disrupted her education:

Alice: I don't think I actually finished a whole year in
primary school . . . I liked school a lot . . . I was just sick of
moving around.

Achieving permanency for children and young people is rare in part
because of the principles enshrined in law and children's rights that
children should be brought up in their birth families as far as possible
(Schofield et al., 2012). Most children will return home when it is deemed
appropriate and safe to do so. However, Ward (2009, p. 1117) notes that
when there are concerns, social workers and courts struggle to 'acknowledge that some parents will not be able to overcome their difficulties sufficiently to resume care of their children within a realistic timescale' and
returning home prematurely can often be more harmful.

Although Alice did find a permanent and stable placement in her
later teenage years, her childhood and early teenage years were transient,
involving movement between temporary and emergency placements and
a brief return to her birth father. She reflected on the impact this return had
on her physical and emotional well-being:

Alice: I was living in an emergency placement on a farm
I loved it because they had loads of animals but then I had to
leave. I went to live with my dad for a while [but] ended up
having alopecia at eight years old because of stress, my dad's
girlfriend would shout at me and blame me for pulling it out
but it used to fall out in my hands.

For Cameron et al. (2015) the last placement before leaving care is the
most crucial for supporting continuing education; and leaving care is both
accelerated and compressed, making it difficult and sometimes impossible
to stay in education (Stein, 2006b). Alice's last foster placement was one
which she felt able to call home and achieved a sense of belonging (Biehal,
2014). She changed her surname by deed poll to reflect the foster family
name and recalled happy experiences as a family unit, including structure,
routine and educational support, which involved 'homework hour' every
day after school.

However, difficulties emerged in the placement when it came to transitioning to university. While she was the first person in her birth family
and foster family to go to university, she received little support in the transition to university, both physically and emotionally.

Alice: They say they are proud of me for going to university . . .
I told them two weeks before I was moving to uni. Mary and
Jim told me they couldn't afford the fuel to take me and my stuff

to halls. That was fine because I have my own car but it would have been nice to have a bit of support. Everyone's parents are coming down to say hello, to see if they have settled in, they [foster carers] haven't done anything.

There was also some confusion around her accommodation status for the holiday period, as the placement was not part of the 'When I'm Ready' scheme and plans had not been discussed during meetings with social services before the start of the academic year. There was also no discussion about the possibility of leaving some personal belongings at the placement or if she was able to return there at weekends. Similar to findings from other studies and wider evidence on leaving care, there is often ambiguity and uncertainty about financial and housing entitlements for those leaving care but remaining in education (Cotton et al., 2014).

Alice did not know where she would live during the Christmas holidays and was in discussion about the possibility of remaining in her student accommodation if necessary, a service offered by the university under the Buttle Quality Mark (Buttle UK, 2015). The availability of university accommodation out of term time has proved to be an essential safety net for many care-experienced young people, offering security and reassurance for those in situations where foster placements or contact with birth family is not an option.

Alice was also complimentary of the support she received from the university through a widening participation scheme. 'Summer University' provides an opportunity to experience university life before making a decision to accept an offer.

> Alice: There are taster lectures, you get given assignments to do and put it on Turnitin [3]. They teach you how to use Blackboard [4] and tell you about university life.

At the time of the interview, Alice did not know if her placement with her foster carers would remain 'open' for her to return on a formal or informal basis. This type of arrangement would ordinarily have been discussed as part of a Pathway Plan, but limited contact with social work staff had made it difficult to make concrete decisions before term commenced. This was a cause of unnecessary concern and upset during a time when she felt she should be enjoying and integrating into university life. Alice discussed how she struggled with managing big changes in her life and stated that her current situation was proving to be a significant adjustment:

> Alice: I don't like change ... and this is proving to be a big change.

These feelings resonate with the experience of many young people transitioning to university and leaving home for the first time, although for most young people they have strong family ties, which may counteract negative feelings. In contrast, those transitioning from care are often doing so on their own and are often solely reliant on university support services to offer emotional and physical support (Cotton et al., 2014).

Self-determination, motivation and challenging stigma

A comparative study of care leavers and young people who lived at home but received social work support found that those leaving care had:

> [a] surprising level of motivation to continue their education despite the fact that in doing so they face formidable obstacles and needed an exceptional degree of determination and self-reliance to succeed. (Cameron, 2013 in Jackson and Cameron, 2014, p. 13.)

Jackson and Ajayi (2007) maintain that one of the main driving forces in academic success is located in the individual motivations of a young person. The determination to prove to carers, birth family, teachers and social workers that they are academically capable can be motivational; for Alice, it was her foster carers who did not believe that she would get into university because of difficulties she experienced in college.

> **Alice:** Before they kicked me out I said I was interested in studying psychology at university and she [foster carer] said 'what do you know, you can't even pass your A levels'. I was like ok I'm going to prove you wrong. The next exam I got 56 out of 60, I told her and she was like 'I'm really proud'.

The determination to prove others wrong motivated Alice to pass the examinations necessary to apply for university. As Mannay et al. (2017) highlight, there is still a perception grounded in professional assumptions that being 'looked after' negates academic success. Such assumptions, while often triggering additional support for learning, have also been associated with 'pity and (sometimes false) sympathy' (Mannay et al., 2017, p. 14). While the intention is to support and recognise the individual learning needs of young people in care, it has been found that allowances given in education such as absences or exclusions from completing homework have downplayed the capabilities of young people to succeed academically. There is also the risk that this approach can limit the opportunities for young people to be academically challenged and realise aspirations. Alice found this to be the case when teachers put her forward for supported learning:

> Alice: I disagreed with them about my reading ability. I can read. I am not dim. I can read. I have a small library at home. I have been reading since I was a child.

The dominant discourse associated with those in care is one characterised by notions of 'trouble' and 'concern' (Mannay et al., 2017) and an identity that is synonymous with failure often burdens those leaving care, adding additional pressure to otherwise difficult transitions. Alice felt the weight of her care status in the first few weeks of university when her peers were receiving visits to halls of residence from parents:

> Alice: Everyone's parents are coming down to visit them. I have heard nothing from them [foster carers], or seen anything of them. Everyone in my halls has support from their families, I don't.

Similarly, when asked about the support she had received from her social worker to transition and settle in university she felt the stigma attached to her care identity even more profoundly:

> Alice: It's just going to be really awkward when he [social worker] comes to do his visit and I have to introduce him. Hello friends, this is my social worker. They will not know what to say and probably ask me questions that I don't want them to know about because I haven't talked about my past.

Support from social work staff was lacking in Alice's narrative, reflecting findings from earlier research (Jackson and Ajayi, 2007). For Alice, communicating with her social worker in the first few weeks of starting university was very difficult, which is a concern as the first few weeks are a critical stage in the settling and transitioning phase, where a great deal of support is required (Cotton et al., 2014). Alice wanted to meet with her social worker as she had been told by another care-experienced student that she could access additional financial support from the local authority. However, when she contacted the social services department she discovered that he had left his post and she would be allocated a new social worker.

Individual determination and motivation to succeed act as powerful enablers for young people transitioning from care to university (Cotton et al., 2014). Alice's circumstances show that despite limited support from foster family and social services, she effectively negotiated transitioning to university from care. Her motivation to succeed academically despite a lack of support from her foster family spurred her on to 'prove people wrong'.

Conclusion

Alice's account illustrates facilitators and barriers to academic success within state care. It is important to consider the subjective experiences of care-experienced young people in providing an informed evidence base that will drive policy and practice changes. For Cameron et al. (2015, p. 191), it is important that social workers 'take the long view' when making decisions about the welfare of a child, ensuring that going to university is a viable option for all and is openly discussed at the earliest opportunity. For university to be considered a normal part of the trajectory after leaving care, a number of issues still need to be resolved.

Of particular concern is the persistent problem with securing long-term placement stability, and challenging the negative perceptions and attitudes to the academic capabilities of those in care. Information and advice regarding university attendance for individuals from a care background is limited, ambiguous and does not explain the authorities' responsibilities clearly enough. Sharing ideas and practices amongst professionals will identify what works, such as 'summer school' programmes, which have proved to be beneficial for some. It should also be noted that those taking on the role of foster carers require specific and targeted training for the provision, support and encouragement of a young person's educational needs.

Alice's account of her care and educational experiences has highlighted that a number of areas of service and support need immediate improvement. Her determination to succeed in the face of adversity merely magnifies the fact that there are too few like her emerging from the care system and succeeding academically. For many, the barriers in accessing higher education, and indeed the risks associated in doing so, are just too great. This is unacceptable in a society where good quality employment calls for a good quality of education. Robust mechanisms and support from all stakeholders need to be in place and readily accessible to ensure that young people who are looked after are able to access and prosper in higher education because of, and not in spite of, the help that is available.

Acknowledgements

I would like to thank all the participants who took part in this doctoral study. Without their valuable contribution, this research would not have been possible. I also extend my gratitude to the All Wales Social Care Collaboration Academy (ASCCA) and Cardiff University for funding and sponsoring the project.

Notes

1. Please note that these figures are not routinely published by HEFCW and were obtained through personal correspondence with HEFCW. The field capturing this information generally includes a large number of unknowns, and therefore care should be taken when citing this figure. Also, due to the requirements of data control methodology this figure has been rounded to the nearest five (HEFCW, 2017).
2. The 'When I'm Ready' scheme has been criticised because unlike young people in foster care, young people are not able to stay in their residential care home past the age of 18 under the 'When I'm Ready' arrangement. For further information see Children's Commissioner for Wales (2017).
3. Turnitin is university software used to detect plagiarism.
4. Blackboard is a forum found on the student intranet in a university where information on student's modules, course details and grades are located.

References

Berridge, D., 'Theory and Explanation in Child Welfare: Education and Looked After Children', *Child and Family Social Work*, 12 (2007), 1–10.

———, 'Reflections on Child Welfare Research and the Policy Process: Virtual Schools Heads and the Education of Looked After Children', *British Journal of Social Work*, 41/1 (2012), 26–41.

Biehal, N., 'A Sense of Belonging: Meanings of Family and Home in Long-Term Foster Care', *British Journal of Social Work*, 44 (2014), 955–71.

Buttle UK, *Quality Mark for Care Leavers* (2015). Available at *http://www.buttleuk.org/areas-of-focus/quality-mark-for-care-leavers* (accessed 11/04/17).

Cameron, C., 'Education and self-reliance among care leavers', in S. Jackson (ed.), *Pathways through Education for Young People in Care: Ideas from Research and Practice* (London: British Association for Adoption and Fostering, 2013), pp. 206–19.

———, Jackson, S., Hauari, H. and Hollingworth, K., 'Continuing Educational Participation among Children in Five Countries: Some Issues of Social Class', *Journal of Education Policy*, 27/3 (2012), 387–99.

———, Connelly, G. and Jackson, S., *Educating Children and Young People in Care. Learning Placements and Caring Schools* (London: Jessica Kingsley Publishers, 2015).

Children's Commissioner for Wales, *Hidden Ambitions: Achieving the Best for Young People Leaving Care* (Llansamlet: Children's Commissioner for Wales, 2017).

Cotton, D., Nash, P. and Kneale, P., 'The Experiences of Care Leavers in UK Higher Education', *Widening Participation and Lifelong Learning*, 16/3 (2014), 5–21.

Forrester, D., 'Is the Care System Failing Children?', The Political Quarterly, 79/2 (2008), 206–11.

Harker, R., Dobel-Ober, D., Lawrence, J., Berridge, D. and Sinclair, R., 'Who Takes Care of Education? Looked After Children's Perceptions of Support for Educational Progress', *Child and Family Social Work*, 8 (2003), 89–100.

Harris, B., 'Overview of Every Child Matters (2003) and the Children Act (2004)', *Pastoral Care in Education*, 24/2 (2004), 5–6.

Higher Education Funding Council, *'Personal Correspondence with Council Secretary HEFCW'* (18 September 2017).

Jackson, S., *The Education of Children in Care* (Bristol: University of Bristol, 1987).

———, 'Reconnecting Care and Education: From the Children Act 1989 to Care Matters' *Journal of Children's Services*, 5/3 (2010), 48–60.

——— and Ajayi, S., 'Foster Care and Higher Education', *Adoption and Fostering*, 31/1 (2007), 62–72.

———, Ajayi, S. and Quigley, M., *Going to University from Care* (London: Institute of Education, 2005).

——— and Cameron, C., 'Leaving Care: Looking Ahead and Aiming Higher', *Children and Youth Services Review*, 34 (2012), 1107–14.

——— and Cameron, C., *Improving Access to Further and Higher Education for Young People in Public Care. European Policy and Practice* (London: Jessica Kingsley Publishers, 2014).

Jackson, S. and Höjer, I., 'Prioritising Education for Children Looked After Away from Home', *European Journal of Social Work*, 16/1 (2013), 1–5.

Johnson, G. and Mendes, P., 'Taking Control and Moving on: How Young People Turn Around Problematic Transitions from out of Home Care', *Social Work and Society*, 12/1 (2014), 1–15.

Mannay, D., Evans, R., Staples, E., Hallett, S., Roberts, L., Rees, A. and Andrews, D., 'The Consequences of Being Labelled "Looked-After": Exploring the Educational Experiences of Looked-After Children and Young People in Wales', *British Educational Research Journal*, 43/4 (2017), 683–99.

———, Staples, E., Hallett, S., Roberts, L., Rees, A., Evans, R. and Andrews, D., *Understanding the Educational Experiences and Opinions, Attainment, Achievements and Aspirations of Looked After Children in Wales* (Cardiff: Welsh Government, 2015).

Mendes, P., Michell, D. and Wilson, J., 'Young People Transitioning from Out-of-home Care and Access to Higher Education: A Critical Review of the Literature', *Children Australia*, 39/4 (2014), 243–52.

O'Higgins, A., Sebba, J. and Luke, N., *What is the Relationship between Being in Care and the Educational Outcomes of Children? An International Systematic Review* (University of Oxford: Rees Centre, Research in Fostering and Education, 2015).

Office For Fair Access., *Topic Briefing: Care Leavers*. Available at *https://www.offa.org.uk/universities-and-colleges/guidance/topic-briefings/topic-briefing-care-leavers/* (accessed 18/09/17).

Schofield, G. and Beek, M., 'Providing a Secure Base: Parenting Children in Long-term Foster Family Care', *Attachment and Human Development*, 7/1 (2005), 3–25.

Schofield, G., Beek, M. and Ward, E., 'Part of the Family: Planning for Permanence in Long Term Foster Care', *Children and Youth Services Review*, 34/1 (2012), 244–53.

———, Ward, E., Biggart, L., Scaife, V., Dodsworth, J., Larsson, B., Haynes, A. and Stone, N., *Looked After Children and Offending: Reducing Risk and Promoting Resilience* (University of East Anglia: Centre for Research on the Child and Family, 2012).

Stein, M., 'Young People Aging out of Care: The Poverty of Theory', *Children and Youth Services Review*, 28 (2006a), 422–34.

———, 'Research Review: Young People Leaving Care', *Child and Family Social Work*, 11/3 (2006b), 273–9.

Ward, H., 'Patterns of Instability. Moves within the Care System, their Reasons, Contexts and Consequences', *Children and Youth Services Review*, 31/10 (2009), 1113–18.

———, Skuse, T. and Munro, E., 'The Best of Times the Worst of Times: Young People's Views of Care and Accommodation', *Adoption and Fostering*, 29/1 (2005), 8–17.

Welsh Government, *When I'm Ready Good Practice Guide* (Cardiff: Welsh Government, 2016a).

———, *Raising the Ambitions and Educational Attainment of Children Who Are Looked After in Wales* (Cardiff: Welsh Government, 2016b).

———, *Care Leavers on their 19th Birthday During the Year Ending 31 March by Local Authority and Number or Per Cent in Touch*. Available at *https://statswales.gov.wales/Catalogue/Health-and-Social-Care/Social-Services/Childrens-Services/Children-Looked-After/Care-Leavers-at-19th-Birthday/careleaversontheir19thbirthdayduringyearending31march-by-localauthority-numberpercent-intouch* (accessed 14/09/17).

II

THE CULTURE OF CARE AND THE EVERYDAY LIVES OF CHILDREN AND YOUNG PEOPLE

7 | The daily lived experiences of foster care

The centrality of food and touch in family life

Alyson Rees

Introduction

THIS CHAPTER DRAWS on the findings from an empirical study that examined the interior world of foster care in Wales. While much research in foster care has not managed to incorporate the voice of the child (Elden, 2013), this chapter focuses specifically on children's and young people's experiences, and on the often taken-for-granted aspects of care. The chapter considers the importance of bodily practices in foster care (with specific attention being paid to self-care, touch and food), as vital aspects of well-being. This study on everyday care helps to illuminate and extend our understandings of bodily practices, and how they contribute to improving the experience of being in foster care and subsequent sense of well-being. The chapter concludes with a section on belonging and argues that bodily practices as constituents of care make a significant contribution to a sense of becoming part of the foster family and should merit far more attention.

Bodily practices

Bodily practices are those practices which families require 'a member to engage in . . . rituals performed by and enacted on the body that create, maintain and display membership of the group' (Davidman, 2011, p. 209);

these might relate to expectations of families eating together, clothing the body and reciprocal touch. Bodily practices are not much discussed in the fostering or social work literature, nor are they widely addressed in social science, which is surprising given their centrality to everyday life (Morgan, 1996, p. 157). Morgan (1996) demonstrates ways in which the sociology of the body can contribute to our understanding of the physical doing of and enacting family. It is widely recognised that physical care, protection and nurturing of children by parents or carers is fundamental to their well-being (Christensen, 2000). Yet notions of the body and embodiment are rarely included in social work assessment materials and debates, nor much invoked in social work's professional standards and procedures (Pithouse and Rees, 2014). It is taken for granted that the foster child can enter a family with relative ease and quickly come to understand the nuances of household relationships and negotiate the boundaries of interpersonal living in the confined space of the family home. This settling into the family is rarely straightforward and much depends upon carers and their birth children being able to articulate family expectations and respond to the child and their needs in ways that allow a trusting intimacy to develop. The child, initially a stranger, becomes a family intimate in a relatively short time, making issues of the body and touch important topics of enquiry.

Touch as a bodily practice is vital for all people as reassurance, as a means of communication and as a vital part of parenting (Cameron and Maginn, 2008). Yet because of the risk of abuse allegations (Inch, 1999; Sinclair et al., 2004; Biehal, 2014; Plumridge and Sebba, 2016) it may be that some children in foster care are rarely touched. The social work profession has become much less likely to view touch as a means of reassurance to children within social care relationships. Current social work practice can be viewed as inhibited by fear of accusation and litigation, rather than an overriding concern for a child's emotional well-being (Piper et al., 2006, p. 151–5). Gilligan (2000, p. 67) noted this fear of allegation when undertaking focus groups with male foster carers and observed that 'the risk of allegations being made against male carers was a frequently cited concern. It can rob the male carers' role and relationship of spontaneity'. Fear of allegations is central to carers giving up their role (Plumridge and Sebba, 2016) but may also be inhibiting their daily family and bodily practices (Morgan, 1996).

With regard to the specific family (and bodily) practice of eating, there is limited guidance in relation to foster care, with the exception of the Caroline Walker Trust's 'Eating well for looked after children and young people' (Caroline Walker Trust, 2001) and 'Promoting the health and well-being of looked-after children' (Department for Education and Department of Health, 2015); what is written highlights the health aspects of eating, rather than its social and relational importance. Children typically learn to structure their understanding of time through the eating of food, thus 'the cycle of breakfast, lunch and supper is the first framework into which they slot their waking experiences' (Ennew, 1994, p. 129).

There is a reported link between child and adolescent well-being and families eating together, which is thought to lead to less conflict, more trusting and helpful relationships and higher life satisfaction (Elgar et al., 2013). Food has a social and symbolic significance, particularly insofar as it involves the relationships of those who partake in the ritual of sharing meals (Emond et al., 2013). Mennell et al. (1992, p. 115) note that those who eat together are also often tied to one another by friendship and mutual obligation: 'Sharing food is held to signify togetherness, an equivalence that defines and reaffirms insiders.' Mealtimes not only allow families to enact and display family life, but are an everyday event through which young people recognise themselves as 'family' (Ashley et al., 2004; Finch, 2007). It is interesting, therefore, to explore how children in foster care experience family eating practices, whether families typically eat together and the significance of this for feelings of belonging (Biehal, 2014) and membership.

Methods

The data in this study are drawn from a small-scale, in-depth qualitative study of a purposive sample of stable foster care placements in Wales (Pithouse and Rees, 2014). The definition of 'stable' was families having provided placements that had not broken down and had lasted as long as needed (Leathers, 2006) for at least one child. All of the children had been living with the family for at least one year. The assumption was that stable placements provided by experienced carers might make for easier access and participation, which in turn could facilitate a more revealing encounter in which the mundane processes of day-to-day care-based relationships could be explored. The study aimed to take a 'worm's eye view' and capture the living, breathing realities of daily life for children and young people in foster care. The study took a strengths-based perspective, focusing on what works well in foster care, particularly relevant in light of the underpinning ethos of the Social Services and Well-being (Wales) Act 2014. Ten foster families took part in the study. There were 16 children in foster care, aged nine to 18 living with the families and one adopted child. The research aimed to gain the perspectives of all members of the foster families, including the birth children, and a variety of data generation techniques were used.

This chapter focuses specifically on the data generated with nine fostered and one adopted participants (n = 10). All children and young people completed eco-maps displaying their networks of relationships and these helped to inform the subsequent interviews (Holland, 2011); some participants (n = 5) also chose to complete audio diaries or written diaries (n = 1) over a one-week period. The creative digital method of audio dairies was used to facilitate freer communication and reflection (Arthur et al., 2014). The audio-recorded interviews and diaries were transcribed and subjected to qualitative methods of coding, categorisation and thematic analysis, alongside the data generated in interviews (Seale, 2012).

Research into children's lives at home is difficult in terms of gaining access to a private social space (Lincoln, 2012). They rarely occupy positions of power within the domestic arena and this is particularly the case for children and young people in foster care, whose position within the family can be precarious. Once the foster carers agreed to take part in the research, accessible information sheets and consent forms were produced for all participants. Children and young people were interviewed in the foster/adoptive home one-to-one and were made aware that their comments would not be shared with carers. Pseudonyms are used throughout the study, and due to the small scale of the study other potential identifiers have been omitted to preserve anonymity. Data have been carefully stored in accordance with the Data Protection Act 1998, and ethical approval for this study was provided by Cardiff University.

The body and touch

The data highlighted the critical importance of bodily care as a basic indicator of warmth and inclusion in the family. The importance and symbolic nature of bodily care appeared to be very important for the participants, and regularly arose in their interview and diary data (see also Cameron and Maginn, 2008). The ordered routine of personal, physical care provided by the families was both comforting and reassuring for the participants and they valued the nurturing aspects of this care. The participants in one family provided a clear demonstration of this; the family home contained three girls (fostered, birth, adopted), and a male and female foster carer. Examples from the girls' audio diaries reflect the significance of bodily caring including the provision and enjoyment of food, which helped in securing a child's sense of security and comfort:

> Had a bath, now I'm going to sort out my clothes for tomorrow . . . I straightened my hair and it looks nice. I changed my belly bar. (Audio diary, Melonie, foster child, age 13)

> Now I'm in bed and after dinner we had some chocolate chip ice cream. Then I went up for a nice warm bath and washed my hair. Then I done my teeth and went downstairs to say goodnight to my dad and then I jumped in bed and my Dad and Mum came up and said goodnight. I am going to have a very nice sleep. Night, night. (Audio diary, Carla, adopted child, age nine)

My food was warm and delicious and the hot bath was lovely,
especially when I lie listening to the rain. Thank you. (Audio
diary, Helen, birth child, age 13)

As suggested in these diary extracts, it was the individualised and
embodied routines of care for each of the girls that, irrespective of their
being fostered, adopted or birth child, demonstrated to them a sense of
warmth and belonging within a nurturing family environment. Similarly,
in another family, Nadia talked about the organisation of washing routines and bodily care:

He [foster carer] always makes us wash our hair and have a
bath or a shower. We don't get out until we've done it, which is
different (from own family experience) really ... I go in the bath
first, then Libby gets in, then Jake. They are really strict about
that. (Nadia, foster child, age 15)

The regularity, ordering and attention paid to bodily care, even when
directed, was greatly valued, especially when this was in contrast to their
previous experiences. A vital aspect of bodily care is that of touch and
physical reassurance; and Callum noted the importance of touch, signifying care and concern over and above that which had been anticipated:

Just small things she said like um (when upset) letting me know
that it would be alright, and comforting me and little gestures
like hugging me ... (Callum, foster child, age 16)

The participants were keenly aware that they could expect to be cared
for from a practical perspective but were less clear about what to anticipate by way of demonstrations of affection through touch or play – they
welcomed this when it occurred but were not sure they had a right to
expect this. Those carers who were willing to enact affection in addition
to good physical care were deemed to be giving more than expected and
to be demonstrating exceptional care. This was the case for all participants, regardless of their gender, and was appreciated from both of the
foster carers:

He [foster carer Josh] is a real people-person. He is a very funny
person and a very serious person as well. I found living with him
he'd mess about 'do you want a fight' just messing around we
just got on so well from the moment I came here. He was very
hands on, he'd put his arms round me and stuff. Again gestures ...
from both Hazel [carer] and Josh ... with Hazel embracing ...
it would be when I needed it whereas with Josh it would often

be as a friendly arm around. Hazel would be a motherly hug.
(Callum, foster child, age 16)

And then I put my [eczema] cream on. Then I said goodnight.
My Mum and Dad came in and gave me a goodnight kiss. Night,
night (Audio diary, Carla, adopted child, age nine)

As highlighted in the background section, a discourse of fear in social work and foster care, the focus of which is often on abusive touch, may well distort fostering practice in that it diminishes the full potential of a nurturing relationship. Many children in the care system will have difficulty in expressing emotion (Bazalgette et al., 2015) and may have come not to expect physical contact with their carers. Additionally, children in care may have experienced physical and sexual abuse (Pithouse and Rees, 2014) and thus may be more anxious about touch, or, conversely, they may be in even more need of positive physical reassurance. Children in such circumstances need positive role models in order to help them understand and experience that touch can and should be reassuring and nurturing.

One young person asked her foster carer 'why people hug' and was suspicious of such alien behaviour, as she did not understand the importance of physical reassurance, but gradually came to understand and enjoy a 'cwtch' (a Welsh language expression describing a cuddle or hug). Children centralised the importance of physical reassurance as playing a significant part of the experience of positive foster care. It is, however, important to recognise that foster carers and birth children do have allegations made against them by children (Plumridge and Sebba, 2016) and this can have a huge negative impact. Thus, it would not be difficult to conceive of some fostering scenarios as arenas of mutual distrust and surveillance, whereby both child and carer warily suspect the motives of the other. None of the children in this study had made allegations against their carers. One of the adult birth children in the study noted that in the past an allegation had been made by a child, and she became very careful about touch. This aspect of 'suspicious care' could potentially be very damaging, inhibiting a healthy approach to physical expressions of warmth.

The participants also discussed various ways in which the presence of pets who jumped on laps and slept on beds was hugely comforting. Nine of the 10 families in the study had pets in the home; and foster carers as a group are reported to have more pets than other families (see Triseliotis et al., 2000). One young person was keen to show me an information letter for children new to the foster home; it introduced all of the five pets by name and included photographs of each, before introducing the adults. Some children chose to place pets in their eco-maps and others referred to them as family members. 'Here is Sam [dog] and I am going to draw a picture of other people too'; the significance of human–pet relationships in children's creation of family has been noted by others (Briheim-Crookall, 2016; Mason and Tipper, 2008). Gabb (2007, p. 9) suggests that affection and touch of pets may not be the same as human-to-human relationships, but nevertheless 'should remain within the intimate equation'. Data, particularly from observation during interviews (where pets were sitting on sofas and running around homes) would suggest that where physical touch and intimacy is restricted for a child, their presence takes on an even greater significance and many lessons can be learnt by children regarding the care of pets.

Food

Although food was not a specific theme of the initial interview schedule, it soon arose across most interviews and recorded diaries and rapidly became a key topic. The meanings and activities associated with food and mealtimes illuminate how families nurture children and signify their inclusion in the foster home. Participants appreciated how the families displayed many of the principles of good parenting through their approach to food, particularly warmth, responsiveness and consistency (Cameron and Maginn, 2008). In this way, a sense of membership and belonging was engendered for children and young people.

Catering to children's 'faddiness' can be seen as part of spoiling and being an indulgent parent. However, this so-called 'spoiling' was well received by some participants in the study and helped to establish a sense of worth and inclusion. Young people's food preferences can be seen in terms of 'food personae' (Brannen et al., 1994, p. 162), that is, those habits and preferences which are seen as an intrinsic part of a young person's identity. We all have a particular history of relationships to food that include our likes and dislikes; similarly, in the foster home the food preferences of children and young people become part of a process of their recognition as an individual. Thus, responding to preferences can act as a source of affirmation, which oils the wheels of family relations and helps embed the foster child's position in the family. Families seemed to be able to strike a balance between indulgence and providing a tailored response to the needs and desires of children and young people, who in turn adapted to the routines and conventions of the foster home, thereby generating harmony. As Nadia explains:

> Yeah. We've all got our own seats, mine is there, Dawn sits there, Libby there, Jake there etc. You have what you feel like. We say we don't mind; we don't all like vegetables, but we do all have soya. (Nadia, foster child, age 15)

The enjoyment of food and the partaking of meals featured as key moments in participants' daily lives, and offering choice about food was seen as particularly important. Knowledge of food preference (food personae) was part of getting to know a child or young person, and catering for their needs. Indeed, it was evident that all the carers, to varying degrees, were catering for the food preferences of the participants, whilst also setting routines and expectations around mealtimes. In this study, most families ate together, with the fostered children and young people being both listened to and contributing to the food agenda. Participants especially talked about the type and amount of food consumed. Food and mealtimes helped them understand the structure of their day and seemed to greatly enhance their enjoyment of it. Melonie recorded her enjoyment of food to which the foster carer had introduced her. She spoke with enthusiasm about trying new foods and developing her food palate:

> We had spaghetti and salad all mixed up. We had coleslaw in a dish and cottage cheese – that was nice 'cos Liz got me on that. (Audio diary, Melonie, foster child, age 13)

Other participants in different families also noted this change to a healthier diet as part of their food repertoire. For example, Carmel, spoke of past and new foods:

> **Researcher:** Is that the kind of food you were used to eating?
> **Carmel:** No, [we used to have] chips, food in the deep fat fryer. (Foster child, age 10)

Food practices

The significance of food practices and routines were frequently noted. For example, when Carmel talked about her first day in the foster home she recalled being asked to take part in the preparation of food and how this had become a memorable and important ritual that continued for some years:

> I remember Grandma [foster carer's mother] here, she lived just round the corner and every Thursday she used to make pasta round here. She was doing pasta for us when [the day] I came. (Carmel, foster child, age 10)

Similarly, Nadia spoke of clear responsibilities with regard to mealtimes that in her view helped promote a sense of expectation and reciprocity:

> We take it in turns to lay the table, clear away and put things in the dishwasher . . . (Nadia, foster child, age 15)

Nadia goes on to observe that mealtimes were a time where particular conduct and contributions were established and normalised. Thus, mealtimes entailed:

> Manners, respect. Everyone, every week takes turn to set the table and clear away, like say if it was my turn I'd be doing it just before dinner and someone dries and someone washes up.

As Greishaber (2004) contends, the significance of clearly defined expectations around food, mealtimes, preparation and clearing up of the dishes is part of being socialised into roles, identities and membership. For the participants, such processes and rituals were profoundly important in establishing a sense of becoming part of the 'production' of family.

The 'proper' meal is at a table, it is 'shared and promotes sociability and talk' (Ashley et al., 2004, p. 125; see also Elgar et al., 2013). Family talk is part of a family eating together, in which mealtimes become a place and time for positive family conversation and interaction. In this study, eating together was a routine but also an important means of communing and interacting. Eating together offers an opportunity for parents to show an interest in the child's day (Fisher and DeBell, 2007) and nearly all the carers, children and young people commented on how they looked forward to the sharing of stories and new experiences at mealtimes. In his diary, Stuart eagerly anticipates sitting down at the dinner table so that he can discuss recent events:

> And now I am waiting for tea to be ready, which is good then we can sit down and talk about what happened today . . . (Written diary extract, Stuart, foster child, age 18)

The participants frequently commented that meals were an important time when they could share news, concerns, problems and, sometimes, secrets:

> Over dinner we had a little chat because some people in my class are misbehaving. (Audio diary extract, Carmel, foster child, age 10)

> We sit at the table and we have to spill it all out when we've got a secret. (Lilly, foster child, age 12)

> We basically get together and sort it out, in the kitchen over the table while having food. (George, birth child, age 15)

Greishaber (2004) argues that eating regimes can be interpreted as disciplinary techniques through which families and the individuals within them are socialised. Mealtimes can provide a site for resistance and can generate frustration for all parties concerned. Consequently, the ways in which carers chose to manage the family eating experience was important. For example, Lilly recalled unpleasant experiences in previous foster homes over the consumption of food:

> In my old house you had to eat everything, every scrap of food. Here they just say leave it … (Lilly, foster child, age 12)

Lilly's current carer caters for her food personae and also allows her to leave food and this was seen as caring and helpful by Lilly, although clearly food intake will in some cases have to be regulated by carers.

Most of the participants spoke of the significance of the traditional Sunday lunch, and the practice of the family gathering for this event:

> We always sit at the table for Sunday lunch and everyone gets together. (Lilly, foster child, age 12)

> We have a cooked dinner every Sunday. (Carmel, foster child, age 10)

This idea of a 'cooked dinner' as a vehicle for family communion is still likely to resonate with a sizeable element of the UK population and a particularly symbolic event for children and young people in foster care. The regularity of mealtimes was a reassuring and comforting structure for some participants, which made them feel safe and cared for. Ashley et al. (2004, p. 124) note the importance that is attached to food because it is symbolic of the significance and respect paid to the consumers of the meal: 'home cooked meals are seen as imbued with warmth, intimacy and personal touch which are seen as markers of the personal sphere'. There is an emotional 'warmth' to food that can signify responsive parenting and reinforce a sense of care and belonging. In eating the food that has been prepared for them, children implicitly display their appreciation of what has been provided. For example, Callum described how his foster carer catered for his food needs and how this experience denoted a significant change in his sense of well-being:

> Dinner – regular 6.30. Almost like clockwork! Food is very important. I do have a very good appetite and that has only happened since I came here. I never used to be able to finish one helping of food and now I can finish about five … Hazel is a really good cook. I do have a miles better appetite here than I do anywhere. When I go out to a restaurant I can eat but when Hazel puts on Sunday lunch and if there is any left overs, I pile them on my plate. (Callum, foster child, age 16)

For several of the participants, food had been a troubling aspect of their past. This was because they simply had not had enough food, or sometimes too much access to unhealthy meals. In either event most had a history of households where they could not anticipate there would be a reliable supply of good food. Such experiences are likely to be linked to neglectful parenting, and Callum described at length how his birth family contrasted with the foster home over this very basic matter of a decent meal eaten in comfort:

> I used to have to eat very quickly because if I didn't there would be hands in, nicking bits of food because there was so many of us [children] living in one house. We grew accustomed to each other and so we used to fight for food and stuff because there was never enough sausage and chips and stuff. Now I don't have to fight for the food but I still eat very, very quickly. Now I've never had it so easy, I get twice as much and I don't have to fight for it. (Callum, foster child, age 16)

In the same way that inconsistent parenting can cause unhappiness and insecurity for a child (Bowlby, 1969), so inconsistent provision of food can generate anxiety for children. In summary, it is evident that the therapeutic potential that resides around the preparation and consumption of regular well-cooked and tasty food can help children and young people feel more at home.

Conclusion

Bodily practices, including food and touch, are mundane aspects of family life, often overlooked and not overtly discussed in the fostering agenda, yet they have the potential to enhance the fostering experience. Food practices, which incorporate the foster child, help them to feel part of the family (Elgar et al., 2013). Similarly, touch and physical nurturing affirm feelings of self-worth and acceptance. These contribute to perhaps some of the most significant aspects of fostering, helping to create a sense of value and belonging (Biehal, 2014). It is the focusing down and understanding of daily life gleaned from the children's worm-eye view that can help illuminate what really matters. Studies of long-term care (Biehal, 2014; Schofield et al., 2012) have identified the need for a sense of belonging and mutual connectedness as 'part of a family' as being vital, and, therefore, these must feature in any understanding of successful care. Importantly, this chapter has illustrated the ways in which bodily practices have huge potential to be utilised therapeutically to support children, develop feelings of belonging and create a sense of family. Consequently, this area would benefit from further research and interrogation, which could inform policy and practice, and thereby improve the everyday lived experiences of children and young people in care.

Acknowledgements

I would like to thank the young people for their patience and for giving freely of their time. Thanks also to the foster carers who facilitated this and supported the aims of the project.

References

Arthur, S., Michell, M., Lewis, J. and McNaughton Nicholls, C., 'Designing fieldwork', in J. Ritchie, J. Lewis, C. McNaughton Nicholls (eds), *Qualitative Research Practice* (London: Sage, 2014), pp. 147–72.

Ashley, B., Hollows, J., Jones, S. and Taylor, B., *Food and Cultural Studies* (London: Routledge, 2004).

Bazalgette, L., Rahilly, T. and Trevelyan, G., *Achieving Emotional Well-being for Looked After Children: A Whole System Approach* (London: NSPCC, 2015).

Biehal, N., 'A Sense of Belonging: Meanings of Family and Home in Long-term Foster Care', *British Journal of Social Work*, 44/4 (2014), 995–71.

Bowlby, J., *Attachment and Loss* (London: Hogarth Press, 1969).

Brannen, J., Dodd, K., Oakley, A. and Storey, P., *Young People, Health and Family Life* (Buckingham: Open University, 1994).

Briheim-Crookall, L., *How Social Workers Can Track and Boost the Happiness of Looked-After Children* (Sutton: Community Care, 2016). Available at: http://www.communitycare.co.uk/2016/03/22/social-workers-can-track-boost-happiness-looked-children/ (accessed 16/04/17).

Cameron, R. and Maginn, C., 'The Authentic Warmth Dimension of Professional Childcare', *British Journal of Social Work*, 38/6 (2008), 1151–72.

Caroline Walker Trust, *Eating Well for Looked After Children and Young People* (2001). Available at: https://www.cwt.org.uk/wp-content/uploads/2014/07/EatingWellChildren2001.pdf (accessed: 16/08/17).

Christensen, P., 'Childhood and the cultural constitution of vulnerable bodies', in A. Prout (ed.), *The Body, Childhood and Society* (Hampshire: Palgrave Macmillan, 2000), pp. 38–59.

Davidman, L., 'The transformation of bodily practices', in C. Bobel and S. Kwan (eds), *Embodied Resistance: Challenging the Norms, Breaking the Rules* (Nashville: Vanderbilt University Press, 2011), pp. 209–21.

Department for Education, *Promoting the Health and Wellbeing of Looked-After Children* (2015). Available at https://www.gov.uk/government/publications/promoting-the-health-and-wellbeing-of-looked-after-children--2 (accessed: 11/05/17).

Elden, S., 'Inviting the Messy: Drawing, Methods and "Children's Voices"', *Childhood*, 20/1 (2013), 66–81.

Elgar, F., Craig, W. and Trites, S., 'Family Dinners, Communication and Mental Health in Canadian Adolescents', *Journal of Adolescent Health*, 52/4 (2013) 433-8.

Emond, R., McIntosh, I. and Punch, S., 'Food and Feelings in Residential Care', *British Journal of Social Work*, 44/7 (2013), 1840-56.

Ennew, J., 'Time for children or time for adults?', in J. Qvortrup, M. Bardy, G. Sgritta and H. Wintersberger (eds), *Childhood Matters: Social Theory, Practice and Politics* (Aldershot: Avebury Press, 1994), pp. 125-38.

Finch, J., 'Displaying Familes', Sociology, 41 (2007), 65-8.

Fisher, M. and DeBell, D., 'Approaches to parenting', in D. DeBell (ed.), *Public Health Care Practice and School-Age Population* (London: Hodder Education, 2007), pp. 84-110.

Gabb, J., 'Stretched to the Limits: Accounting for Contemporary Intimate Relationships'. Paper presented at Centre for Research on Families and Relationships Conference, *Extended and Extending Families*, Edinburgh, June 2007.

Gilligan R., 'Men as Foster Carers: A Neglected Resource?', *Adoption and Fostering*, 24/2 (2000), 63-9.

Greishaber, S., *Rethinking Parent and Child Conflict* (New York: Routledge Falmer, 2004).

Holland, S., *Child and Family Assessment in Social Work Practice* (2nd edn) (London: Sage, 2011).

Inch, L. J., 'Aspects of Foster Fathering', *Child and Adolescent Social Work Journal*, 16/5 (1999), 393-412.

Leathers, S., 'Placement Disruption and Negative Placement Outcomes among Adolescents in Long Term Foster Care', *Child Abuse and Neglect*, 30 (2006), 307-24.

Lincoln, S., *Youth Culture and Private Space* (Basingstoke: Palgrave Macmillan, 2012).

Mason, J. and Tipper, B., *Children Kinship and Creativity* (2008). Available at: *http://journals.sagepub.com/doi/pdf/10.1177/0907568208097201* (accessed 26/07/17).

Mennell, S., Murcott, A. and van Otterloo, A. H., *The Sociology of Food; Eating, Diet and Culture* (London: Sage, 1992).

Morgan, D., *Family Practices* (Basingstoke: Palgrave Macmillan, 1996).

Piper, H., Powell, J. and Smith, H., 'Parents, Professionals and Paranoia. The Touching of Children in a Culture of Fear', *Journal of Social Work*, 6/2 (2006), 151-67.

Pithouse, A., and Rees, A., *Creating Stable Placements: Learning from Foster Children and the Families Who Care for Them* (London: Jessica Kingsley, 2014).

Plumridge, G. and Sebba, J., *The Impact of Unproven Allegations on Foster Carers* (Oxford: University of Oxford, 2016).

Schofield, G., Beek, M. and Ward, E., 'Part of the Family: Planning for Permanence in Long-term Family Foster Care', *Children and Services Youth Review*, 34 (2012), 244-53.

Seale, C., 'Coding and analysing data', in C. Seale (ed.), *Researching Society and Culture* (3rd edn) (London: Sage, 2012), pp. 305–23.

Sinclair, I., Gibbs, I. and Wilson, K., *Foster Carers: Why They Stay and Why They Leave* (London: Jessica Kingsley, 2004).

Social Services and Well-being Act (Wales) 2014. Available at: *http://www.senedd. assemblywales.org/mgIssueHistoryHome.aspx?IId=5664* (accessed 26/07/17).

Triseliotis, J., Borland, M. and Hill, M., *Delivering Foster Care* (London: BAAF, 2000).

8 | The natural environment and its benefits for children and young people looked after

Holly Gordon

Introduction

CONSIDERATIONS OF THE natural environment within social work literature are on the increase. Nature is widely recognised as having both positive and restorative effects on humans (Barton and Pretty, 2010; Townsend and Moore, 2005). Whilst it has been known anecdotally for generations that contact with nature can have positive effects, there is now an established research base which evidences a strong connection between well-being and contact with nature (Kellert and Derr, 1998; Kuo and Taylor, 2004; Louv, 2008). Such research utilised the methods of ethnography, interviews, surveys and observations. However, in recent years, technological advances have led to scientific experimentation: for example, the use of electroencephalography (EEG) has evidenced lower frustration levels when accessing nature (Aspinall et al., 2013).

Whilst the research base for adults outweighs that of children, research that focuses on children's play in the natural environment is well established and should be of great interest to children's practitioners. The right to play has been recognised as a critical part of a child's healthy development and well-being on both a national and a global scale. The focus on well-being in Wales has been significantly enhanced by the introduction of the Social Services and Well-being (Wales) Act 2014. The Act sets out the definition of well-being, which covers several domains including physical, intellectual and emotional well-being, as well as recreation and social well-being; and all of these domains could be considered relevant in relation to children's play in nature.

Additionally, the Welsh Government recognises that play in the natural environment helps children learn about the world they share with others and that play is a behavioural imperative and instinctive desire (Welsh Assembly Government, 2002). The Welsh Government has produced policies recognising play as a right for children in Wales (Welsh Government, 2006; Welsh Government, 2012). Such policies reflect children's play as a right which has been enshrined in the United Nations Convention on the Rights of the Child (UNCRC):

> Children have the right to relax and play, and to join in a wide range of cultural, artistic and other recreational activities.
> (UNCRC, 1989, Article 31: Leisure, play and culture)

To date there has been no primary research into the benefits of nature for children and young people looked after. However, nature appears to have particular benefits for those who are experiencing mental fatigue and stress (Kaplan, 1995; Aspinall et al., 2013). It is therefore possible to transfer this knowledge to the looked after population, whilst considering the differences that alternative care may bring. This chapter explores the potential benefits of outdoor play in nature for children and young people looked after.

It begins with a discussion about how foster carers can promote play in the natural environment by providing opportunities for play, which promote resilience, learning and the promotion of a secure base. An overview of current research and theory will be presented as well as a reflection on the reduction of children's play in nature. Considering the importance of children's play in nature, the chapter then presents a case study relating to a Welsh-based project, 'Fostering outside play', involving Learning through Landscapes [1], Play Wales [2] and the British Association for Adoption and Fostering (BAAF) Cymru [3]. The project aimed to promote the physical and mental well-being of children by engaging with foster carers and practitioners to encourage high-quality outdoor experiences of play in the natural environment and provide a practice-based example of this subject.

The chapter advocates the benefits of a risk-competent approach, which seeks to empower children and maximise on the numerous benefits which play in nature has to offer. A risk-competent approach reflects the work of Schiffer (1993), who argued that risk taking increases a child's competence and actually promotes health rather than endangering health. This approach supports children in becoming risk competent, which is described as a 'process of becoming knowledgeable and skilled in assessing risks and therefore acquiring the competence to take risks more safely' (Eichsteller and Holthoff, 2009, p. 2).

Promoting play in nature

A child's physical, cognitive, emotional and social development is effected by their relationship with others, particularly their attachment to primary carer(s). The development of a secure attachment to a carer can provide the opportunity for positive attachments to be developed in the future (Quiroga and Hamilton-Giachritsis, 2016). Both theorists and practitioners are in agreement about the need for children to have a secure base, which offers reliable, consistent care within a nurturing setting. Schofield's and Beek's (2014) secure base model, drawn from attachment theory, identifies dimensions of caregiving which promote healthy attachments. A secure base is of particular importance for children and young people looked after who are likely to have experienced significant adversity in their early childhood, loss and separation from primary carers and siblings, as well as placement moves and disruptions (Mannay et al., 2015; see also Girling, 2019 [Chapter 10 this volume]).

Whilst attachment can be impacted upon by the child's age when placed and the duration of placement, the relationship-building process between a child and foster carer can support the child in processing loss and trauma (Quiroga and Hamilton-Giachritsis, 2016). The presence of a secure base affords children the ability to explore the world whilst feeling a sense of safety (Schofield and Beek, 2014). In contrast, the absence of a secure base can result in feelings of alienation and anxiety leading to a lack of trust in others, lower levels of confidence and frequent emotional distress. It has been suggested that the perceived continuity (Cobb, 1959) and reciprocity (Abram, 1996) experienced in nature can reflect attributes of a secure attachment (Hordyk et al., 2015). Therefore, this chapter argues that the natural environment can support the development of a positive attachment to others and build resilience. In addition to this, it is also suggested that the natural environment itself can act as a secure base for children.

Researchers have asserted that the natural environment can be used to protect children from life's stressors (Caspi et al., 2000; Wells and Evans, 2003) and to aid in the development of resilience capacities (Corraliza et al., 2011; Ungar and Liebenberg, 2008). Studies have demonstrated the bonding between children as a result of shared experiences of exploration and discovery (Hordyk et al., 2015). This can include the natural environment, which can offer opportunities for excitement, joy and play. It has also been suggested that children are able to explore difficult emotions whilst using nature as a safe space (Hordyk et al., 2015). However, for the natural environment to nurture children, they need to be receptive to the experience. This requires the foster carer to have a strong understanding of the child's background as how the child perceives the outdoors needs to be carefully considered. For example, a child may associate the outdoors with fear and uncertainty if they have previously been sent outside as a punishment prior to their removal (Gordon, 2014).

Foster carers can offer considerable support to children's play in nature through the key areas of permission, time, space and materials, which will now be briefly discussed in turn. The issue of permission is crucial as children who have been removed from families may have missed out on opportunities to play. This may mean that during the initial stages of a child's placement the foster carer may need to offer additional support during the play process. However, this should change once the child becomes more familiar and comfortable with play. Foster carers need to understand the importance of play, and in particular play in the natural environment. Play Wales (2013) suggest that adults may try to over regulate play and attempt to organise how it takes place. Therefore, foster carers need to strike a balance between supporting children and being mindful about not taking the lead in children's play. This involves allowing children to direct their own play and intervening only at specific times. This can include when children directly ask carers to play, when a child is experiencing distress or when a dispute occurs which requires adult intervention. Permission requires a supportive attitude, which avoids dismissing play as a waste of time or implementing needless restrictions based on misplaced fears.

In relation to time, foster carers can promote play by ensuring that children are given time to do so. If foster carers understand the value and importance of play across the developmental domains they are more likely to ensure that time is made available for play – particularly play in nature. There will be benefits for the foster carer when spending time in nature, as well as the whole family unit. Opportunities for play in nature need to be factored in for children, despite the busy schedules with school, contact and hobbies.

Space is also important, and foster carers can support children with accessing natural spaces by accompanying them to green spaces. Foster carers can spend time with children whilst out on nature walks, on the beach or in the woods. They can also support children in accessing green spaces in their local area. Children playing outside in their own communities will be more likely to develop a sense of belonging. In addition to this, foster carers need to be tolerant of how children's play spaces may look. As play can often be messy and noisy, such spaces may appear chaotic to adults (Play Wales, 2013).

Lastly, materials should be considered. In recent years, play has become increasingly commercialised, with parents succumbing to advertising pressure, which targets children. Commercial products often remove the onus of creating play away from children. This can impact on key characteristics of play such as spontaneity and imagination. Foster carers can offer children resources that promote creative play such as 'loose parts', which includes materials such as: water, sand, boxes, wood and tyres, and any other material that can be adapted during play (Play Wales, 2013). The introduction of loose parts into play has the potential to promote problem solving, imagination and spatial awareness. Loose parts can also consist of leaves, grass, sticks, stones, wood, sand, flowers and rope, and are normally found in abundance. These resources are extremely useful in promoting imaginative play and offering a soothing and sensory play experience (Nedovic and Morrissey, 2013).

Research and outdoor play

Proximity and access to green spaces can provide opportunities for children and young people looked after; however, children need support from foster carers and practitioners to be afforded such access. Several studies have considered children's proximity to nature. A Scottish study revealed that children who resided less than 20 minutes away from a green space had better mental health than those who lived further away (Aggio et al., 2015). In another study, children living close to nature had scored themselves higher on self-worth global measures than their peers (Greenleaf et al., 2014). Proximity and access to nature allow children the opportunity to practise and refine skills as they grow older (Little and Wyver, 2008). In addition, this contact can support the formation of friendships (Nedovic and Morrissey, 2013). A research review by Korpela (2002) found that children and young people's descriptions of their favourite places frequently involved the natural environment. These settings were associated with feelings of calmness and relaxation.

Spending time in nature has been associated with improved mental health and behavioural symptoms in children (Chawla, 2015). Psychological difficulties in adolescents are believed to be on the increase, with estimates of depression rates amongst 15 to 16-year-olds doubling from 1980 to 2010 (Nuffield Foundation, 2013). Childhood anxiety and depression have gained recent attention in the United Kingdom (UK). It is known that experiences of early trauma can lead to difficulties in managing stress throughout the life course (Rees, 2010), which places children and young people looked after at an increased risk of poor emotional and mental health. A few studies have explored the impact of the natural environment on Attention Deficit Hyperactivity Disorder (ADHD) symptoms. For example, a study by Taylor et al. (2001) found that the natural environment contributed to the reduction of ADHD symptoms which were exacerbated in non-green settings. Another study which involved 450 children found similar results, with symptoms reducing after outdoor activities in nature compared to activities undertaken in indoor or built outdoor spaces (Kuo and Taylor, 2004). Furthermore, a study by Faber Taylor and Kuo (2009) involved children aged seven to 12 years old with ADHD diagnoses undertaking tests after walking through either a green space, a downtown area or a residential area. The children who had accessed the green space were the only group to show improved concentration, comparable to the effects of ADHD medication.

Whilst the evidence base for reduced stress and restoration in nature is strong, research which specifically focuses on teenagers remains limited (Greenwood and Gatersleben, 2016), with some studies indicating that there are additional considerations for this age group. Attempts to explain this apparent lesser impact have referred to the different adaptive priorities in the adolescent stage of development (Kaplan and Kaplan, 2002). Research in the UK involving 120 young persons aged 16 to 18 explored their stress and mental fatigue levels in both indoor and outdoor settings, either alone or with a friend. Restoration levels amongst those in outdoor settings were higher than the indoor group, and there was also an additional increase in restoration levels for those who were with a friend whilst being outdoors (Greenwood and Gatersleben, 2016). As well as differences in age, there appear to be differences in gender. However, the identified gender differences relate to additional constraints being placed on females by concerned carers as well as societal norms. Natural spaces are not equally available to all children, with restrictive notions of gender roles and safety fears impacting on females' access to nature (Alexander et al., 2015).

Reduction in play in nature

Children are experiencing a decrease in the amount of time they spend outdoors in nature. This appears to be particularly the case for children living in the West, where opportunities for outdoor play have reduced over the last two decades (Hofferth, 2008; Little and Wyver, 2008). Several reasons for this decline have been proffered, including an increase in new technologies, a risk-averse approach by parents, carers and policy makers (Little and Wyver, 2008), as well as a reduction in green space (Bilton, 2005; Little and Wyver, 2008; Louv, 2008). A survey by Worpole (2003) involving 500 children from the general population found that:

- 45 per cent were not permitted to play with water
- 36 per cent were unable to climb trees
- 27 per cent were not permitted to play on climbing equipment
- 23 per cent were not permitted to ride bikes/play on skateboards.

A reduction in time spent outdoors leads to a reduction in exercise, which is associated with increased rates in obesity and related health conditions such as diabetes and heart disease (Carrera-Bastos et al., 2011). This reduction has also been associated with fatigue, a lack of emotional control, depression and increased aggression (Kuo and Sullivan, 2001; Lee and Maheswaran, 2010; Weinstein et al., 2009). A disconnect with nature and the emotional, psychological, and physical consequences it produces, prompted Louv (2008) to coin the term 'nature-deficit disorder' in his book *The Last Child in the Woods*.

The increase in new technologies has led to a shift in how many children and young people spend their free time. Several studies have explored the harmful effects of teenagers' increased usage of technology (David-Ferdon and Hertz, 2007; Oshima et al., 2012; Von Marees and Petermann, 2012). Rikkers et al. (2016) conducted a survey on children's mental health in 2013–14. Levels of internet and gaming usage were high amongst young people with reported behavioural difficulties. The research concludes that there is a link between internet usage and gaming, and mental disorders and risk taking in young people. However, the research could not explain if internet/gaming usage was a precursor to these issues or occurred as a result of them (Rikkers, 2016).

If one was to consider how much time children spend engaging in unstructured play in nature compared to time spent indoors using electronic media, the disconnect between children and nature becomes apparent. For example, Childwise (2013) found that UK children are spending more time in front of a screen each day (around 4.5 hours) than they spend exercising outdoors throughout the entire week. These are important considerations for foster carers and social workers. Whilst it is important for adults to not appear anti-internet, it is also important for foster carers to establish clear household rules on internet use which recognises the value of accessing the internet but also the need to keep children safe online and physically active (Fursland, 2011).

Becoming risk competent

Foster care households are highly regulated in regard to their suitability to care for children who are separated from their families (Nutt, 2006). This involves a lengthy, in-depth fostering assessment, compulsory training, supervision, unannounced visits to their households, annual reviews, and general monitoring and oversight by a fostering service as well as a fostering panel. Foster carers may not only feel accountable towards the fostering service, but also to the children's birth families who often continue to have regular contact with children (see Pye and Rees, 2019 [Chapter 9 this volume]). With this in mind it is not surprising that foster carers can seek to avoid activities which may involve risk:

The natural desire to blame someone when something goes wrong can mean that those who care for children are fearful of allowing them to participate in activities which involve any risk because of fear of litigation (Hewitt-Taylor and Heaslip, 2012).

Adults may restrict or refuse to allow children to engage in play in nature because of concerns for safety, other demands on the children's time, such as school work, and their own lack of familiarity with natural spaces (Louv, 2008). How adults perceive risk impacts on the way they enable learning opportunities for children and a risk-avoidance approach is currently dominant (Hewitt-Taylor and Heaslip, 2012). However, risk also affords the opportunity for empowerment and self-determination, and it has been suggested that exposure to some degree of risk allows children to make judgements and take control of situations, which promotes resilience (Hewitt-Taylor and Heaslip, 2012).

Case study

Reflecting on the literature presented in the previous sections, arguably, outdoor play can engender positive benefits for children looked after; and there are many ways that foster carers and social workers can promote play in nature for children. The case study presented here offers an example of practice that recognised the benefits of play in nature and sought to develop the skills of foster carers, which ultimately sought to improve outcomes for the children they provided care for.

The 'Fostering Outside Play' project emerged from a gap in provision that had been identified during a previous project 'Parents as Partners in Play Cymru'[4], which engaged families with complex needs through outdoor play. Fostering Outside Play aimed to improve the mental and physical well-being of children and young people looked after by supporting foster carers and practitioners to provide them with frequent, high-quality opportunities for play and exploration in the natural environment. In addition, the project sought to demonstrate to social care professionals the rationale for affording such opportunities to children. The course learning outcomes involved developing an understanding of play principles and aimed to ensure foster carers were able to provide appropriate support to children when engaging in outdoor play in nature.

The Fostering Outside Play project was undertaken with Swansea Local Authority fostering service and supported four social care practitioners and nine foster carers for a six-month intervention. The nine carers had 18 children (ranging in age from nine months to 16 years) in placement. The project activities included the development of a training module underpinned by play work principles and no-cost/low-cost activities. Two half-day workshops were delivered, which saw foster carers learn skills from outdoor play workers and an experienced social care practitioner employed by Learning through Landscapes. This supported the foster carers in learning new techniques. As one foster carer noted: 'I thought I knew a lot about outdoor play but this course has helped me see outside the box.'

The course content allowed the foster carers to reflect on their personal memories of childhood outdoor play and the benefits that outdoor play had afforded them. Group discussions were held regarding the ways adults can support child-led play based on the play principles of: time; space; permission; materials; and the value of playfulness. The course provided the opportunity to consider how foster carer competencies could be met through providing children with opportunities for outdoor play in nature. A variety of practical activities which involved the use of using natural materials for creative play were undertaken. The course also included reflective exercises, which focused on implementing change and the learning which had occurred, as illustrated in this foster carer's account:

> I have thoroughly enjoyed these training sessions. I love the outdoors and felt that I didn't really need any training in this area, but I was so wrong! It has helped me go back to my childhood and remember how important play outdoors was for me as I grew up. We all felt a bit silly at times but the way in which everything was done was wonderful, we did stuff together, joined in as much as we felt comfortable with, and shared stories, which was great fun.

The course was supported by a briefing paper to promote an understanding of the theory and research underpinning the course content (Gordon, 2014). Additionally, the foster carers were introduced to a risk–benefit approach (Ball et al., 2012), initially through a case study which they were then able to bring into practice through the undertaking of 'play space audits' during activities.

The foster carers were also given diaries to record outdoor engagement and any observations. Telephone consultations sessions then occurred between the foster carers and the project manager. During these conversations foster carers were encouraged to utilise green spaces, including their garden space, to promote play. A final half-day workshop occurred that gave foster carers the opportunity to share experiences and observations with the other group members. The training was deemed a success and was enjoyed by all. For example: 'Very enjoyable experience that I will remember for a long time and intend to share with others, especially the children I care for.'

A pre- and post-training questionnaire was completed by participants to measure time spent in the nature environment, as well as changes in physical, mental and emotional well-being. This demonstrated that, after the course, children were spending 33 per cent longer outdoors during weekends and more children were cycling and socialising outdoors. Some foster families began new activities including skate-boarding, scootering, climbing trees, outdoor water and sand play, and river and woodland play, and felt more empowerment to adopt a risk-competent approach. In the project one foster carer reported:

> When 14-year-old Joanne came to me for her first respite visit, I just couldn't get her to talk. In the end, I persuaded her to go down to the beach with me for a walk. We didn't need eye contact and could chat side by side as we walked and collected materials for her to do a collage.

This practice example was underpinned by knowledge and research and overall the project upskilled and gave confidence to foster carers in promoting outdoor play in nature, which impacted on the children in their care.

Conclusion

This chapter has provided the reader with insight into how the natural environment can potentially engender benefits for all children, including children looked after. The natural environment is an unexploited resource for foster carers and practitioners who often struggle to support children experiencing overwhelming emotions and difficulties in forming trusting relationships. Taking risks within play is both a need and wish for most children (Ball et al., 2012). The risk-competent approach discussed in this chapter provides the opportunity for a normalisation of care, which builds resilience whilst retaining a nurturing environment.

The academic literature relating to children and nature is well established, however there are several research gaps which remain. For example, the research base would benefit from consideration of how family systems are impacted by experiencing nature together (Chawla, 2015). Whilst no research on the natural environment and children and young people looked after has taken place, other research is transferable to this group and additional considerations highlighted. Furthermore, the example of the 'Fostering Outside Play' practice case study demonstrated the potential opportunities for social care to promote play in nature, which could be replicated by fostering services to promote placement stability by reducing household stress. Ultimately, the natural environment remains an under-used resource and it is hoped that this chapter will encourage further discussion, research and development in nature-based approaches within social care services for children.

Acknowledgements

I would like to thank all of the foster carers who gave their time and commitment to the course, Swansea fostering service who supported the foster carers throughout the course and Learning through Landscapes for leading on this innovative piece of work.

Notes

1. Learning through Landscapes is a UK charity specialising in outdoor learning and play in education.
2. Play Wales is a UK charity which raises awareness of children's need and right to play.
3. BAAF Cymru was an adoption and fostering charity which ceased operations in 2015. AFA Cymru was set up at this time and supports good practice across the breadth of permanency planning.
4. Parents as Partners in Play Cymru involved working with children, their parents/carers and early years practitioners in the most deprived areas of Wales to improve the well-being of vulnerable young children through outdoor play.

References

Abram, D., *The Spell of the Sensuous: Perception and Language in a More-than-human World* (New York: Pantheon Books, 1996).

Aggio, D., Smith, L., Fisher, A. and Hamer, M., 'Mother's Perceived Proximity to Green Space Is Associated with TV Viewing Time in Children', *Preventive Medicine*, 70 (2015), 46–9.

Alexander, J., Cocks, M. L. and Shackleton, C., 'The Landscape of Childhood: Play and Place as Tools to Understanding Children's Environmental Use and Perceptions', *Human Ecology*, 43/3 (2015), 467–80.

Aspinall, P., Mavros, P., Coyne, R. and Roe, J., 'The Urban Brain: Analysing Outdoor Physical Activity with Mobile EEG', *British Journal of Sports Medicine*, 49/4 (2013), 1–6.

Ball, D., Gill, T. and Spiegal, B., *Managing Risk in Play Provision: Implementation Guide* (London: National Children's Bureau, 2012).

Barton, J. and Pretty, J., 'What is the Best Dose of Nature and Green Exercise for Improving Mental Health? A Multi-Study Analysis', *Environmental Science and Technology*, 44/10 (2010), 3947–55.

Bilton, H., *Learning Outdoors: Improving the Quality of Young Children's Play Outdoors* (London: David Fulton, 2005).

Carrera-Bastos, P., Fontes-Villalba, M., O'Keefe, J., Lindeberg, S. and Cordain, L., 'The Western Diet and Lifestyles and Diseases of Civilization', *Research Reports in Clinical Cardiology*, 2 (2011), 15–35.

Caspi, A., Taylor, A., Moffitt, T. E. and Plomin, R., 'Neighborhood Deprivation Affects Children's Mental Health: Environmental Risks Identified in a Genetic Design', *Psychological Science*, 11/4 (2000), 338–342.

Chawla, L., 'Benefits of Nature Contact for Children', *Journal of Planning Literature*, 30/4 (2015), 433–52.

———, Keena, K., Pevec, I. and Stanley, E., 'Green Schoolyards as Havens from Stress and Resources for Resilience in Childhood and Adolescence', *Health & Place*, 28 (2014), 1–13.

ChildWise, *The Monitor Report 2012-13: Children's Media Use* (Bath: Normans Media Ltd, 2013).

Cobb, E., 'The Ecology of Imagination in Childhood', *Daedalus*, 88/3 (1959), 537–48.

Corraliza, J. A., Collado, S. and Bethelmy, L., 'Effects of Nearby Nature on Urban Children's Stress', *Asian Journal of Environment-Behaviour Studies*, 2/4 (2011), 1–12.

David-Ferdon, C. and Hertz, M. F., 'Electronic Media, Violence, and Adolescents: An Emerging Public Health Problem', *Journal of Adolescent Health*, 41/6 (2007), 1–5. Eichsteller, G. and Holthoff, S., 'Risk Competence. Towards a Pedogogic Conceptualisation of Risk', *ThemPra Social Pedogogy C.I.C.* (2009). Available at: *http://www.thempra.org.uk/downloads/risk.pdf* (accessed 02/02/18).

Evans, G. W., Jones-Rounds, M. L., Belojevic, G. and Vermeylen, F., 'Family Income and Childhood Obesity in Eight European Cities', *Social Science and Medicine*, 75/3 (2012), 477–81.

Faber Taylor, A. and Kuo, F. E., 'Children with Attention Deficits Concentrate Better after Walk in the Park', *Journal of Attention Disorders*, 12/5 (2009), 402–9.

Fursland, E., *Foster Care and Social Networking. A Guide for Social Workers and Foster Carers* (London: BAAF, 2011).

Girling, R., 'Yet another change: The experience of movement for children and young people looked after', in D. Mannay, A. Rees and L. Roberts (eds), *Children and Young People 'Looked After'? Education, Intervention and the Everyday Culture of Care in Wales* (Cardiff: University of Wales Press, 2019), pp. 127–39.

Gordon, H. L., *Looked After Children and the Natural Environment: The Fostering Outside Play Project* (London: Learning through Landscapes/BAAF, 2014). Available at *https://www.ltl.org.uk/resources/results.php?id=771* (accessed 21/11/17).

Greenleaf, A. T., Bryant, R. M. and Pollock, J. B., 'Nature-Based Counselling: Integrating the Healing Benefits of Nature Into Practice', *International Journal for the Advancement of Counselling*, 36/2 (2014), 162–74.

Greenwood, A. and Gatersleben, B., 'Let's Go Outside! Environmental Restoration Amongst Adolescents and the Impact of Friends and Phones', *Journal of Environmental Psychology*, 48 (2016), 131–9.

Hewitt-Taylor, J. and Heaslip, V., 'Protecting Children or Creating Vulnerability?', *Community Practitioner*, 85/12 (2012), 31–3.

Hofferth, S. L., 'American children's outdoor and indoor leisure time', in E. Goodenough (ed.), *A Place for Play. A Companion Volume to the Michigan Television Film "Where Do The Children Play?"* (Carmel Valley: The National Institute for Play, 2008), pp. 41–4.

Hordyk, S. R., Dulude, M. and Shem, M., 'When Nature Nurtures Children: Nature as a Containing and Holding Space', *Children's Geographies*, 13/5 (2015), 571–88.

Kaplan, R. and Kaplan, S., 'Adolescents and the natural environment: A time out?', in P. H. Kahn, Jr and S. Kellert (eds), *Children and Nature: Psychological, Sociocultural, and Evolutionary Investigations* (Cambridge, MA: MIT Press, 2002), pp. 227–58.

Kaplan, S., 'The Restorative Benefits of Nature: Toward an Integrative Framework', *Journal of Environmental Psychology*, 15 (1995), 169–82.

Kellert, S. R. and Derr, V., *National Study of Outdoor Wilderness Experience* (Washington DC: Island Press, 1998).

Korpela, K., 'Children's environments', in R. Bechtel and A. Churchman (eds), *Handbook of Environmental Psychology* (Hoboken: John Wiley, 2002), pp. 363–73.

Kuo, F. E. and Sullivan, W. C., 'Aggression and Violence in the Inner City: Effects of Environment via Mental Fatigue', *Environment and Behavior*, 33/4 (2001), 543–71.

——— and Taylor, F. A., 'A Potential Natural Treatment for Attention-Deficit/Hyperactivity Disorder: Evidence from a National Study', *American Journal of Public Health*, 94/9 (2004), 1580–6.

Lee, A. C. K. and Maheswaran, R., 'Health Benefits of Urban Green Space: Review', *Journal of Public Health*, 33/2 (2010), 1–11.

Little, H. and Wyver, S., 'Outdoor Play: Does Avoiding the Risks Reduce the Benefits?', *Australian Journal of Early Childhood*, 33/2 (2008), 33–40.

Louv, R., *Last Child in the Woods: Saving our Children from Nature-deficit Disorder* (Chapel Hill: Algonquin, 2008).

Mannay, D., Staples, E., Hallett, S., Roberts, L., Rees, A., Evans, R. and Andrews, D., *Understanding the Educational Experiences and Opinions, Attainment, Achievement and Aspirations of Looked After Children in Wales* (Cardiff: Welsh Government, 2015).

Nedovic, S. and Morrissey, A. M., 'Calm Active and Focused: Children's Responses to an Organic Outdoor Learning Environment', *Learning Environments Research*, 16/2 (2013), 281–95.

Nuffield Foundation, *Social Trends and Mental Health: Introducing the Main Findings* (London: Nuffield Foundation, 2013).

Nutt, L., *The Lives of Foster Carers: Private Sacrifices, Public Restrictions* (London: Routledge, 2006).

Oshima, N., Nishida, A., Shimodera, S., Tochigi, M., Ando, S. and Yamasaki, S., 'The Suicidal Feelings, Self-injury, and Mobile Phone Use After Lights Out in Adolescents', *Journal of Paediatric Psychology*, 37/9 (2012), 1023–30.

Play Wales, *The Role of Adults in Children's Play: Why Play Matters and What We Can All Do about It* (Cardiff: Play Wales, 2013).

Pye, J. and Rees, P., 'Factors that promote positive supervised birth family contact for children in care', in D. Mannay, A. Rees and L. Roberts (eds), *Children and Young People 'Looked After'? Education, Intervention and the Everyday Culture of Care in Wales* (Cardiff: University of Wales Press, 2019), pp. 113–26.

Quiroga, M. G. and Hamilton-Giachritsis, C., 'Attachment Styles in Children Living in Alternative Care: A Systematic Review of the Literature', *Child Youth Care Forum*, 45/4 (2016), 625–53.

Rees, C. A., 'All They Need is Love? Helping Children to Recover from Neglect and Abuse', *Archives of Disease in Childhood*, 96/10 (2010), 969–76.

Rikkers, W., Lawrence, D., Hafekost, J. and Zubrick, S. R., 'Internet Use and Electronic Gaming by Children and Adolescents with Emotional and Behavioural Problems in Australia – Results from the Second Child and Adolescent Survey of Mental Health and Wellbeing', *BMC Public Health*, 16/399 (2016), 1–16.

Schiffer, E., *Warum Huckleberry Finn Nicht Süchtig Wurde* (Weinheim, Germany: Beltz, 1993).

Schofield, G. and Beek, M., *The Secure Base Model* (London: Coram BAAF, 2014).

Taylor, A. F., Kuo, F. E. and Sullivan, W. C., 'Coping with ADD: The Surprising Connection to Green Play Settings', *Environment and Behavior*, 33/1 (2001), 54–77.

Townsend, M. and Moore, M., *Research into the Health, Wellbeing and Social Benefits of Community Involvement in the Management of Land for Conservation* (Melbourne: Deakin University, 2005).

Ungar, M. and Liebenberg, L., *Resilience in Action: Working with Youth Across Cultures and Contexts* (Toronto: University of Toronto Press, 2008).

Unicef, UNCRC, 1989, Article 31: Leisure, Play and Culture.

Von Marees, N. and Petermann, F., 'Cyberbullying: An Increasing Challenge for Schools', *School Psychology International*, 33/5 (2012), 467–76.

Weinstein, N., Przybylski, A. K. and Ryan, R. M., 'Can Nature Make Us More Caring? Effects of Immersion in Nature on Intrinsic Aspirations and Generosity', *Personality and Social Psychology Bulletin*, 35/10 (2009), 1315–29.

Wells, N. M. and Evans, G. W., 'Nearby Nature', *Environment and Behavior*, 35/3 (2003), 311–30.

Welsh Assembly Government, *Welsh Assembly Government Play Policy* (Cardiff: Welsh Assembly Government, 2002). Available at *http://gov.wales/dcells/publications/policy_strategy_and_planning/early-wales/playpolicy/play policy.pdf?lang=en* (accessed 21/11/17).

Welsh Government, *Play in Wales: The Assembly Government's Play Policy Implementation Plan* (Cardiff: Welsh Government, 2006).

———, *Creating a Play Friendly Wales: Statutory Guidance to Local Authorities on Assessing for Sufficient Play Opportunities for Children in Their Areas* (Cardiff: Welsh Government, 2012).

Worpole, K., *No Particular Place to Go? Children, Young People and Public Space* (Birmingham: Groundwork, 2003).

9 | Factors that promote positive supervised birth family contact for children in care

Joanne Pye and Paul Rees

Introduction

INTERNATIONALLY, THE FAMILY is recognised as the 'fundamental group of society and the natural environment for the growth and well-being of all of its members and particularly children' (United Nations Convention on the Rights of the Child, UNCRC, Preamble, p. 3). Unsurprisingly, therefore, the right to family life and direct contact with birth parents is enshrined in international law and conventions. The UNCRC (Article 9) states that when a child is separated from one or both of their parents, the child has the right to maintain personal relations and direct contact with them on a regular basis. However, for many children in the care system, contact is restricted and takes place less frequently than they would like (Timms and Thoburn, 2006).

The duty to promote birth family contact is set out in legislation (see section 8 of the Children and Families Act 2014 and the Social Services and Well-being (Wales) Act 2014, section 95). The Code of Practice (Part 6: Looked After and Accommodated Children, Welsh Government, 2015) that accompanies the Welsh legislation notes that continued contact between a child in care and their family is a 'key principle' of the Act (paragraph 50), reminding local authorities of their duty to 'endeavour to promote contact between the child and their parents . . .' (paragraph 51).

Yet the legally imposed duty is not without qualification. Legislation and guidance repeatedly states that this duty does not apply if contact would be contrary to the child's best interests. Practitioners have to balance the child's right to contact with their own professional judgement on the best interests of the child. This requires a thorough knowledge of the child, the birth family and a multitude of other factors. It is often highly emotive for all involved (Macaskill, 2002) and may come under the close scrutiny of the courts.

In addition to fulfilling the caveat that governs the fundamental right of children to see their parents, contact can serve many other purposes (Taplin, 2005), and be used as a tool or practice resource (Neil and Howe, 2004). Given that children in care are at risk of a range of poor outcomes (Welsh Government, 2016; Fernandez, 2013), the finding that contact can be a positive influence is of considerable interest to policy makers and practitioners (Boyle, 2017; Berridge and Cleaver, 1987; Sinclair, 2005; Rees, 2013). Conversely, some have highlighted the potentially adverse impact of contact (Moyers et al., 2006; Loxterkamp, 2009). Although legislation suggests that the weight of evidence is in favour of the importance and potential benefits of contact, research literature on the subject is limited.

Evaluating research on contact is challenging precisely because it takes many different forms, and researchers often consider a range of distinct types of contact within one study. Contact can be supervised or unsupervised; face-to-face or indirect (telephone or post); and, with a single parent, both parents, and/or other family members. Similarly, contact varies in respect of frequency, duration and location. Knowledge of these factors, and others, are needed when making comparative statements on impact. Another possible reason why the research is inconclusive is that there remains a lack of clarity on how to define 'positive' contact (Triseliotis, 2010). Positive contact is likely to be the goal of all involved and their perspectives on what this 'looks like' is an important consideration.

This chapter draws on a Swansea University and Economic and Social Research Council funded study carried out in Wales that explored the views of a large number of individuals (N = 165) who were actively engaged in supervised contact (Pye, 2017). Participants fell within five discrete categories: young people, birth family members, carers, contact supervisors and social workers. The chapter summarises what these key stakeholders considered positive contact to be and explores five interrelated themes that were prominent in the participants' discourse around positive supervised contact, namely communication, support, knowledge, context and consistency. More themes emerged but these were selected given their perceived level of importance and utility. The chapter demonstrates how relatively small changes in practice have the potential to promote positive supervised contact.

Methods

A mixed method design was employed to gain the views of the key participant groups (young people, birth family members, carers, contact supervisors, social workers) who were involved in supervised contact at a single contact centre in south Wales. Their views were gathered in two sequential phases.

In Phase 1, which was primarily quantitative, general views on the importance of contact, training and support were explored through structured questionnaires (N = 165). These were completed by nine young people, 38 birth family members, 72 carers, 31 social workers, and 15 contact supervisors. We also collated the views of respondents on their own experience of supervised contact in relation to the family unit that they were a part of, or working with (each discrete family unit consisted of a child or sibling group, at least one birth parent, a carer and associated professionals). No child or parent belonged to more than one family unit, but clearly some social workers and contact supervisors (and to a much lesser extent carers) were involved with several families. Social workers, contact supervisors and carers working with more than one family were asked to respond in respect of each family unit, accounting for the larger number of responses collected. Therefore, in all, we collected views on the experience of 90 discrete family units (N = 477 responses). The responses of the different groups were compared.

In Phase 2, which was primarily qualitative, bespoke semi-structured face-to-face interviews were undertaken with participants connected to 22 of the 90 family units. These 22 family units were chosen as they had recently commenced supervised contact and were likely to be experiencing the final stages of contact within the duration of the study. Multi-perspective thematic analysis (Braun and Clarke, 2006) was used to explore their responses: this included data from two young people, 17 birth family members, 17 carers, 16 social workers and 12 contact supervisors (N = 64).

What is positive contact?

While subtle differences in emphasis were observed between participant groups, analysis of the quantitative and qualitative data suggested a large degree of consistency in how they defined positive contact. Above all, it was clearly felt that contact needs to be purposeful. For some, purpose and meaning was thought to be the achievement of major goals such as successful rehabilitation or the stabilisation of an alternative form of permanence, but for others the facilitation of emotionally warm interactions during contact appeared to be the primary purpose. Despite reported differences over the perceived purpose, clarity around the purpose of contact appeared to be valued by all.

Participants contended that for contact to be positive, arrangements had to match the purpose. If the purpose was, for example, to assess parenting capacity or quality of familial relationships, then ill-prepared, haphazard sessions of limited duration were unlikely to provide a realistic and holistic picture. For many of the participants, contact was positive if it was well matched to the purpose, timely, sufficient in quantity and consistent.

Participants also suggested that for contact to qualify as positive, it needed to be stimulating. This necessitated a session that was engaging, focused and allowed for natural play and conversation between the child and the birth family. In addition, adults considered the extent to which children enjoyed contact to be a major indicator of quality. For example, one social worker commented:

> [It's] positive if I can see that he's laughing and chuckling, he's playing with his toys, he is going up and down as he does, I know he has enjoyed himself.

This view was confirmed by a young person who stated that the most positive thing for her was 'that I spend time with them and we have a whale of a time'.

For many professionals and carers, the extent to which the child's safety and well-being was protected featured highly in their definition of positive contact. Professionals and carers were less concerned, given the tightly controlled environment, over the physical safety of the child and more concerned about their emotional security. They were fearful that comments made by birth family members about, for example, their care plan might disrupt the child's sense of security outside the contact. Birth family members had very limited concern about safety within contact sessions, but acknowledged using the sessions to gain an insight into the child's safety in their care placement, so for them, too, assurance of the child's safety featured within their own definition of positive contact.

This research was able to explore participants' views on supervised contact over several months, typically from the commencement. The views of each participant group illustrated a perception that contact sessions change and can become more positive or negative over time. The following discussion highlights salient factors that influenced such shifts in views, emphasising their importance during the initial stages of contact in promoting positive supervised contact.

Salient factors which can promote positive supervised contact

From the responses of the participant groups, a number of common themes emerged which provide a useful framework when reflecting on the promotion of positive contact. These themes include: the quality of communication between all involved; the availability of formal and informal support (including training); knowledge of contact; the setting; consistency of contact; and, the attitude of each participant toward supervised contact. We now briefly examine each of these themes in turn.

Communication

Almost without exception participants viewed effective communication between themselves and others as critical to the achievement of positive contact. However, the ways in which the various participant groups saw their own and others' communication did not always match the views of the other participant groups. Social workers, for example, generally perceived the quality of their communication and relationship with birth family members, carers and contact supervisors more positively than other groups did. The mismatch of views was most pronounced in respect of social workers and birth family members, where social workers perceived the quality of their communication and relationship with birth family members far more positively than did birth family members. A mismatch in views highlights potential difficulties in communication in terms of expectations and experiences.

Social workers believed that they involved birth family members, carers and contact supervisors in planning supervised contact to a greater extent than these groups felt they had. Birth family members, carers and contact supervisors felt they should have been consulted and involved in planning arrangements to a greater extent. They also felt that limited attention had been paid by social workers to their wishes and feelings. Examples of poor communication and consultation generated negative feelings and inappropriate arrangements. In contrast, some non-social worker participants who had, in their view, experienced good communication with the relevant social worker considered many of the arrangements made to be suitable. These preferred arrangements considered and respected the established routines of the children, the importance of which was emphasised especially in respect of high-frequency contact. Good communication also avoided unrealistic contact arrangements which could lead to parental non-attendance and, ultimately, to contact being restricted or stopped.

Effective communication between participant groups was also considered to be essential for the development of relationships between adults involved in supervised contact. Participants felt that the setting in which supervised contact took place often inhibited more open dialogue. For example, carers and birth family members noted the absence of any dedicated space within the contact centre for them to develop a working rapport. The presence of birth family members at initial contact planning meetings, and the point of handover following contact, was felt to hinder open communication for carers and contact supervisors respectively.

For carers, a source of anxiety and another perceived barrier to communication was the hostility they felt birth family members directed towards them, demonstrated through reflections such as 'working myself up all morning have I done everything right' and 'what are they going to pick on today?'. A number of carers had decided that the best option was to have minimal contact. Many participants recognised this to be the case in their own family unit, and regretted how the gulf between the carers and birth family members had prevented the exchange of valuable knowledge and insights, all of which could have made the supervised contact more profitable and positive.

There was some recognition that although social workers had, at times, understood communication from other participant groups, they did not always act on what they had been told. Some groups were accepting that social workers were trying to balance the multiple, and sometimes conflicting, views and needs of all those involved. There was a clear impression among many participants that arrangements were frequently geared towards the birth family's needs, and sometimes at the expense of the young person. Some participants felt that all needed to be regularly reminded that supervised contact is for the benefit of the child, not the parent.

It was evident from the interviews that effective communication and relationships supported the promotion of positive supervised contact. Effective communication and amicable relationships were seen as powerful in alleviating the anxiety of the child. Carers in particular stressed the importance of communicating an encouraging and positive attitude towards contact 'even if you don't feel like that'. Carers noted that children carefully read the interactions of all those involved and had a remarkable ability to 'pick up any vibes so, you just make it a positive event rather than be negative about it'. The carers considered their own outlook and behaviour around supervised contact to be crucial in making it a positive experience for the children. They felt the children enjoyed contact more and found it easier to interact with their family if they, as carers, adopted a positive and open approach to communication and supervised contact generally. A positive working relationship also defined how comfortable birth family members felt within contact which, in turn, was thought to aid the quality of interaction with the child:

> Contact Supervisor: If they are feeling uncomfortable in a
> contact and feeling intimidated by me or anything, that's going
> to impact on their interactions with their children.

The establishment of open communication and relationships was influenced by the knowledge base of individuals. For example, carers' willingness to engage with birth family members was closely tied to their knowledge of the family. Inaccurate or inadequate knowledge around the prescribed roles, related responsibilities and expectations (due to inadequate communication) was a common barrier to effective communication and positive relationships. Conversely, open communication and positive working relationships facilitated access to mutual support.

Through experience, many of the participants had come to appreciate that the quality of communication between themselves and others involved in supervised contact had changed over time, often for the better. Many suggested that the greater the frequency of supervised contact, the more positive the working relationship became. Greater frequency seemed to make birth family members less anxious during contact, enhancing their ability to seek and receive support from contact supervisors and subsequently improving the quality of contact sessions:

> **Birth Family Member:** I feel I can talk to her a lot better now, in the beginning I was very wary, but now I feel like I can talk to her about anything.

Support

The complexity, emotional sensitivity and potential consequences of supervised contact demands that appropriate support be provided to all involved. Understandably, in this study the focus of much of this support was often on the child. However, professionals also discussed the emotional and practical support they were providing to birth family members before and after contact. Conversely, birth family members reported a lack of emotional support and often felt that they had been left to process powerful emotions alone. This need for emotional support among the birth family members, if met, may have helped to make the experience of supervised contact more positive for all involved.

The support needs of contact supervisors, carers and social workers differed. Contact supervisors felt they had received good training and had a clear sense of being part of a structured and supportive team. However, carers and social workers were often critical about the lack of support they had received. They reported receiving only minimal training and for some this contributed to a lack of clarity about their role. The feeling that they were unsupported and ill-informed engendered feelings of negativity towards supervised contact sessions and undermined the quality of contact in many cases.

Some systems put in place to support contact were also considered by social workers to be detrimental. For example, social workers' experience of formal support through staff supervision was said to focus on the most pressing risk factors within children's cases. As a result, detailed consideration of birth family contact was sometimes not deemed to be a priority, but, as noted by one participant, had the potential to store up problems for the future:

> Social Worker: Supervision is concentrating on the more
> complicated stuff which is worrying because sometimes the
> easier stuff . . . is a ticking time bomb.

The mode of operation of the supervised contact team was also perceived by some to be, at times, a barrier to promoting positive supervised contact. Lengthy referral and gate-keeping procedures, threshold criteria, resource limitations and a lack of assumed responsibility were felt to limit the ability of social workers to arrange timely, consistent and appropriate contact.

Knowledge

Professionals considered a sound knowledge of the principles of supervised contact to be essential for the facilitation of positive contact. However, as discussed earlier, some social workers reported that their knowledge base was limited due to inadequate training. They described an organisational outlook that social workers simply 'do what has always been done' when arranging contact. Some social workers questioned this practice, with one commenting, 'Is that good enough for the child? Is that really the best way to decide on contact?'

Many social workers felt they did not possess the necessary knowledge to promote positive contact. Newly appointed social workers, in particular, were concerned that their knowledge of contact was weak, as one confided: 'It is a terrifying responsibility when in truth you do not know what you are doing'. Financial cuts and resource limitations were felt to be a barrier to accessing formal training. However, while having knowledge of one's own role is essential, having knowledge of the role of others participating in the same supervised contact is equally important, and participants were often unclear on the role that others were performing. Birth family members in particular were often confused about the role of the carer, social worker and contact supervisor, but there were also some contrasts between how contact supervisors and social workers saw their respective roles.

Knowledge of the child, birth family members and case history were also seen as important for positive contact. Inadequate or out-of-date knowledge compromised the contact supervisors' ability to support children and young people, manage overt risks (physical harm, dealing with challenging behaviour), as well as more covert risks which could re-traumatise children:

> Contact Supervisor: it could be a really closed down contact
> . . . we don't know if there's triggers, we don't know if there's
> any words that that child's been sexually abused and using
> words to trigger off things, we just don't know, do we, if we
> haven't been told?

A number of social workers emphasised their limited personal experience of caring for infants and felt this inhibited their ability to assess:

Social Worker: Not having children of my own ... I know the basics, I know if you know a bottle is too hot, how a bottle is sterilised I don't really know ... so parents could be doing it wrong but because it looks ok to me, you know then it is frightening. You know the responsibility is huge.

Knowledge of what was expected of all involved in the contact session was also seen by many as pivotal in achieving positive contact. Overwhelmingly, birth family members felt that minimal preparatory work had been undertaken with them and they simply did not know what to expect. For many, this lack of knowledge had led to emotional upset, fear and anxiety. Birth family members reported that the lack of information provided to them in advance had directly impacted on their behaviour and interaction with the child, and one commented, 'I just didn't know what I wasn't and what I was allowed to do'.

The few birth family members who did report having been given information in advance noted that it was brief and very basic, 'obvious, common sense stuff', focusing upon what they could not do rather than 'positive things'. Professionals acknowledged that a lack of preparation could leave birth family members feeling anxious and the provision of more positive information would enhance interactions and contact more generally.

Some birth family members and professionals said they did not know why the contact was being supervised, or the purpose of the contact. This may reflect inadequate or misinterpreted communication; nevertheless, a lack of clarity about the need for supervised contact could hinder the ability of contact supervisors to ensure the safety of the child. For birth family members, this may lead to feelings of resentment and hinder the establishment of positive relationships. The absence of a shared knowledge could also result in the creation of false beliefs and unnecessary restrictions that hamper child–parent interactions being implemented. However, the acquisition of knowledge over the course of several sessions changed the feel of supervised contact for many participants. For example, birth family members having acquired meaningful knowledge around what to expect and what was expected of them resulted in a more positive view of supervised contact. However, the acquisition of such knowledge stemmed from the experience of supervised contact over time rather than information being formally imparted:

Birth Family Member: Now it's okay but in the very beginning it was absolutely horrendous because I was frightened that if I'm doing something wrong or I was being watched all the time,

but it's nice, it's alright now because like I've just got to forget
they're sitting, I've got to forget where I am, I've got to forget
that it's supervised and I've got to, you know, I just get on with it.
But it's better now.

Context

The environment within which contact takes place has the potential to
influence the interaction between a child and their birth family. In the
contact centre in which this study took place, the children, birth family
members, carers and social workers repeatedly highlighted the physical environment as restrictive, artificial and sterile. For example, a social
worker commented that they were 'trussed up and stuck in a little box'.
Similarly, birth family members used the adjectives 'grim' and 'claustro-
phobic'. There was a general acceptance that meaningful engagement
was difficult to achieve in this context. It also hindered the ability of
birth family members to manage their children's challenging behaviour
and impacted upon the families' general frame of mind. As one social
worker remarked:

> If you put somebody in a black room they are going to have
> a black mood, if you put somebody in a yellow room they are
> going to be a bit happier.

However, the restrictive nature of the environment was felt by a minority
to provide privacy, with one young person noting, 'nobody else knows what
you're doing in the rooms . . . so nobody can butt in your business'. Nevertheless, there was a general consensus that age-appropriate resources
and outdoor facilities would alleviate boredom, stress, tiredness and promote a more enjoyable, engaging and dynamic setting. Many participants
accepted that a lack of finance restricted what could be done, but there
remained a view that professionals needed to be creative.

Supervised contact necessitates the presence of a contact supervisor
and this resulted in many birth family members feeling judged, uncomfortable, anxious and disempowered. Some professionals recognised the
impact this had on how they interacted with their children. For example, a
contact supervisor commented:

> Some parents cannot be themselves . . . I know parents who have
> said they are too embarrassed to even read their child a story
> because I am sitting in the room.

Parents were often highly anxious about making mistakes. At times, birth
family members also felt contact supervisors over-involved themselves
and this detracted from their ability to engage with their child. Some birth

family members found it difficult to control their emotions and found themselves behaving in a cautious and unnatural way with their children. It was felt that a system of monitoring, which did not necessitate the physical presence of a supervisor, may be more beneficial in terms of promoting positive interactions. For example, one social worker suggested:

> Two way mirrors would improve it to observe it and you could even go I suppose if you spent money the video kind of monitoring possibly an observation room as well where you could observe behind a two way mirror? . . . I think it would give a very different session.

However, some social workers acknowledged that they rarely thought about the impact of the setting on all involved:

> Sometimes you can get into a position where you see people as clients or parents and you don't consider the environment that you are putting them and the child in and how that affects everybody.

Consistency

Consistency influenced the acquisition of knowledge, the quality of communication and the availability of support, all of which impacted upon the quality of interactions. For example, conflicting knowledge provided to birth family members by different professionals led to confusion and anxiety during contact. Consistency in arrangements (facilitated by communication) was important to ensure disrupted routines did not lead infants to be 'tired' (Carer) or 'cross' (Contact Supervisor). With regard to older young people, consistency was important to ensure activity routines and free time was respected:

> I've got lots of things going on all week . . . I've got after school club, Tuesday, contact, Wednesday, nature club and after school club. Thursday, contact. Friday, after school club.

Furthermore, consistently arranged contact promoted parental attendance. This was reinforced by one young person who stated a contact session was positive if 'they [parents] turn up and have fun' and negative 'if they don't come'. Consistency in the form of a familiar adult undertaking the role of transportation was also felt to lessen young people's anxiety so they 'don't have an extra face because they see a lot of people' (Carer). Similarly, consistency of the contact supervisor aided the development of positive relationships and resulted in birth family members feeling more comfortable during contact and being able to access more support. However, the logistics of contact, the number of individuals who need to be accommodated and the work commitments of key individuals made consistency in supervised contact difficult to achieve.

Attitudes towards contact

Despite all participant groups feeling contact was important, young people and birth family members valued it most highly; and birth family members often felt that the child's social worker valued the supervised contact far less than they did. Although social workers repeatedly claimed to see the critical importance of contact for a child, they also readily acknowledged that it was difficult to prioritise due to volume of work. They also felt that the social work processes paid insufficient attention to contact:

> Social Worker: We do all these assessments and we talk about a child's health, we talk about their development, we talk about all of that in-depth, but supervised contact is just an add-on.

Social workers also acknowledged that due to the many other pressures on them, and a lack of training, they found contact generated anxiety, frustration, vulnerability, and stress. These feelings of anxiety and frustration by all involved led to a sense of disempowerment for many participants but especially birth family members, carers and contact supervisors. These feelings appeared to consolidate over time and contributed to a lack of communication and poor relationships with social workers.

An awareness of the potential for negative preconceptions about birth family members to contribute to unproductive contact was frequently acknowledged. Preconceptions appeared to impact heavily and adversely on communication, the establishment of positive relationships and the interpretation of the quality of contact sessions. Similarly, birth family members often held negative attitudes regarding social workers at the outset, due to the perception that they were responsible for the child's situation and the need for contact to be supervised.

Implications and concluding remarks

This study has underlined the importance of promoting positive contact rather than contact per se. However, there is insufficient guidance on the definition of positive contact and what factors promote it. Whilst acknowledging the individuality of children and their circumstances, the inclusion of such information within guidance would promote a more coherent, unified, integrated and consistent approach to contact. A greater mutual understanding and appreciation of each other's experiences, roles, responsibilities, expectations and aspirations is needed. Within practice this could be achieved through more effective communication and greater collaboration between carers, professionals and birth family members. Tailored inductions, training prior to and after commencing roles, joint training, effective supervision, formal and consistent guidance and reflective practice are recommended.

Individuals tasked with promoting, arranging and monitoring contact have a responsibility and obligation to make this experience as positive as possible. A failure to promote positive contact can impact not only upon the immediate well-being of the child, but upon assessments and longer-term care plans. However, the diversity, interrelatedness and complexity of factors which define positive contact highlight that achieving positive supervised contact is a complex and challenging task. This is further compounded by striking differences in views and experiences between groups, which illustrate conflicting expectations, different agendas and unique standpoints. Given the individuality of children and young people and their circumstances, it is not possible to create detailed prescriptive guidance on contact for all cases. However, a number of factors outlined in this chapter have the potential to enhance relationships and promote positive supervised contact.

References

Berridge, D. and Cleaver, H., *Foster Home Breakdown* (Oxford: Basil Blackwell Ltd, 1987).

Boyle, C., 'What Is the Impact of Birth Family Contact on Children in Adoption and Long-term Foster Care? A Systematic Review', *Child & Family Social Work*, 22 (2017), 22–33.

Braun, V. and Clarke, V., 'Using Thematic Analysis in Psychology', *Qualitative Research in Psychology*, 3/2 (2006), 77–101.

Fernandez, E., *Accomplishing Permanency: Reunification Pathways and Outcomes for Foster Children* (London: Springer, 2013).

Loxterkamp, L., 'Contact and Truth: The Unfolding Predicament in Adoption and Fostering', *Clinical Child Psychology & Psychiatry*, 14/3 (2009), 423–35.

Macaskill, C., *Safe Contact? Children in Permanent Placement and Contact with their Birth Relatives* (Dorset: Russell House Publishing Ltd, 2002).

Moyers, S., Farmer, E. and Lipscombe, J., 'Contact with Family Members and Its Impact on Adolescents and their Foster Placements', *British Journal of Social Work*, 36/4 (2006), 541–59.

Neil, E. and Howe, D., 'Conclusions: A transactional model for thinking about contact', in E. Neil and D. Howes (eds), *Contact in Adoption and Permanent Foster Care: Research, Theory and Practice* (London: British Association for Adoption and Fostering, 2004), pp. 224–54.

Pye, J., *The Experience and Impact of Supervised Birth Family Contact with 'Looked After Children': Perspectives, Roles and Purposeful Use* (unpublished PhD thesis, Swansea University, 2017).

Rees, P., 'The Mental Health, Emotional Literacy, Cognitive Ability, Literacy Attainment and "Resilience" of "Looked After Children": A Multidimensional, Multiple-rater Population Based Study', *British Journal of Clinical Psychology*, 52/2 (2013), 183–98.

Sinclair, I., *Fostering Now: Messages from Research* (London: Jessica Kingsley Publishers, 2005).

Taplin, S., *Is All Contact between Children in Care and Their Birth Parents Good Contact? Discussion Paper* (New South Wales: Centre for Parenting & Research, 2005).

Timms, J. E. and Thoburn, J., 'Your Shout! Looked After Children's Perspectives on the Children Act 1989', *Journal of Social Welfare & Family Law*, 28/2 (2006), 153–70.

Triseliotis, J., 'Contact Between Looked After Children and Their Parents: A Level Playing Field?', *Adoption & Fostering*, 34/3 (2010), 59–66.

Welsh Government, *Adoptions, Outcomes and Placements for Children Looked After by Local Authorities in Wales, 2015–2016 – Revised* (Cardiff: Welsh Government, 2016). Available at *http://gov.wales/docs/statistics/2016/161018-adoptions-outcomes-placements-children-looked-after-local-authorities-2015-16-revised-en.pdf* (accessed 11/03/18).

———, *Social Services and Well-being (Wales) Act 2014, Part 6 Code of Practice (Looked After and Accommodated Children)* (Cardiff: Welsh Government, 2015). Available at *http://gov.wales/docs/phhs/publications/160106pt6en.pdf* (accessed 11/03/18).

10 | Yet another change

The experience of movement for children and young people looked after

Rebecca Girling

Introduction

OUR CARE SYSTEM is home to some of the most vulnerable children in the United Kingdom (UK), most of whom have experienced abuse, neglect, family dysfunction or are disabled (Berridge et al., 2012). Having been removed from their families, authorities need to provide an environment that will offer both physical and emotional permanence. Children who change placement frequently often lack this permanence and can continue to face significant challenges later in life. Longitudinal research has evidenced this: for example, Biehal et al. (2010) found children who have been in stable placements for over three years have significantly better behavioural outcomes and make greater educational progress than children whose placements are unstable. Sinclair et al. (2007) also found that children who entered care when they were 11 years or older, and experienced three or more placements in a year had more challenging behaviour, more difficulties at school, lower ratings for emotional well-being and were also less likely to have formed an attachment to an adult or be settled in placement. To help improve these outcomes, and consequently give the chance of better futures to children from care backgrounds, it is important to aim to minimise placement moves by finding stable placements.

Finding a stable placement for a child can be a challenge, particularly as children can demonstrate new behaviours and needs as they settle into a placement. Measuring the success of placements based upon outcomes such as a child's behaviour is not always reliable, as behaviour can be both a cause and a consequence of a child being moved. Indeed, Biehal et al. (2010) found children in stable placements had better behavioural outcomes, whereas the review by Oosterman et al. (2007) found that behaviour was a robust predictor of placement breakdown, as was age, with older children being far more likely to experience multiple placements. However, it is often factors external to the child that trigger placement moves. The analysis by Koh et al. (2013) of case files found that the primary reason for children changing placement was related to the foster family they were living with. Factors such as whether there are other children in the home or whether it was a kinship placement have been found to influence placement stability. Children also move placements as part of local authority care plans. Sinclair et al. (2007) found that most placements actually matched their planned length and most moves are planned moves (Ward, 2009; Berridge et al., 2012). These findings are significant as decisions around placement length and transition are factors which are to an extent controllable and therefore can be adapted to better manage children's care experiences. However, what remains unclear is whether a child's prior knowledge and understanding around the reasons for a placement move also affects the success of its outcome.

Whilst a child in care experiences an average of five placements, the majority of children do only have one placement (Ofsted, 2014). In Wales, 10 per cent of children in care experienced three or more placement moves in 2015/16 (Welsh Government, 2016). It appears that it is a minority of children who experience the majority of placement moves (Rosenthal and Villegas, 2010) and the children who are most likely to move tend to have had the most traumatic childhoods and longest care histories (Elliott et al., 2016). This suggests that children experiencing greater movement are particularly vulnerable, and therefore managing the elements of movement that can be controlled should be a priority.

Residential homes in the UK tend to have high levels of movement. Berridge et al. (2012) found that less than 56 per cent of children remained in the same home for longer than six months. Children in residential care are more likely to move with less than a week's notice, and they are less likely to report having a choice compared to children in foster care (Ofsted, 2014). Additionally, children in residential placements appear to be particularly vulnerable, with most entering a unit following placement breakdown, or due to plans for permanence failing rather than through plans not being made (Schofield et al., 2007). Residential care in the UK is often seen as a last resort placement (Boddy, 2013). These placements are used less in Wales than in England (Elliott et al., 2016), yet 15 per cent of children in care still stay in a residential placement for a period of time (Department for Education, 2011). Research on children's opinions tells us that their comparisons of foster to residential care vary, with many children reporting they had negative experiences in foster care where they were heavily disciplined, did not feel cared for or like part of the family (Children's Commissioner for Wales, 2016).

Children in residential care tend to have high levels of need. The residential care population is predominantly male adolescents (Elliott et al., 2016), often with special educational needs, mental health problems (Berridge et al., 2012) and high levels of risk behaviour preceding their placement into residential care (Stanley, 2007). A large number have displayed violent and sexually aggressive behaviour and have engaged in self-harm and criminal activity (Schofield et al., 2007; Berridge et al., 2012). Boddy's (2013) review of permanence for children in care found residential care has the highest risk of poorest outcomes compared to other placements. The 18-month review by Berridge et al. (2012) of children in residential homes found a wide variation between homes, but on average a third of children were excluded from school, more than half had unexplained overnight absences and 40 per cent had been reported to the police. With residential care having such a vulnerable population, and a high turnover of placements, it is not surprising that on the whole outcomes for children in residential care are poor. It is important that the elements over which we have control, such as finding suitable placements to minimise unnecessary movement, are managed to give the most vulnerable children the best opportunities. This chapter is based upon a Masters dissertation which looked at how children in residential care viewed their life stories, with the aim of understanding their experiences in order to make improvements to practice.

Methods

Semi-structured interviews were carried out with seven young people from private residential homes in Wales. They were five males and two females, ranging between 15 and 17 years of age. The young people had experienced between two and ten placement moves each, averaging 5.57. The interviewees were volunteers, recruited by sending age-appropriate information sheets to a large number of homes, asking managers to arrange interviews when interest was shown. Interviews were conducted in the residential homes, recorded on a dictaphone with the young person's consent, and then transcribed. The interview schedule was developed using key questions and themes gleaned throughout the literature review, but the structure remained flexible, following themes raised by the interviewees with the aim of understanding their lived experiences

(Barbour and Schostak, 2011). Thematic analysis of the interview transcripts was undertaken in two phases: first, total immersion in the data including the use of fieldnotes, creating headlines to sum up content and coding to create categories. The second phase of analysis focused on the construction of the accounts, looking at the language used by interviewees (Schutt, 2011).

Findings

Broader concept of movement

The consistent theme that emerged from each young person's narrative was that the concept of movement expands beyond a physical change in placement. This can be demonstrated using the information shared by two of the young people interviewed. Going by standard measures of stability, that being changes in placement, both young people would have been considered to have experienced three placement moves each. However, Figure 10.1 demonstrates that from the interviewees' perspective they experienced six and twelve periods of change respectively, as in the second diagram the young person reported running away for at least three periods of time. These diagrams help to demonstrate the underlying theme that ran through these interviews: that movement and flux are not only experienced at a physical level, but also through relationships,

Figure 10.1: *Movement maps of two interviewees' narratives*

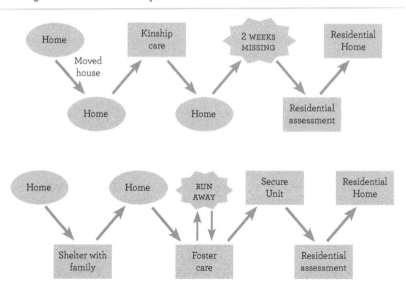

differing expectations and changes in a sense of control. Each of these factors will subsequently be discussed. These findings broaden the discourse around reducing placement moves set out by policy and government guidance.

In sharing their narratives the young people spoke about early life changes such as moving home with their family, birth of siblings and death of family members. These events are not unique to individuals within the care system; however, they set the scene for a sense of flux that is potentially harder to manage within an abusive or dysfunctional environment. Most of the young people had experienced foster placements prior to residential placements, and they described this change as more than a physical movement. Residential care tends to be a more structured environment with a greater number of rules to follow, which for some young people created a feeling of loss of freedom. However, others appreciated the structure as a positive change from their previous environments, feeling that the rules had been created properly and were fair, making them feel equal to the other residents. The young people's narratives did not focus on the change in placement type but tended to discuss the impact of differing rules and expectations:

> John: With [previous carers] I wouldn't have a TV or x-box in my room ... when I moved to [new carer] she was like, there you go, here is your x-box, put that in your room ... I was getting confused with lots of different thing happening around me. Different rules ... I've never been able to pick what we eat in the week, she gave me so many options and stuff. And I told her, why are you giving me all these options. She told me this is life.

For John, the change goes beyond a physical movement between two foster placements. The way he conducted his daily life also changed and, although these changes were considered positive, psychological adjustment was still required. His experience of movement extended beyond a physical change and change in relationships to one which challenges his understanding of 'life', likely increasing his sense of instability. Other than a change in routine, different expectations and consequences for behaviour appeared to also be affecting how well young people coped with the physical movement between placements. For example:

> Sam: I found it really different because there it was like all chilled out. It was a big house, there was a lot of staff ... they would always take you out ... even if you were grounded ... Then I come here ... and you have to do chores, start independent stuff ... the groundings a lot different because you can't go out.

The functional differences between two residential homes meant a great adjustment for Sam; being grounded had different consequences, and there were different expectations placed upon her. Again, her sense of normality needed to adjust, enhancing feelings of instability. Research has taught us that routine is associated with social skills, academic and language development (Spagnola and Fiese, 2007). Therefore, when physical movement is coupled with a drastic change in routine and expectations, the opportunity for a young person to feel settled and learn to manage their behaviour and perform academically is further reduced.

Relationships and movement

Another prominent theme impacting perceptions of movement and placement experience is relationships. Schofield and Beek (2005) found just one specific change, such as a new positive relationship, or discovery of a child's talent, can alter their life significantly. Good quality, consistent relationships are essential for helping create security and a feeling of stability, and this was reflected in the way that the young people spoke about their placements. Within each narrative were experiences of rejection by various professionals and adults close to them. Some spoke of how the lack of expectations or positive outlook for their future held by staff in previous placements had impacted them, so they were then glad to move on. However, on the whole young people spoke of building positive relationships with staff despite a changing workforce, and appeared to understand the boundaries of their role as staff, not parents or friends. Young people wanted respect from staff, and responded positively to receiving this. Many interviewees expressed the importance of staff sharing a joke with them, but they also wanted to be taken seriously:

> **Tyler:** They treated us like we were adults, they weren't talking down to us like we were five year old kids. They respected you and you respected them.

This notion of mutual respect can facilitate decision making as well as building the young person's confidence and teaching them life skills for independent living. Positive relationships with staff fostered a sense of belonging and hope for the future:

> **Grace:** They believe in you. They help you the best they can.

> **John:** They all seem like they care, properly care. Everyone works hard.

Within each narrative the young people spoke of their ambitions, the value that they now placed on education and the jobs or further study that they wanted to undertake. The flux of staff did not emerge as a concern for these young people. Rather, it was evident that the ability to think positively about their future and to have goals and aspirations came from staff members who had believed in them, been encouraging and fostered a stable environment where the young people felt that they were cared for. Placement change, therefore, can also cause a loss of these key, established sources of support for young people.

A further prominent influence on movement was peer relationships. Other young people moving into and out of the placement affected perceived stability in both foster and residential placements. One young person's foster carers regularly looked after children for short periods:

> **Michael:** Well I felt like, why aren't I going home now? Why can't I go home? I kept asking my social worker can I go live with my Dad and she was like you have to wait till you're 16 ... it really really annoyed me. I was like they are getting to go home at the age of 7/8 and I was 14.

The comparisons this young person makes between his placement length and others' appears to be coupled with a lack of understanding about his own situation. In addition, movement of other children was likely creating feelings of abandonment and being treated differently. This extract highlights his perceived lack of stability as his persistent request was to go home, and also highlights the importance of good communication.

Many interviewees first lived in an assessment centre before moving into their current residential placement, meaning they experienced regular changes in their environment. One perceived benefit of living in an assessment centre was having peers in similar situations who they could enjoy living with, without having to discuss their pasts. It was evident that not feeling judged was important to them, and living with other young people in care facilitated this. Young people discussed how they could support each other through the tough days, and share common interests. However, comorbid with having positive peer relationships was the feeling of loss created when one young person moved on.

> **Grace:** No-one cared about my past, no-one judged me ... I got along with a lot of people and staff and everyone ... but the thing with there is the atmosphere changes a lot coz you have kids moving out ... and then you have a new kid coming in that you have never met before. The atmosphere always changed in that house ... Four of us we got along so well and then slowly [others moved out] and there was completely new kids and I was the only one left ... I was not always comfortable with some kids that were living there at that time.

Although this young person initially had a positive experience with her peers, it was underpinned by themes of abandonment and instability as they moved on, leaving her behind. The nature of her environment changed as this movement happened around her, so whilst she was not physically moving placement, feelings of change and instability were still present. Additionally, as suggested in the quote above, peer relationships were not always positive. Each narrative described another individual with whom they had resided but had not experienced a positive relationship. The interviewees shared how this had negatively impacted their functioning. One used the term 'living hell', and when a young person is in this environment it is going to be hard to feel a sense of permanence. Emond (2014) found that, despite peer relationships being a source of both stress and support, it is an area that adults who support individuals in residential care tend to overlook. These findings suggest, and the Children's Commissioner for Wales' (2016) research with young people in residential homes supports the idea, that matching residents in a placement is vital to increase perceived stability and create a happy living environment.

Agency within movement

Within each narrative, placement moves were perceived differently, depending on the young people's experience at each placement. Sometimes they had not wanted to move and did not understand why movement was forced upon them:

> David: I said to my social worker, why can't I stay? Why can't there be a different alternative?

This sense of helplessness was not uncommon. Some young people did not voice their opinion as they felt it would make no difference. They felt that their opinions did not matter and they would just be wasting the social worker's time. Similarly, the Children's Commissioner for Wales (2016) found that some young people felt moving to residential homes was a punishment. However, other young people had positive experiences of being listened to in residential care. These narratives described changes that they felt they had been consulted about, or described times they had remained informed whilst attempts to action their requests were ongoing. In those situations, even when decisions were made against their requests, young people had a positive outlook:

> Sam: It wasn't my choice . . . it was the best thing that could have happened really.

On the whole, these young people were able to look back and reflect upon past decisions, and see them differently, particularly if the decisions were associated with a sense of agency. Whether this is through therapy, their need to positively reframe situations, or the benefit of hindsight, it is hard to tell. However, the knowledge that young people can look back at an event they once considered negatively and understand why it happened, demonstrates the value in communicating with young people.

Agency is defined as the capacity of a person to exercise control (Bandura, 2001). Phase two analysis of transcripts revealed that the language used and the manner with which young people constructed their accounts conveyed a greater or lesser sense of agency associated with each move. This sense of agency affected their view of the placement. Most young people had experienced unwanted moves which were beyond their control, and they described these transitions using terminology such as the following (author's own emphasis):

Grace: They were gonna secure me ... but instead of **securing me** they put me ...

Stuart: They **shipped me** off up here. They didn't tell me or nothing.

Sam: Me and [name] **got placed** into a foster home.

Tyler: [foster carers] was like we can't keep you here if you are messing up your school work so they **kicked me** out of that placement.

The verbs used indicate that the young people felt that they lacked agency in the decisions being made around starting or changing placements. This created a sense that movement was being *done to* rather than in *consultation with* them. Furthermore, the verbs used in the above extracts are powerful, associated with a strong and definite action. The choice of verb could be seen to further reflect the powerlessness felt in these situations.

The language used when moves are anticipated is very different, and the young people spoke with a sense of agency around the placement change in these circumstances. This is seen clearly when the young people describe transitioning between the assessment centre and their current placement, because they enter the assessment centre with the knowledge they will move within six months.

John: I moved here.

Stuart: Then I come here.

Language of agency is also seen when young people have expressed their views to their social worker about moving prior to the transition:

> **Michael:** I don't want to live anywhere down south. They was like, right then you are not moving anywhere down south . . . I come up here. And this is the best place ever.

This young person evidently felt that he had been listened to and had some influence over where he was placed. This sense of ownership is often associated with a more positive experience within the new placement. However, it is important to recognise that even if a young person does not want to move or initially dislikes the placement, they can still retain a sense of agency if moving was anticipated or discussed with them.

> **Grace:** I used to stay in me room, didn't used to eat because I didn't like it here because I was in my other place [assessment centre] for six months.

Here, although a negative situation is described there is no negative agency associated with the act of moving. This extract does, however, demonstrate that whilst communication is vital, there is more to facilitating positive placement moves than a young person having prior knowledge and expectation of the change.

Creating movement

Young people spoke predominantly with a language of agency about moves that were planned: for example, moving on from an assessment centre or knowing they were in a short-term foster placement. Some placement change was a result of circumstances beyond the young people's control, such as foster carers getting new jobs or foster carers' family situations changing. A number of interviewees spoke about placements ending because of a foster carer's abusive behaviour towards them. This was again associated with a sense of powerlessness. Many narratives revealed the young people's perception that placement change was triggered by their own behaviour:

> **David:** I was only there for a week and then I f**ked things up.

> **John:** At one point I was in so much trouble I could have been killed or sent to prison, so that's why I got, why I ended up here.

Whilst their behaviour may have been a contributing factor to the placement move, the young people placed a large emphasis on it being their fault, without also considering external factors. The term 'placement breakdown' is used frequently within policy, literature and among professionals. However, it was not a term the young people used. They gave more specific reasons. The nature of the term implies a sense of failure, which reflects negatively on the young person and their view of that situation. For young people to be able to process what is happening and why, clarity of communication is vital.

Finally, some narratives revealed that young people forced their own movement by absconding as a method of expressing their views and ensuring that they were heard. Having run away repeatedly due to the abuse happening in foster care, a few narratives detailed the relief at being found by the police. Movement through absconding was a form of control or a coping mechanism and, whilst it contributed towards instability, by absconding young people were forcing their own agency. One interviewee, who absconded because her reports of abuse were being ignored, later said she would tell others in a similar situation not to abscond because you 'end up back in secure [unit]'. This statement suggests that this individual has learnt an association between her coping mechanism and negative consequences. She demonstrates agency by absconding, which is a cry for help as she feels that no one is listening to her. However, this chosen act of movement is met with a restriction on her freedom, causing her to feel punished. The concept of sensemaking (Weick, 1993) needs to be applied in these situations. Sensemaking is defined as the ongoing viewing and interpretation of everyday reality to make sense of situations and direct our responses. Here, young people and professionals see a different reality, which leads to different interpretations of the behaviour. It is essential that consideration be given to the reasons behind elected movement, as well as young people's understanding behind forced movement.

Conclusion

A placement in residential care is part of the journey for many young people who go through the care system. Despite best efforts to provide stability for all children who are looked after, movement and change are part of the culture of care and play a significant role in shaping children's life experiences. The research this chapter has summarised explored the idea that placement change is a broader concept than physical movement between placements. Between any two placements, young people can experience a change in routine, expectations around their behaviour or consequences for their actions, all of which require substantial adaptation. Significant changes can also trigger questions about what 'normality' is, further creating a sense of psychological instability alongside the physical movement.

Relationships are key in creating a sense of stability and belonging but can also cause instability. Young people value being respected by carers and staff members. Knowing that the adults supporting them believe in their capability to succeed fosters similar belief in the young people. Peer relationships need to be carefully managed; experiencing movement of peers into and out of their homes can greatly affect young people's sense of stability and their experience of the placement. Young people need to understand the reasons for and timescales around being in placement, so that comparison with others is minimised. Placement of new peers should be matched so that a stable environment is not unsettled, and when young people move on, awareness is needed around feelings of loss or abandonment.

Movement between placements is often necessary and is sometimes forced by young people themselves. This can be through behaviours such as absconding and it is vital that understanding of triggers behind such behaviours is explored so that responses by adults are a solution not a punishment. A sense of agency held by the young person tends to help a positive transition between placements, even when the movement is against their wishes. Young people want to feel listened to, be given advanced warning and be kept informed. Immediately finding the right initial placement for every child in our care system may be an unrealistic ideal but giving consideration to the broader concept of movement and how it can best be managed will hopefully provide greater stability and thus improve the chance of success in other areas of our vulnerable children's lives.

Acknowledgements

I would like to thank all the young people who gave up their time to share their stories with me, the staff who work tirelessly to support them and individuals within the Care Provider Network who made this research possible.

References

Bandura, A., 'Social Cognitive Theory: An Agentic Perspective', *Annual Review of Psychology*, 52 (2001), 1–26.

Barbour, R. S. and Schostak, J., 'Interviewing and Focus Groups', in B. Somekh and C. Lewin (eds), *Theory and Methods of Social Research* (London: Sage, 2011), pp. 61–8.

Berridge, D., Biehal, N. and Henry, L., *Living in Children's Residential Homes* (London: Department for Education, 2012).

Biehal, N., Ellison, S., Baker, C. and Sinclair, I., *Belonging and Permanence: Outcomes in Long Term Foster Care and Adoption* (London: British Association of Adoption and Fostering, 2010).

Boddy, J., *Understanding Permanence for Looked After Children: A Review of Research for the Care Enquiry* (London: The Care Enquiry, 2013).

Children's Commissioner for Wales, *The Right Care: Children's Rights in Residential Care in Wales* (Cardiff: Children's Commissioner for Wales, 2016).

Department for Education, *Children in Children's Homes in England Data Pack* (London: Department for Education, 2011).

Elliott, M., Staples, E. and Scourfield, J., *Residential Care in Wales: The Characteristics of Children and Young People Placed in Residential Settings* (Cardiff: Care Council for Wales, 2016).

Emond, R., 'Longing to Belong: Children in Residential Care and their Experiences of Peer Relationships at School and in the Children's Home', *Child and Family Social Work*, 19/2 (2014), 194–202.

Koh, E., Rolock, N., Cross, T. and Eblen-Manning, J., 'What Explains Instability in Foster Care? Comparisons of a Matched Sample of Children with Stable and Unstable Placements', *Children and Youth Services Review*, 37 (2013), 36–45.

Ofsted, *Children's Care Monitor 2013/14: Children on the State of Social Care in England* (London: Ofsted, 2014).

Oosterman, M., Schuengel, C., Slot, W., Bullens, R. and Doreleijers, T. A., 'Disruptions in Foster Care: A Review and Meta-analysis', *Children and Youth Services Review*, 29/1 (2007), 53–76.

Rosenthal, J. and Villegas, S., 'Living Situation and Placement Change and Children's Behaviour', *Children and Youth Services Review*, 32/12 (2010), 1648–55.

Schofield, G. and Beek, M., 'Risk and Resilience in Long-Term Foster-Care', British *Journal of Social Work*, 35/8 (2005), 1283–301.

———, Thoburn, J., Howells, D. and Dickens, J., 'The Search for Stability and Permanence: Modelling the Pathways of Long-stay Looked After Children', *British Journal of Social Work*, 37/4 (2007), 619–42.

Schutt, R. K., *Investigating the Social World: The Process and Practice of Research* (London: Sage, 2011).

Sinclair, I., Baker, C., Lee, J. and Gibbs, I., *The Pursuit of Permanence: A Study of the English Child Care System* (London: Jessica Kingsley Publishers, 2007).

Spagnola, M. and Fiese, B. H., 'Family Routines and Rituals – A Context for Development in the Lives of Young Children', *Infants and Young Children*, 20/4 (2007), 284–99.

Stanley, N., 'Young People's and Carers' Perspectives on the Mental Health Needs of Looked-After Adolescents', *Child and Family Social Work*, 12/3 (2007), 258–67.

Ward, H., 'Patterns of Instability: Moves within the Care System, their Reasons, Contexts and Consequences', *Children and Youth Services Review*, 31 (2009), 1113–18.

Weick, K., 'The Collapse of Sensemaking in Organisations: The Mann Gulch Disaster', *Administrative Science Quarterly*, 3 (1993), 628–52.

Welsh Government, *Adoptions, Outcomes and Placements for Children Looked After by Local Authorities, Year ending 31 March 2016, revised* (Cardiff: Statistics for Wales, 2016).

11 | 'A family of my own'

When young people in and leaving state care become parents in Wales

Louise Roberts

Introduction

THIS CHAPTER CONSIDERS early parenthood for young people in and leaving state care in Wales. Currently, little is known about how many young parents are themselves parented by the state, the support that is available to those who need it, or the outcomes experienced by families with one or both parents in or leaving the care system. This includes how many children remain in the care of their parents, how many are subject to Children's Services intervention and how many are separated from their parents and subject to court orders. This chapter provides details of an ongoing research study undertaken within the Children Social Care Research and Development Centre (CASCADE) at Cardiff University. The origins of the research will be outlined, together with some emerging findings of the research to date. Drawing on qualitative interviews with parents and leaving care professionals, the chapter will highlight some key barriers facing young parents in and leaving care: namely experiencing stigma, being vulnerable to discrimination and having inadequate access to support. It will argue that continued policy and practice development is required to give young people in and leaving state care the best chance of preventing cycles of intergenerational care experience and of 'having a family of their own'.

Early parenthood for young people in and leaving care

National and international evidence suggests that young people in and leaving state care are more likely than their peers to experience early pregnancy and parenthood (Biehal and Wade, 1996; Dixon et al., 2004; Del Valle et al., 2008; Vinnerljung and Sallnäs, 2008; Mendes, 2009; Roca et al., 2009; Oshima et al., 2013; King et al., 2014; Courtney et al., 2011). In Wales, an audit of teenage pregnancy by Craine et al. (2014) found that more than five times as many young people in state care presented as pregnant (five per cent) compared to the general population of under 18-year-olds in Wales (0.8 per cent). Reducing teenage pregnancy is a long-established policy goal within England and Wales (Welsh Assembly Government, 2010; Welsh Government, 2012). For young mothers, it is associated with a range of disadvantage, including living in poverty, lower educational attainment and economic activity, poor housing and health inequalities (Public Health Wales, 2016). The likelihood of such disadvantage may be compounded for young parents in and leaving care, who by nature of their care status already face a heightened risk of poor outcomes (Social Care Institute for Excellence, 2004).

Despite such concerns, early parenthood may be perceived favourably by some young people in and leaving care. As Stein (2006, p. 274) has discussed, young people leaving care experience an 'accelerated and compressed journey to adulthood'; moving to independence at an earlier age than their non-care-experienced peers. In this way, the idea of 'settling down' and starting a family may be experienced at a comparatively early stage. In a review of the US literature, Svoboda et al. (2012) noted that young people have high hopes for family life and want better parenting experiences for their children than they had themselves. This resonates with Connolly et al.'s (2012) international review of qualitative research, which observed that young people in care may associate having a baby with stability, family, closeness and love.

For young people with limited economic prospects, parenthood may be a positive aspiration, offering a socially accepted role and status (Haydon, 2003). Similarly, pregnancy may be considered 'a force for good' (Mantovani and Thomas, 2014), signifying positive change and/or hope for the future in otherwise chaotic lives (Barn and Mantovani, 2007). Indeed, the positive impact of parenthood on young people's lives has been observed in several studies. For example, Wade (2008) reflected that parents interviewed as part of a leaving care study for the Department of Health were largely positive about their new family lives and reflected warmly on being needed and having a sense of purpose. Similarly, Maxwell et al. (2011) noted the potential for motherhood to be a positive and repairing experience while Chase et al. (2006, p. 442) observed that parents in their study frequently attributed children as having 'turned their lives around'.

Despite being a positive life event for some young people, emerging evidence suggests that young parents in and leaving care are at increased risk of compulsory child welfare intervention and intergenerational experiences of family separation. In North America an examination of social work records, concerning 2,487 children born to young people in foster care in Illinois, concluded that parents in state care were more likely than other adolescent parents to experience child welfare involvement (Dworsky, 2015). Jackson Foster et al.'s (2015) large cohort study found that adults who had previously been in state care were more likely to report having a child placed in foster care in comparison to the general population (nine per cent versus 1.1 per cent). Moreover, Courtney et al.'s (2011) longitudinal study found care leaver mothers were six times more likely to report living apart from at least one biological child by age 25/26. In England, the Centre for Social Justice (2015) highlighted a worrying number of care leavers' children being taken into care, with 10 per cent of parents having experienced their own child entering state care within the preceding year. Emerging evidence also suggests that women with experience of state care are over-represented amongst women who are subject to repeat care proceedings (Broadhurst et al., 2017).

In terms of research in Wales, with the exception of Craine et al. (2014), little of what is known about young parents in and leaving care originates from a Welsh context. There are no official statistics detailing the numbers of young people who are pregnant and/or who are parents. There is also no published data on outcomes for families where one or both parents is in or leaving care and it is unknown how many are 'successfully' parenting or how many experience compulsory child welfare intervention. The post-doctoral research project discussed in the following sections was designed to investigate the experiences and outcomes of families where one or both parents is a young person in or leaving state care (up to the age of 21 or 25 if in education, training or employment) in Wales.

Methods

The idea for the research came from young people and adults associated with Voices from Care. CASCADE has a close working relationship with young people connected to the organisation and is committed to their experiences being at the heart of the Centre's work and shaping the research that is undertaken (see Staples et al., 2019 [Chapter 15 this volume]). Young people and adults connected to the organisation had discussed their concerns about support availability and outcomes for young parents who were care-experienced. While for some the experience was positive, in too many instances young parents had encountered significant difficulties and challenges, including occasions where they had been subject to compulsory safeguarding assessment and intervention. Over the course of developing the research idea with both voluntary and statutory professionals, there was widespread agreement that this was a challenging area of practice and one which would benefit from research attention. Funded by Health and Care Research Wales, the study has several stages. At the time of writing the project was ongoing and scheduled for completion in 2019.

Stage one involved initial exploratory interviews with care-experienced parents. The interviews were designed to provide insight into the experiences of parents in Wales and highlight the salient issues to inform future parts of the fellowship project. Two third sector agencies, with a support remit spanning south and west Wales, recruited eight parents to take part in a qualitative interview. Two parents were the primary carers for their children but six had experienced the permanent and compulsory removal of their child or children. At the point of interview, 12 of the 16 children born to the participants were in state care or had been adopted. Further details about this phase of the study are outlined in Roberts (2017).

Stage two was a review of the international literature. A scoping approach was adopted which combines systematic search techniques with a relatively broad subject focus including both published and unpublished literature (Arksey and O'Malley, 2005). The review identified a range of evidence including examinations of parent experience, risk and protective factors in respect of early pregnancy and parenthood and an emerging evidence base concerned with outcomes for families where one or both parents is care-experienced. Concerns have been raised by third sector organisations in Wales about responses and support provision available for parents in and leaving state care (Voices from Care et al., 2016). Yet despite 'many calls to action' (Fallon and Broadhurst, 2015, p. 4) there is a dearth of evidence in respect of 'what works' when seeking to support care-experienced young people as parents.

Stage three aimed to investigate the current numbers, support provision and outcomes for families where one or both parents is in or leaving care in Wales. Qualitative interviews were undertaken with representatives of leaving care services from each of the twenty-two local authorities across Wales. The interviews were designed to explore practice experience, as well as consider local responses to young people in and leaving care who are expecting a child or who are parenting. In addition, local authorities were asked to complete a survey requiring non-identifiable data about each young person currently expecting a child or who was a parent. The survey was designed to examine current numbers of young parents, professional perceptions of risk and protective factors in respect of parenting, as well as the extent of additional support and intervention by statutory social services.

During this phase of the research, the author collaborated with colleagues working on the Wales Adoption Study (see Anthony et al., 2016 for further details). The study comprised the records of all children placed for adoption by every local authority in Wales between 1 July 2014 and 31 July 2015. This involved the review of 374 Child Assessment Reports for Adoption records (Roberts et al. 2017). Analysis concluded that care leavers were over-represented amongst birth parents whose children were placed for adoption. Despite less than 1 per cent of children being in state care (Welsh Government, 2016), 27 per cent (n = 96) of birth mothers and 19 per cent (n = 45) of birth fathers were recorded as care leavers (Roberts et al., 2017).

Stage four was an in-depth prospective case study of young people nearing the birth of their child. Qualitative interviews were conducted with the mother and/or father, and if appropriate with key professionals including social workers, personal advisers and carers. Follow-up interviews approximately three and twelve months later were also planned. This stage was intended to generate rich data on barriers and enablers to successful outcomes for this group in the early stages of parenting.

In the final stage of the study (stage five), an advisory group consisting of key stakeholders, namely parents, statutory and third sector professionals, will review the study findings. The group will assess current needs and consider whether current services and responses across Wales are adequate. Where appropriate, recommendations regarding further policy and service development will be made to Welsh Government. The remainder of this chapter provides an overview of the key themes emergent from the research to date and draws upon qualitative interview data generated with parents in stage one and leaving care professionals in stage three.

Barriers to 'a family of my own'

When faced with the prospect of parenthood, the vast majority of parents that participated in the project or whose stories have been told by professionals, wanted to be 'good' parents and build close relationships with their children. Outcomes for these families varied, with some thriving in their parenting role, with others experiencing compulsory Children's Services intervention. However, over the course of the research recurrent themes have emerged in respect of the barriers faced by young people in and leaving care in respect of parenting: namely the potential for them to experience stigma and discrimination because of their care histories, and the limited support young people can access, if needed, to help them in their parenting role.

Stigma and discrimination

Goffman's (1963) conceptualisation of stigma explored the potential for assumptions or expectations to be made about an individual's social identity based on personal characteristics or attributes. While young parents face a range of negative labelling associated with teenage pregnancy (Ellis-Sloan, 2014), young people in and leaving care can also be stigmatised as a result of their care status. A 'presumed incompetency' (Mantovani and Thomas, 2014) has been identified in previous research, as has a professional tendency to perceive intergenerational patterns of care to be 'inevitable' (Rutman et al., 2002). Over the course of this research, the impact of previous experiences, either before care or during care, on parenting capacity was repeatedly questioned:

> I mean their experience is going to obviously impact on their ability to parent ... most relationships and experiences of parenthood is skewed or is dysfunctional so it's not going to have a good impact. There are some young people that do absolutely brilliantly and you think oh my gosh where did they learn that from because they come from households of neglect or sexual abuse (Leaving care professional)

> We were both in care for similar reasons. Violence was a massive part of it, that's what's made them [social workers] a bit nervous, the fact that whether or not we would treat him [son] the same way. (Parent)

These quotes suggest young people face assumptions that their ability to parent is inhibited or damaged by their previous experiences. In sentiments not uncommon within the study, professionals often expressed surprise if young people demonstrated positive parenting ability. As described by the parent, more commonly there was concern or suspicion that parents would replicate abusive behaviours and/or had not experienced good parenting, and therefore did not know how to be a good parent themselves.

Related to stigma, the potential for young parents in and leaving care to be discriminated against has also been raised within the research. As a 'known name' within the authority, professionals acknowledged that young people were more likely to come to the attention of Children's Services. The majority of leaving care professional respondents stated that there was no official policy for responding to young people who presented as pregnant. Some stated there had been a general move away from automatically referring young people for pre-birth assessment. However, a minority of respondents acknowledged that there was 'an unspoken policy of every looked after child needs to be referred' (Leaving care professional) for a pre-birth assessment.

> I don't think you'll find it written down anywhere but there's an expectation that they will be referred onto children's services as unborn yeah. I don't agree with that because I think each case

should be assessed on its own merits but there is ... a blanket expectation that they should all be referred onto children's services ... I think that there is a long held view that looked after children who become parents will inevitably fail, or struggle, and will need additional services put in. (Leaving care professional)

In an effort to resist expectations to make a formal referral to the safe-guarding team, one professional respondent discussed how the leaving care service had opted to undertake their own parenting assessments:

We'll do the [parenting] risk assessment to, that's really to justify why we're not referring ... we use that to like I say to justify why we're not referring because I think some people feel that well they're looked after they must have a referral you know and I don't think that should be always be the case. (Leaving care professional)

While the sentiment of this team's response was well meaning, young parents in and leaving care are nevertheless subject to assessment that other parents would not expect from those supporting them. Moreover, the practice is motivated by efforts to identify and manage risk as opposed to identifying if and in what ways the young person can be supported.

For parents who are subject to a safeguarding assessment, professionals also have access to a wealth of historical information, which is not available for families with little or no previous involvement with statutory services. The influence of such information, regardless of concerns for accuracy or continued relevance, has been criticised by some respondents:

Once they [Children's Services] found out I'd been in care that was it, they went back pulled up all the files, read them all seen what had happened ... they read those records some of which had been written ten years previously. They judged me and used it against me. (Parent)

Our bottom line really is 'would you say that for any other child'? And if the answer is 'well actually probably not but we know the history', well that shouldn't be the case then. (Leaving care professional)

Such comments imply that records previously used to record a young person's support needs have the potential to be re-framed in terms of risk when transitioning to parenthood.

Support

The availability and adequacy of support for parents in and leaving care has been a recurrent focus of discussion over the course of the research. Local initiatives described by participants included therapeutic support during pregnancy, mother and baby foster placements, short breaks for children with foster carers, as well as support groups and parenting courses facilitated by leaving care professionals. However, the availability of such initiatives across local authority areas is highly variable, with some initiatives described as 'one off' interventions, as opposed to ongoing support provision. Efforts to develop a model of good practice and create greater parity of provision across Wales are hampered by a lack of evidence in terms of impact and efficacy of specialist initiatives (Finnigan-Carr et al., 2015). Significant challenges also exist in developing service responses which can meet the range of potential needs of both parents and children, as well as ensure accessibility in rural and urban areas. Discussing the potential development of peer support groups, one respondent commented:

> The geography of the county doesn't help with doing group work, it takes you all your time to get young people into one place. (Leaving care professional)

Moreover, service development and sustainability can be inhibited by fluctuating demand for parenting support provision, with variable and changeable numbers of parenting young people within and across local authorities. As noted by one respondent:

> We go through little cohorts ... so at some point we'll have you know maybe x number of parents going on at the same time and then at other times we might have you know a couple of pregnancies ... it's not like you have such significant numbers that you can systematically think this is a service that we're going to need to provide now. And I think that's probably one of the stumbling blocks. (Leaving care professional)

Key tensions emerged regarding attempts to improve supportive responses. These included debates about what support should be offered, for how long and for what purpose. The development of support specifically aimed at care leavers was a contentious issue; for some, a recognition of a young person's previous experiences was important and opportunities for parents to meet others with shared understanding of the care system provided valuable opportunities for peer support.

> [Young parents in and leaving care] feel a bit conscious about attending some of those [universal services] because they are

generally older parents who have got a good social network and they feel as though everyone is looking at them if they turn up and feel as though they're being judged and watched. (Leaving care professional)

Yet for other respondents, targeted support was viewed as stigmatising and compounded notions that parents in and leaving care were likely to be struggling and in need of monitoring. Similarly, the time-limited nature of support from the state as parent/grandparent was criticised by some respondents:

we stop working with people at either 21 or 25 and I think even sort of 20, 21 is still very young ... to be able to manage the realities of having a child then, even if there were no other concerns attached to that. (Leaving care professional)

some of the needs of young people and children who have been through the care leavers system are way past the sort of 21 mark (Leaving care professional)

Extending support availability has links to wider social work tensions about supporting independence or encouraging dependency. Moreover, support provision post age 21/25 may be neither wanted nor needed for some parents in and leaving care. As noted in Roberts (2017), some parents within the study were desperate for support but none was forthcoming, while others were offered comprehensive packages of support but found these were intended to assess or monitor parenting capacity as opposed to providing meaningful help. Such concern was subsequently recognised by one professional respondent:

Young parents coming through the system it doesn't feel like support, it sounds awful, yeah it does feel almost like policing, [they are] being watched and it's token positive; 'oh she is engaging well with social services BUT...' (Leaving care professional)

Despite such tensions, several respondents believed that service responses should seek to better replicate the type of support that non-care-experienced parents would typically expect from extended family:

I think we'd have to look at the sorts of services that normal everyday grandparents provide, general support, kind of babysitting, helping out financially now and again, just the sort of stuff that we, as a council, don't do. (Leaving care professional)

Yeah I think [corporate parents] need to have a better
understanding and recognition in terms of what they would
do for their own children when they're a parent, the support
that they would provide, the babysitting on a weekend so they
could go away or have a night out or go out for a meal. I guess
it's those little things that a lot people take for granted that care
leavers don't have the opportunity to have really which makes it
twice as hard for them. (Leaving care professional)

Conclusion

Young people in and leaving care face significant barriers as they transition to parenthood. There is potential for them to face stigma and discrimination, and to have inadequate access to support. In highlighting the
potential for disadvantage, it is not the intention of this research study to
add to the perception that all parents in and leaving care will have support needs or experience difficulties as parents. Many examples of young
people parenting successfully, with and without the assistance of support, have been provided over the course of the research. The range of
parenting support needs that have been discussed during this study are
commonly shared by all parents, regardless of age and care-experience.
However, what tends to be different for parents in and leaving state care is
the limited resources they have available to them and the judgements and
perceptions of those around them.

Of particular concern is the vulnerability of those young people who
do require support with parenting. The findings suggest that not only
is the available support inconsistent and/or insufficient, the potential
to improve such provision is inhibited by a range of factors, not least
underdeveloped ideas about the nature of the role and responsibilities
of the state as grandparent. Further policy and practice development
is required, including local and national policies which make explicit a
commitment to supporting young parents with their children, to ensure
that young people in and leaving care are provided with the best chance
of preventing cycles of intergenerational care-experience and of 'having
a family of their own'.

Acknowledgements

The project was funded by Health and Care Research Wales and has been supported by a wide variety of individuals across both statutory and third sector
organisations. I am very grateful to the professionals who gave up their time to
contribute to the research and deeply appreciative of parents' willingness to share
their experiences.

References

Anthony, R., Meakings, S., Doughty, J., Ottaway, H., Holland, S. and Shelton, K., 'Factors Affecting Adoption in Wales: Predictors of Variation in Time between Entry to Care and Adoptive Placement', *Children and Youth Services Review*, 60 (2016), 184–90.

Arksey, H. and O'Malley, L., 'Scoping Studies: Towards a Methodological Framework', *International Journal of Social Research Methodology*, 8 (2005), 19–32.

Barn, R. and Mantovani, N., 'Young Mothers and the Care System: Contextualizing Risk and Vulnerability', *British Journal of Social Work*, 37 (2007), 225–43.

Biehal, N. and Wade, J., 'Looking Back, Looking Forward: Care Leavers, Families and Change', *Children and Youth Services Review*, 18/4–5 (1996), 425–45.

Broadhurst, K., Mason, C. and Bedston, S., *What Are Our Obligations to Care Leavers Who Lose Their Own Infants and Children to the State?* (2017). Available at *http://wp.lancs.ac.uk/child-and-family-justice/2017/03/01/care-leavers-children/* (accessed 08/04/17).

Centre for Social Justice, The, *Finding Their Feet: Equipping Care Leavers to Reach Their Potential* (2015). Available at *http://www.centreforsocialjustice.org.uk/UserStorage/pdf/Pdf%20reports/Finding.pdf* (accessed 09/10/15).

Chase, E., Maxwell, C., Knight, A. and Aggleton, P., 'Pregnancy and Parenthood Among Young People in and Leaving Care: What Are the Influencing Factors, and What Makes a Difference in Providing Support?', *Journal of Adolescence*, 29/3 (2006), 437–51.

Connolly, J., Heifetz, M. and Bohr, Y., 'Pregnancy and Motherhood among Adolescent Girls in Child Protective Services: A Meta-synthesis of Qualitative Research', *Journal of Public Child Welfare*, 6 (2012), 614–35.

Courtney, M., Dworsky, A., Brown, A., Cary, C., Love, K. and Vorhies, V., *Midwest Evaluation of the Adult Functioning of Former Foster Youth: Outcomes at Age 26* (Chicago, IL: Chapin Hall at the University of Chicago, 2011).

Craine, N., Midgley, C., Zou, L., Evans, H., Whitaker, R. and Lyons, M., 'Elevated Teenage Conception Risk amongst Looked After Children: A National Audit', *Public Health*, 128/7 (2014), 668–70.

Del Valle, J. F., Bravo, A., Alvarez, E. and Fernanz, A., 'Adult Self-Sufficiency and Social Adjustment in Care Leavers from Children's Homes: A Long-term Assessment', *Child & Family Social Work*, 13 (2008), 12–22.

Dixon, J., Wade, J., Byford, S., Weatherly, H. and Lee, J., *Young People Leaving Care: A Study of Outcomes and Costs* (York: Social Work Research and Development Unit, 2004).

Dworsky, A., 'Child Welfare Services Involvement among the Children of Young Parents in Foster Care', *Child Abuse & Neglect*, 45 (2015), 68–79.

Ellis-Sloan, K., 'Teenage Mothers, Stigma and their "Presentations of Self"', *Sociological Research Online*, 19/1 (2014), 9.

Fallon, D. and Broadhurst, K., *Preventing Unplanned Pregnancy and Improving Preparation for Parenthood for Care-Experienced Young People* (London: Coram, 2015).

Finnigan-Carr, N. M., Murray, K. W., O'Connor, J. M., Rushovich, B. R., Dixon, D. A. and Barth, R. P., 'Preventing Rapid Repeat Pregnancy and Promoting Positive Parenting among Young Mothers in Foster Care', *Social Work in Public Health*, 30 (2015), 1-17.

Goffman, E., *Stigma: Notes on the Management of Spoiled Identity* (New Jersey: Prentice Hall Inc., 1963).

Haydon, D., *Teenage Pregnancy and Looked after Children/Care Leavers* (London: Barnardo's, 2003).

Jackson Foster, L. J., Beadnell, B. and Pecora, P. J., 'Intergenerational Pathways Leading to Foster Care Placement of Foster Care Alumni's Children', *Child & Family Social Work*, 20 (2015), 72-82.

King, B., Putnam-Hornstein, E., Cederbaum, J. A. and Needell, B., 'A Cross-sectional Examination of Birth Rates among Adolescent Girls in Foster Care', *Children and Youth Services Review*, 36 (2014), 179-86.

Mantovani, N. and Thomas, H., 'Choosing Motherhood: The Complexities of Pregnancy Decision-making among Young Black Women "Looked After" by the State', *Midwifery*, 30 (2014), 72-8.

Maxwell, A., Proctor, J. and Hammond, L., '"Me and my Child": Parenting Experiences of Young Mothers Leaving Care', *Adoption and Fostering*, 35/4 (2011), 29-40.

Mendes, P., 'Improving Outcomes for Teenage Pregnancy and Early Parenthood for Young People in Out-of-home Care: A Review of the Literature', *Youth Studies Australia*, 28/4 (2009), 11-18.

Oshima, K. M., Narendorf, S. C. and McMillen, J. C., 'Pregnancy Risk among Older Youth Transitioning out of Foster Care', *Children and Youth Services Review*, 35/10 (2013), 1760-5.

Public Health Wales, *Reducing Teenage Conception Rates in Wales: Project Report* (2016). Available at *http://www.wales.nhs.uk/sitesplus/documents/888/Teenage %20conceptions%20in%20Wales%20%2OFINALv1.pdf* (accessed 12/03/17).

Roberts, L., 'A Small Scale Qualitative Scoping Study into the Experiences of Looked After Children and Care Leavers Who Are Parents in Wales', *Child & Family Social Work*, 22/3 (2017), 1274-82.

————, Meakings, S., Smith, A., Forrester, D. and Shelton, K., 'Care Leavers and their Children Placed for Adoption', *Children and Youth Services Review*, 79 (2017), 355-61.

Roca, J. S., García, M. J., Biarnés, A. V. and Rodríguez, M., 'Analysis of Factors Involved in the Social Inclusion Process of Young People Fostered in Residential Care Institutions', *Children and Youth Services Review*, 31/12 (2009), 1251-7.

Rutman, D., Strega, S., Callahan, M. and Dominelli, L., ' "Undeserving" Mothers? Practitioners' Experiences Working with Young Mothers in/from Care', *Child & Family Social Work*, 7 (2002), 149-59.

Social Care Institute for Excellence, *Preventing Teenage Pregnancy in Looked After Children* (2004). Available at *http://www.scie.org.uk/publications/briefings/briefing09/* (accessed 08/04/17).

Staples, E., Roberts, L., Lyttleton-Smith, J. and CASCADE Voices, 'Enabling care-experienced young people's participation in research: CASCADE Voices', in D. Mannay, A. Rees and L. Roberts (eds), *Children and Young People 'Looked After'? Education, Intervention and the Everyday Culture of Care in Wales* (Cardiff: University of Wales Press, 2019), pp. 196–209.

Stein, M., 'Research Review: Young People Leaving Care', *Child & Family Social Work*, 11 (2006), 273–9.

Svoboda, D. V., Shaw, T. V., Barth, R. P. and Bright, C. L., 'Pregnancy and Parenting among Youth in Foster Care: A Review', *Children and Youth Services Review*, 34 (2012), 867–75.

Vinnerljung, B. and Sallnäs, M., 'Into Adulthood: A Follow-up Study of 718 Young People Who Were Placed in Out-of-home Care During Their Teens', *Child & Family Social Work*, 13 (2008), 144–55.

Voices from Care, NYAS, Family Rights Group and Tros Gynnal Plant, *Joint Statement of Concern* (2016). Available at *http://www.voicesfromcarecymru.org.uk/sites/default/files/joint_statement_of_concern.pdf* (accessed 11/01/17).

Wade, J., 'The Ties that Bind: Support from Birth Families and Substitute Families for Young People Leaving Care', *British Journal of Social Work*, 38/1 (2008), 39–54.

Welsh Government, *Sexual Health and Wellbeing Action Plan for Wales 2010–2015* (2010). Available at *http://www.shnwales.org.uk/Documents/485/Strategy%20(English).pdf* (accessed 08/04/17).

———, *Tackling Poverty Action Plan 2012–2016* (2012). Available at *http://www.senedd.assembly.wales/documents/s500001880/CELG4-2014%20Paper%205.pdf* (accessed 08/04/17).

———, *Adoptions, outcomes and placements for children looked after by local authorities* (2016). Available at *http://gov.wales/statistics-and-research/adoptions-outcomes-placements-children-looked-after/?lang=en* (accessed 08/04/17).

III

PARTICIPATORY, QUALITATIVE AND COLLABORATIVE APPROACHES

---

12 | Positionality and reflexivity

Conducting qualitative interviews with parents who adopt children from foster care

Claire Palmer

Introduction

THIS CHAPTER FOCUSES on qualitative interviewing as a method of eliciting data from parents [1] who have adopted older children (aged four and over) from the looked-after system. The chapter is drawn from my PhD study [2] on the transition to parenthood for adopters of older children. Data for my study were collected as part of a national study of adoption, the Wales Adoption Study [3]. In the wider study, mixed methods were used and data were drawn from three sources: social services documentation on every Welsh child placed for adoption in a 13-month period; questionnaires completed by adoptive parents; and qualitative interviews with adopters. However, in this chapter the method of qualitative interviewing will be centralised.

The chapter first outlines the context of adoption in the looked-after system in Wales, using quantitative data to illustrate the experiences of those placed for adoption at older and younger ages. The motivations of parents who adopt older children and the processes by which they decided to adopt an older child are also explored. The latter part of the chapter reflects on my experience of interviewing adoptive parents who had recently had a former looked-after child placed with them for adoption. Methodological considerations arising from the interview process are discussed, including the impact of the researcher on the research setting.

I also reflect on the emotional impact of conducting research and how researchers can be affected by the process.

Adoption from foster care in Wales

Since the late 1960s, social changes such as the increased availability of contraception, the legalisation of abortion, the reduced stigmatisation of single and same-sex parents, and welfare payments for single parents have changed adoption practice in England and Wales. The Adoption and Children Act 2002 (ACA 2002) (implemented in 2005) reflected the shift in circumstances of the children waiting for adoption, to older children who had been in local authority care, rather than relinquished babies (Ball, 2002, 2005). Importantly, the ACA 2002 made provision for children to be adopted without the consent of their birth parents (Doughty, 2015). The ACA 2002 remains the key legislation regarding adoption in England and Wales, but there has been some recent divergence in policy between countries as adoption is a devolved area. A key development in adoption provision in Wales is the establishment of the National Adoption Service, which was launched in November 2014, in response to Welsh Government's Social Services and Well-being Act 2014.

A minority of children leave local authority care through adoption. On the 31 March 2015, there were 5,615 Welsh children in the looked-after system (Stats Wales, 2017). During the 13-month period from 1 July 2014 to 31 July 2015, the Wales Adoption Study identified that 374 Welsh children were placed for adoption. My study focuses on those who parent children who are older at the point of adoptive placement, as research has indicated that members of this group are more at risk of experiencing adoption disruption than children placed at a younger age (Selwyn and Meakings, 2015; Selwyn et al., 2014). Adoption disruption is the term used when a child prematurely leaves the adoptive family home. I define older children as children aged four and over at the time of placement. Out of the 374 children placed in Wales in the study period, 86 were aged four and over. The oldest child placed for adoption in the study period was aged nine (n = 1) and the youngest were under the age of one (n = 94).

An analysis of pre-adoption experiences shows that older-placed children had experienced more abuse in all categories, more neglect, more significant injuries and had been exposed to more domestic violence (except for prenatal domestic violence) than younger children. Older-placed children spent longer on average living with birth parents (meaning they were likely to have spent longer in an abusive environment), experienced longer periods in the care system, were subject to a higher number of placement moves, on average, than younger children, and had more failed reunifications than younger-placed children. These trends in pre-adoption experiences are illustrated in Figure 12.1.

Figure 12.1: *Pre-adoption experiences in Wales, 1 July 2014 to 31 July 2015 – Wales Adoption Study*

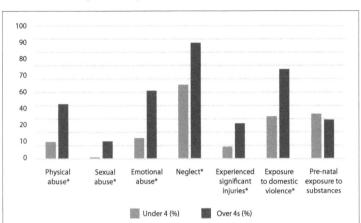

There is evidence to suggest that cumulative exposure to Adverse Childhood Experiences (ACEs) has negative long-term consequences for the individual, such as poor physical health (Felitti et al., 1998), and can increase the likelihood of risk-taking behaviours (such as drug taking and sexual promiscuity) and poor anger control (Anda et al., 2006). An exploration of Adverse Childhood Experiences (ACEs) within the Wales Adoption Study found that a greater percentage of children who were placed for adoption at age four or over had experience of each indicator of adversity, with the exception of parental mental illness (Anthony and Shelton, 2017).

The long-lasting impact of increased exposure to early adversity experienced by older adoptees, may mean that this group could prove more challenging to parent, perhaps accounting, at least in part, for the higher level of family breakdown for older-placed children (Selwyn et al., 2015, 2014). In the Wales Adoption Study, adopters responded to questionnaires which asked how well they felt they were adjusting to adoptive family life approximately a year after the child had been placed. Those who had adopted children who were older at time of placement were experiencing more difficulties than those who had adopted younger children. For example, 46.2 per cent said they were facing unexpected or many difficulties, whereas this was true of only 11.1 per cent of parents who had adopted younger-placed children (χ^2 (1) = 12.359, p = < .001). These figures are indicative of the potential challenges associated with parenting an older child. Through qualitative interviewing it has been possible to move beyond the figures, and gain a nuanced understanding of the subjective experiences and motivations of parents who adopt an older child.

Interviewing adopters of older looked-after children

This section presents some findings from the qualitative interviews conducted with adopters of older children, foregrounding both the usefulness of the interview approach and the sensitive nature of the research topic. The interviews enabled insights into the multiple factors that influence the decision to adopt a child, which, in some instances, may not have been available to the social workers who were assessing the adoptive parents, due to the power dynamics involved in the adoption assessment process. It is notable that the interviewee below felt that, to some extent, prospective adopters answer social work questions in ways that reflect what they think social workers want to hear. The 'home study' referred to below is the series of home visits, in which the assessing social worker gets to know prospective adopters, to decide whether to recommend them as potential adoptive parents:

> **Rebecca:** I think the home study is contrived, a lot of it is utterly pointless and if you are bright you know what they want to hear … don't get me wrong we were very honest, but if you were clever you would know.

Although parents in the study generally stated that they had been open and honest with their assessing social worker, the power imbalance implicit in the adoption process, whereby the social worker is the key gatekeeper in securing a child, could be a barrier to frank discussions. Arguably, there is also a power imbalance in the interview setting – the interviewer sets the topic, asks the questions, chooses what to probe further and decides when the conversation is over (Brinkmann and Kvale, 2015). However, the different dynamic of the research interview, combined with the anonymity offered to interviewees, may have allowed for adoptive parents to more openly reflect on the adoption process, without worrying about potential repercussions. Therefore, through qualitative interviewing, different information is brought to light than that which is available to social work professionals.

Fourteen parents of older children were interviewed in the study. Eleven out of the fourteen families who participated cited infertility or health issues as the primary reason for pursuing adoption. During the interviews, several parents explained how they had tried fertility treatments or had experienced multiple miscarriages. For the remainder, in two instances, the parents did not mention health or infertility issues, but had considered (and decided against) fostering as a route to parenthood. In the final family, the parents' motivations were altruistic and linked with their religious beliefs.

Many of the adopters had a long-held desire to become a parent, and described the family that they had 'always wanted'. This suggests a role played by fantasy in the transition to adoptive family life, as the longed-for child is imagined by the prospective parent, as illustrated in the following interview extracts;

> Sophie: I *always wanted* a little girl so I had, I really wanted ... an 18-month-old ideally, like, I don't know, I had a picture of a little blonde 18-month-old [laughs].

> Jennifer: And we've bought a caravan to go away on the weekends now and ... yeah, it's just being a family now and that's what we've *always wanted* and yeah, it's hard but we certainly wouldn't change it.

As prospective adopters, the interviewees had been asked by social workers to give their preferences about their future child. Several adopters noted that they ideally wanted the 'perfect child', who had not experienced prior-adversity or who did not have ongoing high-level health or emotional needs, but they knew this was highly unlikely due to the nature of adoption from care in the UK context. Adopters expressed preferences regarding the child's age, gender and appearance. The adopters were also asked what they felt they could not cope with, in terms of the child's needs and past experiences. Some felt that they would be unable to cope with the potential challenges presented by a child who has experienced certain types of abuse. Notably, several parents felt they would be unable to support a child who had been sexually abused. These conversations and decisions were a difficult part of the process. Some adopters explained that they were mindful when they were expressing their preferences that they were still undergoing assessment and so felt pressured to say that they would be happy with certain attributes that they felt concerned about. Due to this, several parents detailed how their preferences had changed considerably through the process, to ensure that they would be successful in procuring a child.

The interviews enabled an opportunity for adoptive parents to share nuanced, detailed and experiential accounts, which provided fascinating insights into the process of adoption, from their initial thoughts on their future child to the point that the match was decided and agreed. In several families, multiple and, at times, overlapping reasons were given for accepting a match with an older child. Most commonly, adoptive parents had initially hoped to adopt a younger child, but through the process of assessment had altered their preferences regarding the child's age.

Adopters were sometimes encouraged early in the process by their social worker to widen the age bracket that they would consider. Adoptive parents were often receptive to the suggestions of the assessing social worker and, in many cases, altered their preferences accordingly. In other cases, the adopter decided to consider older children due to lack of links being made with younger children, thereby widening their criteria to secure a match. Several parents who did not fit the normative model of the 'perfect' parent (single or older parents), felt they had been overlooked for matches with younger children in favour of those who did fit the model. Several parents felt aware that they were effectively competing for children with other prospective adopters.

A key motivation was the altruistic notion of rescuing a child who may not otherwise have had the opportunity of a stable home. This thinking was pertinent as prospective adoptive parents were aware that older children were less likely to secure an adoptive home. For others, the primary reason for choosing an older child was due to their own age, as they did not want to be considered the 'elderly' parent of a very young child. Another common theme in decision making was the idea that by adopting an older child this meant that developmental issues would already be apparent. There was a sense that, by adopting an older child, there would be less developmental uncertainty. Phillip provides an example of this type of thinking:

> Phillip: ... To be honest with you I think in the end we ended up broadening our age bracket you know? I think we were comfortable with around [age] two and I think we sort of like set it at a window of around about [age] six because we felt that that sort of cut off any ... medical issues and by then we probably know behaviourally where things were at as well.

Some adopters had been encouraged by social workers to think in this way. Evidence suggests that developmental issues are particularly prevalent in the looked-after population (Ford et al., 2007), and therefore, as prospective adopters, interviewees were keen to have a clear understanding of their future child's developmental needs.

Reflecting on the interview data, for most parents interviewed, infertility or health issues were the main initial motivation for deciding to pursue adoption. For many, the desire to become a parent was a long-held one and parenthood was something about which they had fantasised. The main reasons for adopting an older child involved: a widening of criteria to secure a match; altruism – the idea of giving a child a chance for permanency that they may not have had otherwise; a consideration of the ages of current family members; and to guard against developmental and behavioural uncertainties. Arguably, all of these factors are emotive and emotional, and experiences which necessitate a relational aspect, the interview conversation, to explore parents' subjective understandings of the adoption process. However, interviewing is not always straightforward and the following section offers reflections on the fieldwork process.

Qualitative interviewing and reflexivity

The use of qualitative interviews made it possible to gain understandings of the complex processes through which adopters negotiated their decision to adopt an older child. As Brinkmann and Kvale (2015) note, 'through conversations we get to know other people and learn about their experiences, feelings, attitudes, and the world they live in', and can attempt to 'understand the world from the subject's point of view'. Similarly, for May (2001), 'interviews yield rich insights into people's biographies, experiences, opinions, values, aspirations, attitudes and feelings'. In qualitative interviews, the researcher is the instrument; they are an active respondent, who shapes the way the interview is conducted and influences the responses that are elicited (Pezalla et al., 2012). Researchers bring their own identity (Berger, 2015) and preconceptions, and reveal things about themselves, both verbally and non-verbally within the interview process (Abell et al., 2006; Jordon, 2006). Consequently, it is important to consider the interview context and the impact of the individual researcher upon the interview data.

Coffey (1999, p. 17) stresses the importance of 'locating the self' by recognising the impact that the researcher's identity has on the research setting, as well as the impact of fieldwork on the individual. Some relevant issues to consider in relation to researcher positionality include gender, race, age, sexual orientation, immigration status, personal experiences, linguistic tradition, beliefs, biases, preferences, theoretical/political/ideological stance, and one's emotional response to the participant (Berger, 2015). It is therefore important that researchers reflect upon their impact on the data they collect and the way in which they interpret that data. Researchers are not neutral or objective, they are 'imperfect social actors' (Ellingson, 2006, p. 299). One way to recognise the impact of the researcher is through self-awareness and reflexive thinking throughout the research process (Koch, 1994). Reflexivity can be defined as:

> The process of continual internal dialogue and critical self-evaluation of researcher's positionality as well as active acknowledgement and explicit recognition that this position may affect the research process and outcome. (Berger, 2015, p. 220)

Accordingly, researchers should critically assess their interactions within the research setting, to engage with their embodied and emotional placement in the research (Ellingson, 2006; Ezzy, 2010). There are several ways in which researchers can increase self-awareness, such as keeping a reflexive journal about the process, writing themselves into fieldnotes, recording analytic and methodological decisions in memos, and being reflexive about each decision made (Barry et al., 1999; Koch, 1994). Reflexivity adds quality to research by accounting for the researcher's own biases and therefore adding to the trustworthiness of the research (Berger, 2015; Koch, 1994). As discussed in the following section, in this research I was careful to reflect on my positionality, and its impact on the data produced.

Similarity, difference and self-disclosure

In examining the impact that I had on the interviews, I considered my own identity and the points of similarity and difference between myself and the interviewees. My identity is multifaceted. There are several aspects that I could focus on (for example, as a social worker/research novice/white/middle-class person), but the element of my identity which I have chosen to focus on here is my identity as a pregnant woman. At the time of interviewing, I was between 14 and 30 weeks pregnant with my first child. As stated earlier in the chapter, most adoptive parents within this study had come to the decision to adopt due to infertility, miscarriage or other pregnancy-related health issues. I was therefore cautious about how I approached this point of difference, as I was worried that it may cause friction in my relationship with the adoptive parents, or serve as a painful reminder of the grief and loss that they had experienced.

The concepts of the researcher as an 'insider' or 'outsider' and the impact of this on the setting have been widely discussed (see Daly, 1992; Mannay, 2010; Morriss, 2015; Wiederhold, 2014). There are possibilities and pitfalls associated with both positions. Outsiders may miss key factors or lack understanding because they do not have lived-experience of the research topic (Berger, 2015). Insiders, in contrast, may risk overfamiliarity with the area and therefore need to find ways to 'make the familiar strange' to study it (Mannay, 2010). A further problem for insiders is that participants may not explain their experience as fully, assuming that, due to their shared experience, explanation is unnecessary (Daly, 1992; Morriss, 2015).

However, the binary categories of insider/outsider are simplistic. Our identities are far more complex than this. As Wolf contends (1996, p. 16), 'A number of feminist researchers reject this simplistic dichotomy of insider–outsider. Some feminists say they felt they were neither insider or outsider or both simultaneously'. As an interviewer, in many ways I was an insider. For example, as a well-educated, middle-class, professional person, I was from a class background similar to that of most of my participants. I live in the same city as some of them. I understood the cultural references made by my participants and I understand what it is to live in the Welsh context. I am a white, married, heterosexual – similarities shared by many participants. Furthermore, I was also embarking on the journey to parenthood. Simultaneously, I am an outsider. I am not an adoptive parent and I have not experienced the process of becoming an adoptive parent. My participants had been recipients of social work services as prospective adopters, and later, as adoptive parents, whereas I, as a former social work practitioner, have only ever been the deliverer of services and never the recipient.

It is worth considering here the issue of what is disclosed, both purposely and unintentionally by researchers and how this can influence the responses elicited at interview. Participants were likely to respond to me in particular ways because of things I cannot help but reveal about myself – such as my ethnicity, age, gender and accent. Furthermore, I chose to reveal some things about myself: for example, participants could see my marital status as I chose to wear my wedding ring. My pregnant status was something that I was eager to hide, as I felt that it was unlikely to be helpful in establishing my relationships and building rapport with participants. My body betrayed me, and, as the weeks progressed, my pregnant form became increasingly evident. I actively tried to conceal my pregnancy by choosing my clothing carefully and by trying not to communicate my pregnancy through my posture or body language. For example, in one interview, the interviewees suggested that we sat on bar stools around the kitchen counter. Sitting at the kitchen counter for three hours whilst pregnant was uncomfortable, but I did not want to reveal my discomfort to the couple, in case this prompted a further consideration of why I was uncomfortable. In this instance, I am certain that I was overthinking the matter, but the example serves to illustrate the 'performance' that I was giving to the participants and the lengths I was going to in order to manage the impression I was giving to others (Goffman, 1959).

I felt uncomfortable about the ethical implications of concealing my pregnancy. There is a long-established tradition in feminist research whereby self-disclosure is encouraged to conduct research in a non-hierarchical manner (Oakley, 1982; Yeo et al., 2014). However, it is common for researchers to downplay or emphasise elements of their identity to build rapport (Reich, 2013). As I was conducting the interviews as novice researcher in a multidisciplinary research team, I felt a sense of corporate responsibility for the data, and this impacted the ways in which I conducted the interviews and how I dealt with ethical issues in the research (Rogers-Dillon, 2005). Whilst in many ways I felt an affinity with adopters who had made the recent transition to parenthood, as I was considering the prospect of my own journey to parenthood, I did not know if this view would be reciprocated. I felt slightly less anxious about my pregnant state around adopters who already had a birth child, although this may have been misguided, as several participants had experienced secondary infertility and may have found it insensitive to be interviewed about this by a pregnant researcher. It is difficult to know how I would have been perceived had I been more willing to openly display my pregnant state.

I do not know if most of my participants had any inclination that I was pregnant. If they did, it is not possible to know what impact this had on their responses to the interview or their feelings about me as an interviewer. During the process of interviewing, only one adopter asked me about my pregnancy, and this happened at the beginning of the interview. The participant did not seem to be upset or overly concerned about the fact I was pregnant, but my sensitivity to the issue made me feel flustered, and meant that I did not probe about the couple's reasons for adopting as I may have done had my pregnancy not been mentioned. At the end of a subsequent interview, I was asked whether I had any children. The participant had several birth children, had been a foster carer and had chosen to adopt a child in her care. Due to the circumstances of the adoption and having completed the interview itself, I felt less concerned about revealing my pregnant state than I did with the previous adopter.

The desire for sensitivity to my participants had a profound impact on my own perception of myself as a pregnant person. I was intensely aware of my changing body and my desire not to upset adoptive parents leaked into my everyday experience of pregnancy. I reacted irritably to friends and family members who commented on my changing figure. I became anxious about my growing bump and made every effort to hide it, not just during interviews, but at all times. The nature of the research impacted my perception of my situation. I felt enormous guilt about having been able to conceive easily whilst feeling ambivalent about the prospect of parenthood. The injustice of fertility weighed heavily on me, especially when comparing myself to those who had been desperate to become parents, and yet had been unable to conceive. Although I had been looking forward to conducting interviews, I was eager to finish the interviews before my pregnancy became too visible. I was aware throughout the fieldwork that I was negotiating my own sense of parenting identity whilst talking to new (adoptive) parents about their experiences of the transition to parenthood.

These feelings were often unwelcome; however, emotional responses can be helpful in the process of research. As Coffey (1999, p. 158) maintains:

> Emotional connectedness to the process and practices of fieldwork, to analysis and writing is normal and appropriate. It should not be denied or stifled. It should be acknowledged, reflected upon, and seen as a fundamental feature of well-executed research.

Reflexivity, then, can enable the researcher to understand their emotions throughout the research process and can be beneficial in terms of protecting them from experiencing negative consequences because of emotionally identifying with research subjects (Benoot and Bilsen, 2016). It can be difficult to acknowledge the emotions caused by research as 'it goes against the image of dispassionate science' (Rogers-Dillon, 2005, p. 445). However, reflexivity is important in terms of ensuring researcher safety and to conduct 'ethical and emancipatory' research (Malacrida, 2007, p. 1339). Experiences in the field can shape how data are interpreted, and 'failure to name these emotions and responses might lead them to become expressed in other ways such as in how we write about that person' (Mauthner and Doucet, 2003, p. 419). However, there are limits to what it is possible to access through reflexivity, as our understandings of what influences the process of meaning making is only ever partial and may become clearer with the passing of time and distance (both emotional and intellectual) from a research project (Mauthner and Doucet, 2003).

Conclusion

Through using qualitative interviews, I could explore the motivations and complex decision-making processes of adopters who had older children placed with them for adoption. Adoption is one way by which children leave the care system, and most children available for adoption from Wales have experienced the looked-after system. Children who are older (aged four and over) when placed for adoption have been found to be more likely to experience difficulties in the adoptive family home when compared to those placed at a younger age. Therefore, it is important to examine the subjective experience of adoptive parents, and this chapter has illustrated the ways in which the qualitative interview can be an effective tool to gain an understanding of adoptive parents' views in relation to the care-experienced children that they parent. Qualitative interviewing has the potential to elicit different responses than the insights which are gleaned from social work interactions, due to the differing power dynamics in each situation.

This chapter has also argued that all researchers shape the research that they conduct through their positionality and biographical experience, and by the ways in which they are perceived by the participants. The data gathered from interviews, and how that is interpreted, reflect the co-constructed experiences of both researcher and the researched. Consequently, researchers need to think reflexively to gain insights into their own performative interactions and subjective meaning making. As a pregnant researcher exploring the motivations of adopters, many of whom had experienced infertility and health-related issues, I was mindful of how adoptive parents may have perceived my pregnant form when I explored this sensitive topic. I encountered a strong emotional response to conducting the interviews, which not only impacted how I perceived participants, but also how I perceived myself as a parent-to-be. Acknowledging emotions is an important part of the research process and reflexivity is important in helping the researcher to manage the emotional impact of conducting research. The process of reflection strengthens data analysis and adds quality to research. Qualitative interviewing allowed for new insights into the lived experiences of adoptive parents of care-experienced children and these insights facilitate further understanding around the support needs of newly formed adoptive families.

Acknowledgements

Sincere thanks go to the staff from the Local Authority adoption teams in Wales, who kindly assisted with contacting families, and all members of the research advisory group for their guidance; and, most, importantly, the families who participated.

Notes

1. All names given in the above account are pseudonyms.
2. My PhD research project is funded by the Wales School for Social Care Research.
3. The Wales Adoption Study was funded by Health and Care Research Wales, a Welsh government body that develops, in consultation with partners, strategy and policy for research in the NHS and social care in Wales. The team who worked on the study were as follows: Katherine Shelton (Principal Investigator), Sarah Meakings, Julie Doughty, Heather Ottaway, Amanda Coffey, Sally Holland, Rebecca Anthony, Claire Palmer and Janet Whitley. For further information on the study please see: *http://sites.cardiff.ac.uk/adoptioncohort/*.

References

Abell, J., Locke, A., Condor, S., Gibson, S. and Stevenson, C., 'Trying Similarity, Doing Difference: The Role of Interviewer Self-disclosure in Interview Talk with Young People', *Qualitative Research*, 6 (2006), 221–44.

Anda, R. F., Felitti, V. J., Bremner, D., Walker, J. D., Whitfield, C., Perry, B. D., Dube, S. R. and Giles, W. H., 'The Enduring Effects of Abuse and Related Adverse Experiences in Childhood: A Convergence of Evidence from Neurobiology and Epidemiology', *European Archives of Psychiatry and Clinical Neuroscience*, 256 (2006), 174–86.

Anthony, R. and Shelton, K., 'Technical Summary 5: The Prevalence of Adverse Childhood Experiences and the Relationship with Children's Mental Health Post-adoption', (Wales Adoption Study, Cardiff: Cardiff University, 2017).

Ball, C., 'Regulating Inclusivity: Reforming Adoption Law for the 21st Century', *Child and Family Social Work*, 7 (2002), 285–96.

———, 'The Adoption and Children Act 2002: A Critical Examination', *Adoption & Fostering*, 29 (2005), 6–17.

Barry, C. A., Britten, N., Barber, N., Bradley, C. and Stevenson, F., 'Using Reflexivity to Optimize Teamwork in Qualitative Research', *Qualitative Health Research*, 9 (1999), 26–44.

Benoot, C. and Bilsen, J., 'An Auto-Ethnographic Study of the Disembodied Experience of a Novice Researcher Doing Qualitative Cancer Research', *Qualitative Health Research*, 26 (2016), 482–9.

Berger, R., 'Now I See It, Now I Don't: Researcher's Position and Reflexitivity in Qualitative Research', *Qualitative Research*, 15 (2015), 219–34.

Brinkmann, S. and Kvale, S., *InterViews: Learning the Craft of Qualitative Research Interviewing* (London: SAGE Publications, 2015).

Coffey, A., *The Ethnographic Self: Fieldwork and the Representation of Identity* (London: Sage, 1999).

Daly, K., 'Parenthood as problematic: Insider interviews with couples seeking to adopt', in J. Gilgun, K. Daly and G. Handel (eds), *Qualitative Methods in Family Research* (California: Sage, 1992), pp. 103–25.

Doughty, J., '"Where Nothing Else Will Do": Judicial Approaches in England and Wales', *Adoption and Fostering*, 39 (2015), 105–18.

Ellingson, L., 'Embodied Knowledge: Writing Researchers' Bodies into Qualitative Health Care Research', *Qualitative Health Research*, 16, (2006), 298–310.

Ezzy, D., 'Qualitative Interviewing as an Embodied Emotional Performance', *Qualitative Inquiry*, 16 (2010), 163–70.

Felitti, V. J., Anda, R. F., Nordenberg, D., Williamson, D. G., Spitz, A. M., Edwards V., Koss, M. P. and Marks, J. S., 'Relationship of Childhood Abuse and Household Dysfunction to Many of the Leading Causes of Death in Adults: The Adverse Childhood Experiences (ACE) Study', *American Journal of Preventative Medicine*, 14 (1998), 245–58.

Ford, T., Vostanis, P., Meltzer, H. and Goodman, R.,'Psychiatric Disorder Among British Children Looked After by Local Authorities: Comparison with Children Living in Private Households', *British Journal of Psychiatry*, 190 (2007) 319–25.

Goffman, E., *The Presentation of Self in Everyday Life* (London: Penguin, 1959).

Jordon, A. B., 'Make Yourself at Home: The Social Construction of Research Roles in Family Studies', *Qualitative Research*, 6 (2006), 169–85.

Koch, T., 'Establishing Rigour in Qualitative Research: The Decision Trail', *Journal of Advanced Nursing*, 19/5 (1994), 976–86.

Malacrida, C., 'Reflexive Journaling on Emotional Research Topics: Ethical Issues for Team Researchers', *Qualitative Health Research*, 17 (2007), 1329–39.

Mannay, D., 'Making the Familiar Strange: Can Visual Research Methods Render the Familiar Setting more Perceptible?', *Qualitative Research*, 10, (2010), 91–111.

Mauthner, N. S. and Doucet, A., 'Reflexive Accounts and Accounts of Reflexivity in Qualitative Data Analysis', *Sociology*, 37 (2003), 413–31.

May, T., *Social Research: Issues, Methods and Process* (Berkshire: Open University Press, 2001).

Morriss, L., 'Dirty Secrets and Being "Strange": Using Ethnomethodology to Move Beyond Familiarity', *Qualitative Research*, 16/5 (2015), 1–15.

Oakley, A., 'Interviewing women: a contradiction in terms', in H. Roberts (ed.), *Doing Feminist Research* (London, Boston and Henley: Routledge and Kegan Paul, 1982), pp. 30–61.

Pezalla, A. E., Pettigrew, J. and Miller-Day, M., 'Researching the Researcher-as-Instrument: an Exercise in Interviewer Self-Reflexivity', *Qualitative Research*, 12 (2012), 165–85.

Reich, J. A., 'Emerging breasts, bellies, and bodies of knowledge: how pregnancy and breastfeeding matter in fieldwork', in T. Mose Brown and J. Dreby (eds), *Family and Work in Everyday Ethnography* (Philadelphia: Temple University Press, 2013), pp. 41–60.

Rogers-Dillon, R. H., 'Hierarchal Qualitative Research Teams: Refining The Methodology', *Qualitative Research*, 5 (2005), 437–54.

Selwyn, J. and Meakings, S., *Beyond the Adoption Order (Wales): Discord and Disruption in Adoptive Families* (Bristol: University of Bristol, School for Policy Studies, 2015).

———, Wijedasa, D. and Meakings, S., *Beyond the Adoption Order: Challenges, Interventions and Adoption Disruption* (Bristol: University of Bristol, 2014).

Stats Wales, 'Children Looked After at 31 March by Local Authority, Gender and Age' (2017). Available at *https://statswales.gov.wales/catalogue/health-and-social-care/social-services/childrens-services/children-looked-after/children-lookedafterat31march-by-localauthority-gender-age* (accessed 08/08/17).

Wiederhold, A., 'Conducting Fieldwork At and Away from Home: Shifting Researcher Positionality with Mobile Interviewing Methods', *Qualitative Research*, 15/5 (2014), 1–16.

Wolf, D. L., 'Situating feminist dilemmas in fieldwork', in D. L. Wolf (ed.), *Feminist Dilemmas in Fieldwork* (Colorado and Oxford: Westview Press, 1996).

Yeo, R., Legard, R., Keegan, J., Ward, K., McNaughton-Nicholls, C. and Lewis, J., 'In-depth interviews', in J. Richie and J. Lewis (eds), *Qualitative Research Practice* (Thousand Oaks and London: SAGE Publications, 2014), pp. 177–210.

13 | Sandboxes, stickers and superheroes

Employing creative techniques to explore the aspirations and experiences of children and young people who are looked after

Dawn Mannay and Eleanor Staples

Introduction

A S A COMMITMENT TO children's and young people's participation in research about them has become steadily more mainstream, there has been a simultaneous increase in the variety of methods used to attempt to promote that participation, particularly with groups whose perspectives have traditionally been marginalised in policy and research (Abrahams and Ingram, 2013; Lomax et al., 2011; Mannay, 2016). In these studies, the basis of participants' involvement in research has shifted from something that is done to them to one in which they have 'designed, enacted and interpreted inquiries and been honoured as an authentic critical voice' (Groundwater-Smith et al., 2015, p. 2). Consequently, within social and policy research, creative methods are often positioned as facilitating participatory relationships, whilst also being seen as 'effective ways to address increasingly complex questions in social science' (Kara, 2015, p. 3).

This chapter draws on a study that explored the educational experiences and aspirations of children and young people in public care in Wales. Children and young people who are looked after are often subject to formal social care and legal processes that involve some form of social work encounter in which their accounts inform decisions about their lives. Consequently, in the study discussed here, participatory and creative techniques were introduced to resist the recreation of the social work interview, and attempts were made to empower participants to take part in the research in a meaningful way. The chapter explores the strengths and limitations of these approaches for working with children and young people, and gaining an insight into their perspectives, aspirations and everyday lives.

Background

The number of children and young people in the care system has been steadily increasing (see Elliott, 2019 [Chapter 2 this volume]). In Wales, the number of children and young people in care at the time of this study, 2015, stood at 5,415, with this figure having increased by 20 per cent in the preceding 10 years (Welsh Government, 2015). Nationally and internationally, care-experienced children, young people and care leavers are reported to perform less well than the general population across a range of educational outcomes (Jackson and Cameron, 2010; Sebba et al., 2015; Matheson, 2015; see also Allnatt, 2019 [Chapter 6 this volume]).

To gain an insight into these differentiated patterns, some studies (Holland et al., 2010; National Fostering Framework, 2016; Ross et al., 2009; Wilson and Milne, 2016) have employed research methods, which centralise care-experienced children's and young people's subjective accounts of their experiences. However, the majority of studies are weighted towards the words and ideas of researchers, professionals and policy makers, rather than those of the children and young people themselves (Winter, 2006; McLeod, 2007). By relying on the accounts of adults who work with (or on) children and young people, it is unlikely that meanings made by children and young people about their education will be understood. Consequently, structural and organisational changes which meaningfully benefit their lives are not likely to be realised.

Importantly, listening to the views of children and young people can potentially inform prevailing discourses around care and education, and contribute to informed policy making and practice. The significance of this becomes clear when considering the range of government initiatives in Wales and the United Kingdom (see the Children Act 2004, the Children and Young Persons Act 2008, the Social Services and Well-being (Wales) Act 2014), which have yet to significantly improve educational outcomes for care-experienced children and young people. This raises the fundamental question of whether current policies adequately respond to the complex causes of the attainment gap (Berridge, 2012; Stein, 2012). Consequently, research approaches need to consider how best to work with children and young people to enable their views to be communicated, heard and acted upon.

Methods

The data presented in this chapter were generated as part of a Welsh Government commissioned study to explore the educational experiences, attainment and aspirations of care-experienced children and young people in Wales (Mannay et al., 2015, 2017). The study was conducted through the collaboration of Cardiff University's Children's Social Care Research and Development Centre (CASCADE), the Fostering Network [1], Voices from Care Cymru [2] and Spice Innovations [3]. The research team at Cardiff University analysed existing statistics on educational attainment in England and Wales, reviewed literature on the educational experiences of the care-experienced population; and conducted a full systematic review of effective educational interventions with children and young people who are looked after (see Rees et al., 2019 [Chapter 3 this volume]).

Alongside the analysis of existing data, it was important to include the views of care-experienced children and young people. We worked with 67 participants; 22 in primary school (aged six–11); 17 in secondary school (aged 11–16); 26 who had completed compulsory education with mixed engagement with further education (aged 16–27); and two in higher education. Of the participants, 27 (40 per cent) were female and 40 (60 per cent) were male. This sample did not directly reflect the gender balance of the public care population. At the time of the study, there were 2,595 girls (46.3 per cent) and 3,020 boys (53.7 per cent) in public care in Wales (Welsh Government, 2015). However, the sample aligned relatively closely with this distribution as well as including children from a wide range of care circumstances: foster care (n = 52); foster, residential and kinship care (n = 4); foster and residential care (n = 7); foster and kinship care (n = 1); foster care and semi-independent (n = 1); residential care only (n = 1); and unspecified (n = 1).

The fieldwork with young people living independently or having left care (n = 26) included focus groups, organised in conjunction with Voices from Care Cymru, and a range of creative activities developed with Spice Innovate. The research team recruited, trained and worked with care-experienced peer researchers from CASCADE Voices [4] to facilitate these research events (see Mannay et al., 2015; and Staples et al., 2019 [Chapter 15 this volume]). However, this chapter is concerned with the fieldwork with younger participants (n = 39), which consisted of activity days. These events were developed with the Fostering Network, and involved a number of creative and sports-based activities such as jewellery making, clay modelling, T-shirt and bag design, wall climbing, and ball games.

The data production was embedded within these activity days, and children and young people had the choice of contributing to the research or only taking part in the accompanying activities. The research techniques included sticker activities, sandboxing and traditional interviews;

and children and young people who wanted to be involved in the study pegged a piece of card with their name on to a string. These participants (n = 39) were given a choice about whether to create a sand-scene, which some undertook (n = 19). Others selected a traditional interview (n = 14) or the option to take part in an emotion sticker activity followed by an interview (n = 6). We offered a range of activities, in the recognition that some approaches are not necessarily appropriate to use with some participants or may not suit their individual preferences (see Johnson et al., 2012; Smith, 2019 [Chapter 14 this volume]).

Ethical approval for the study was granted by Cardiff University and all participants and their carers were provided with information about the study and completed age-appropriate informed consent sheets. While researchers make efforts to gain active consent from older children and young people (Shaw and Holland, 2014), with younger children 'assent' is often sought (Cocks, 2006). However, in this research, younger children were also asked to sign or mark a consent form. While no arguments are made about the validity of this as an exercise in gaining active consent, the children appeared to enjoy being asked to sign their name and to be given the opportunity to display their 'signature' on a document.

Sandboxes, stickers and superheroes

Using the emotion sticker and sandboxing activities provided a way to rebalance the interview dynamic because participants could lead the discussions around their visual productions and take some control over the direction of the interview. This participant-directed model also acted to limit the propensity for the researchers' own knowledge and experiences to overshadow the participants' accounts: 'fighting familiarity' (Delamont and Atkinson, 1995), as discussed in previous visual studies (Mannay, 2010; Richardson, 2015). Additionally, the activities facilitated discussions around feelings and emotions, as researchers did not need to ask direct questions about children's and young people's emotional lifeworlds (Gabb and Fink, 2015). Being non-intrusive was important, because we sought to resist recreating the experience of a formal interview or intervention, which participants would have been subject to as part of their journey into public care.

In the emotion sticker activity, children were provided with card, paper, coloured pencils and pens, and emoticon stickers representing happiness and sadness, to create a mind-map of salient aspects of their school life. Where appropriate, depending on the age of the children, researchers helped with writing the verbal cues, and participants were encouraged to use the stickers to show which parts of the school and the school day they liked and disliked, as well as their favourite times or places. The emotion sticker activities elicited discussions about feelings and emotional

Figure 13.1: *Emotion Sticker Activity*

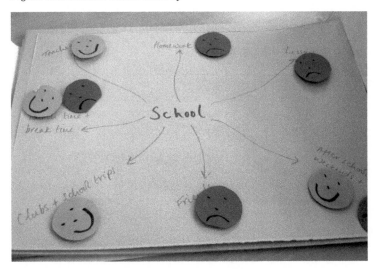

interactions that children experience during the school day. For example, when discussing the sad faces placed on her school map in relation to playtime and friends, Ruby [5] commented:

> **Ruby:** When the children get sad they don't really do anything about it, they just say have you told the people on the, have you told the people on the yard? And I say no because the teachers are doing other things. So that's why it is really.

The stickers and maps also contributed to knowledge about care-experienced children's social worlds in relation to placement moves, and allied issues such as changing schools, which characterise the experiences of many care-experienced children and young people (Jackson and Cameron, 2010):

> **Jack:** I don't want to be, to go away from [name of foster carer]. I don't want to go to another foster home.

Accordingly, the maps enabled the children to both situate their feelings in the interactional and institutional contexts of their school life, and construct narratives about themselves as a school child, in the past, the present and an imagined future.

In relation to Ruby's comments, the 'normative cruelties' of school yard and classroom interactions have been well documented (Thorne,

1993; Renold, 2005). However, the lack of response or action from school staff was considered at different points in Ruby's interview and, arguably, coping with the difficulties arising from a feeling that teachers do not 'deal with things' can be more problematic for children in care because of associated feelings of 'difference' (see Mannay et al., 2017). Jack discussed his fear of moving to a different foster home, and children's placement moves are often accompanied by school moves. These can be characterised by inadequate information transfer between agencies, the disruption of learning opportunities, and the need to build new peer relations and adjust to different school regimes and practices (Zetlin et al., 2004; Jackson and Cameron, 2010; Pecora, 2012).

Therefore, the visual evidence of the feelings that children experienced and managed at school is important child-led knowledge about the emotional landscapes in the school, which could be more actively and responsively managed by teachers and lunchtime supervisors. It also highlights ongoing, pervasive anxieties about stability that care-experienced children negotiate as part of their educational lives and identities. In this way, these visual materials facilitated a productive dialogue that enabled an engagement with the mundane, yet important, aspects of schooled lives, which may not have been possible using a more traditional, purely verbal-answer interview approach.

In the 'sandboxing' activity, participants either created sand-scenes representing what school was like, or focused on their future aspirations; with an elicitation interview following the creation of the sand-scenes. The activity consisted of building a scene with a tray filled with sand and miniature figures and objects, including trees, gates, fences, cars and trucks, superheroes, work roles, fantasy figures, animals, shells and jewels. The sandboxing activity drew on 'the world technique' (Lowenfeld, 1979), which has been used extensively in play therapy and psychoanalytical approaches. However, here it was applied as a tool of data production, not as a therapeutic activity (see Mannay, Staples and Edwards, 2017). The researchers also made their own sand-scenes, where appropriate, and this was done concurrently, to engender a more collaborative exchange where the contents and meanings of the scenes could be shared. This aligned with an attempt to foster a participatory approach (O'Kane, 2008), and to assist in building rapport over a relatively short period of time.

Like the emotion stickers activity, the sandboxing also provided a platform for exploring the hopes, fears and emotional lifeworlds of care-experienced children and young people without asking direct questions about participants' feelings. For example, a desire to foster security and safety for themselves and others featured in many of the participants' accounts, as illustrated in Figure 13.2.

Sandboxing allowed children and young people to create complex visual representations of their future aspirations like the battle scene

Figure 13.2: *John's sandbox* – 'help everyone'

using soldiers and wild animals (Figure 13.2). This scene represented John's desire to join the army 'because there's some little wars which are going on and people are trying to fight for their country to keep it . . . I want to help them and keep them going'. There was an emphasis on the importance of doing a job where he could keep people safe, and in gaining recognition for doing this work to protect people. John talked about the role that the army plays in disaster relief, explaining that he could 'help everyone . . . if there was an earthquake'; alternatively, if he joined the fire brigade he reflected that he could 'save some people and actually be a hero'.

Many participants spoke of altruistic future selves where they would help others in their work by becoming superheroes, social workers, vets or teachers (see Mannay et al., 2015, 2017). However, John's battle scene also illustrated an understanding that safety and security were not necessarily automatically conferred, rather that they were things that involved some form of negotiation, struggle or fight. This theme transferred to the participant's discussion of his employment and how his wages would be related to ensuring his future family's security:

> John: I wouldn't mind anything that I could make a lot of money, just in case I have a family so we're actually able to look after them and to keep them safe.

As discussed earlier, a desire for stability and safety are often central in the experiences of care-experienced children and young people, which can be characterised by instability, family separations and placement moves (Jackson and Cameron, 2010). The creation of the sand-scene, and the mirroring activity in which the researcher made a representation of their aspirations, along with the ensuing conversation, enabled a discussion of these sensitive issues, which moved beyond the boundaries and form of the traditional social work interview.

Importantly, sandboxing also allows scenes to be easily made-and-remade. Many visual methods lack this level of fluidity as they become fixed once stickers are stuck, collage pieces are glued or when ink comes into contact with paper. Arguably, Lego Serious Play [6] encourages experiential forms of expression and reflection that can help participants see familiar situations in a new way (Gauntlet and Holzwarth, 2006; Hinthorne and Schneider, 2012). However, although Lego bricks have the potential to be built and rebuilt, they do not necessarily have the flexibility of sandboxing; and to some extent, unlike sandboxing, they are reliant on particular spatial and coordination skills, which could exclude some participants.

The sandboxing figures are not pliable or open to physical change, although metaphorically they can take on multiple and unrestricted meanings. However, even where the figures and objects were not actually malleable, they were placed and moved or removed and structures were built and destroyed both prior to and during the interviews. The sand-scenes were often decorated by the imprints of other pieces that were inserted

Figure 13.3: *Tracey's sandbox* – 'that means bad'

and later taken out, and live enactments featured in interviews with children and young people, with one participant creating a complex dramatised play with the figures. The sandboxing activity was also useful in the creation of physical boundaries due to the flexible nature of the sand, as illustrated in Figure 13.3.

Tracey demarcated a good and bad section, using the sand to clearly stake out a division between her two possible imagined futures. The importance of pets was notable in many of the care-experienced children's and young people's accounts of their past and current experiences, and their future lives. Pets are significant, as although they play an active role in fostering well-being (Briheim-Crookall, 2016), they are often left behind in the process of separation from the family home and later in placement moves to different foster cares.

Here, Tracey has put snakes on the left-hand side to represent the horrible pets she would have in a bad future:

> **Tracey:** There will just be like horrible, like, I don't like snakes so then that means bad … they are really mean pets, and I don't really like meanness.

Tracey also used the sand to partially bury a yellow snake, emphasising their sneakiness. The ability to demarcate and bury objects provided understandings about how care-experienced children and young people visualise their futures within conflicting narratives of the positive and the negative, and a lack of choice and agency, which often reflects their everyday experiences. In line with previous research (Welbourne and Leeson, 2012; Sebba et al., 2015), many participants in the study had experienced a disrupted education due to difficulties in their family home and subsequent placement moves. Therefore, having an open activity, where participants could create representations of their future, on their own terms, allowed space for exploring the complexities and uncertainties faced by care-experienced children and young people.

Conclusion

Whilst they are not a guarantee of full and active participation, the use of visual, creative and material methods do have the potential for more collaborative and participant-led data production. In this way, the visual offers the potential to 'question, arouse curiosity, tell in different voices or see through different eyes' (Edwards, 1992, p. 54). Additionally, in this study, sandboxing and the emotion sticker activity were specifically chosen to resist the recreation of the social work interview.

The formal social care and legal processes involved in placing a child or young person into public care mean that all of the participants would have experienced some form of social work encounter, which may have informed fundamental decisions about their lives (Jackson and Cameron, 2010; Mannay et al., 2015). Therefore, although semi-structured interviews have proved effective in previous studies (Jackson and Höjer, 2013), and they generated important data within this study, particularly with older participants (Mannay et al., 2015, 2017), they partially mirror social work practice. Arguably, this question and answer format could inhibit some participants from producing an account of their educational experience, lest what they say be used to determine a decision about their life.

Enabling participants to lead the research by centralising their selected visual data activity also stood in contrast to a social work interview, in which they would have had no choice about how or whether to participate. Moreover, previous work with care-experienced children and young people has noted how arrangements directing gaze forwards, not toward each other, in car journeys, engendered a less hierarchical and more relaxed research encounter (Ross et al., 2009; Ferguson, 2008). Similarly, the visual activities shifted the gaze to the creative product, allowing less intensive and invasive forms of conversation and communication, enabling a creative way of interviewing that is 'responsive to participants' own meanings and associations' (Bagnoli, 2009, p. 547). Therefore, arguably, adopting less formalised interview techniques, and introducing more flexible approaches, could prove beneficial in both social science research and social work practice (see Crow et al., 2008; Woodcock, 2011).

However, there were limitations to these approaches and they should not be seen as a panacea. For example, the open nature of the sandboxing activity often meant that, although child-led, the conversations moved in multiple directions, which were interesting and important but not related to the central research questions. Conversely, despite the introduction of creative data production, some of the interviews, particularly in the emotion sticker activity, reverted to a researcher-led question and answer style, which sometimes acted to close down opportunities for children to express their own ideas and experiences. These elicitation interviews illustrate the tensions between how best to centralise the voices of children and young people in a participatory framework, whilst at the same time addressing the requirements of researchers and funding bodies (Lomax, 2015).

However, despite their limitations, these activities went some way towards facilitating care-experienced children's and young people's engagement with researchers on their own terms, and provided a space in which they could articulate their experiences and imagine their futures. Importantly, this more collaborative and 'partially participatory' (Mannay, 2016) approach elicited a nuanced data set in which children and young people were able to articulate their educational experiences and aspirations; and what they felt should change and be improved. These reflections and suggestions formed the basis of 17 recommendations for practice (Mannay et al.,

2015), which in turn informed policy strategy (Welsh Government, 2016). Therefore, it is important to develop creative research approaches that engage care-experienced children and young people to share their stories and ideas, which can potentially inform policy and practice, and improve their future educational experiences and outcomes.

Acknowledgements

We would like to acknowledge the participants who made this chapter possible. We also thank the doctoral and peer researchers who assisted with the fieldwork, Louisa Roberts who administered the project, Professor Sally Holland for conceptualising the study, and our project partners, the Fostering Network, Voices from Care Cymru and Spice Innovations. The study was based in the Children's Social Care Research and Development Centre (CASCADE), whose work is concerned with all aspects of community-based responses to social need in children and families. The research project from which this chapter is drawn was commissioned and supported by the Welsh Government.

Notes

1. The Fostering Network is a fostering charity, providing support and campaigning to improve foster care.
2. Voices from Care Cymru is a charity led and inspired by looked-after children and care leavers.
3. Spice Innovations provides a system for organisations and individuals to exchange their skills and resources.
4. CASCADE Voices a collaboration between Voices from Care Cymru and the Children's Social Care Research and Development Centre (CASCADE). Members of the group have been involved in a range of research-related activities.
5. Children and young people chose or were allocated pseudonyms.
6. For further information on Lego Serious Play see *https://www.lego.com/en-gb/ seriousplay/background*.

References

Abrahams, J. and Ingram, N., 'The Chameleon Habitus: Exploring Local Students' Negotiations of Multiple Fields', *Sociological Research Online*, 18/4 (2013), 21.

Allnatt, G., 'Transitions from care to higher education: A case study of a young person's journey', in D. Mannay, A. Rees and L. Roberts (eds), *Children and Young People 'Looked After'? Education, Intervention and the Everyday Culture of Care in Wales* (Cardiff: University of Wales Press, 2019), pp. 69–82.

Bagnoli, A., 'Beyond the Standard Interview: The Use of Graphic Elicitation and Arts-based Methods', *Qualitative Research*, 9/5 (2009) 547–70.

Berridge, D., 'Educating Young People in Care: What Have We Learned?', *Children and Youth Services Review*, 34/6 (2012), 1171–5.

Briheim-Crookall, L., *How Social Workers Can Track and Boost the Happiness of Looked-After Children* (Sutton: Community Care) (2016). Available at *http://www.communitycare.co.uk/2016/03/22/social-workers-can-track-boost-happiness-looked-children/* [accessed: 16/04/17].

Cocks, A., 'The Ethical Maze: Finding an Inclusive Path towards Gaining Children's Agreement to Research Participation', *Childhood*, 13/2 (2006) 247–66.

Crow, J., Foley, P. and Leverett, S., 'Communicating with children', in P. Foley and S. Leverett (eds), *Connecting with Children: Developing Working Relationships* (Bristol: Policy Press in association with the Open University, 2008), pp. 9–39.

Delamont, S. and Atkinson, P., *Fighting Familiarity: Essays on Education and Ethnography* (Cresskill, NJ: Hampton Press, 1995).

Edwards, E., *Photography and Anthropology 1860–1920* (London: Royal Anthropological Institute, 1992).

Elliott, M., 'Charting the rise of children and young people "looked after" in Wales', in D. Mannay, A. Rees and L. Roberts (eds), *Children and Young People 'Looked After'? Education, Intervention and the Everyday Culture of Care in Wales* (Cardiff: University of Wales Press, 2019), pp. 15–28.

Ferguson, H., 'Liquid Social Work: Welfare Interventions as Mobile Practices', *British Journal of Social Work*, 38/3 (2008), 561–79.

Gabb, J. and Fink, J., 'Telling Moments and Everyday Experience: Multiple Methods Research on Couple Relationships and Personal Lives', *Sociology*, 49/5 (2015), 970–87.

Gauntlett, D. and Holzwarth, P., 'Creative and Visual Methods for Exploring Identities', *Visual Studies*, 21/1 (2006), 82–91.

Groundwater-Smith, S., Dockett, S. and Bottrell, D., *Participatory Research with Children and Young People* (London: Sage, 2015).

Hinthorne, L. and Schneider, K., 'Playing with Purpose: Using Serious Play to Enhance Participatory Development Communication in Research', *International Journal of Communication*, 6 (2012), 2801–24.

Holland, S., Renold, E., Ross, N. J. and Hillman, A., 'Power, Agency and Participatory Agendas: A Critical Exploration of Young People's Engagement in Participative Qualitative Research', *Childhood*, 17/3 (2010), 360–75.

Jackson, S. and Cameron, C., *Final Report of the YiPPEE Project WP12: Young People from a Public Care Background: Pathways to Further and Higher Education in Five European Countries* (London: Thomas Coram Research Unit, 2010).

——— and Höjer, I., 'Prioritising Education for Children Looked After Away from Home', *European Journal of Social Work*, 16/1 (2013), 1–5.

Johnson, G. A., Pfister, E. A. and Vindrola-Padros, C., 'Drawings, Photos, and Performances: Using Visual Methods with Children', *Visual Anthropology Review*, 28/2 (2012), 164–77.

Kara, H., *Creative Research Methods in the Social Sciences: A Practical Guide* (Bristol: Policy Press, 2015).

Lomax, H., 'Seen and Heard? Ethics and Agency in Participatory Visual Research with Children, Young People and Families', *Families, Relationships and Societies*, 4/3 (2015), 493–502.

———, Fink, J., Singh, N. and High, C., 'The Politics of Performance: Methodological Challenges of Researching Children's Experiences of Childhood through the Lens of Participatory Video', *International Journal of Social Research Methodology*, 14/3 (2011), 231–43.

Lowenfeld, M., *The World Technique* (London: Allen and Uwin Press, 1979).

Mannay, D., 'Making the Familiar Strange: Can Visual Research Methods Render the Familiar Setting more Perceptible?', *Qualitative Research*, 10/1 (2010), 91–111.

———, *Visual, Narrative and Creative Research Methods: Application, Reflection and Ethics* (Abingdon: Routledge, 2016).

———, Evans, R., Staples, E., Hallett, S., Roberts, L., Rees, A. and Andrews, D., 'The Consequences of Being Labelled "Looked-After": Exploring the Educational Experiences of Looked-after Children and Young People in Wales', *British Journal of Educational Research*, 43/4 (2017), 683–99.

———, Staples, E. and Edwards, V., 'Visual Methodologies, Sand and Psychoanalysis: Employing Creative Participatory Techniques to Explore the Educational Experiences of Mature Students and Children in Care', *Visual Studies*, 32/4 (2017), 345–58.

———, Staples, E., Hallett, S., Roberts, L., Rees, A., Evans, R. and Andrews, D., *Understanding the Educational Experiences and Opinions, Attainment, Achievement and Aspirations of Looked After Children in Wales* (Cardiff: Welsh Government, 2015).

Matheson I., *Slipping Down Ladders and Climbing Up Snakes: The Experiences of University Students formerly in OOHC, and Research Challenges to Current Policy and Practice* (PhD thesis, University of Otago, Dunedin, 2015).

McLeod, A., 'Whose Agenda? Issues of Power and Relationship when Listening to Looked-After Young People', *Child and Family Social Work*, 12/3 (2007), 278–86.

National Fostering Framework, *National Fostering Framework. Phase One Report 2015–2016* (2016). Available at *http://www.adsscymru.org.uk/media-resources-list/national-fostering-framework-phase-one-report/* (accessed 04/04/17).

O'Kane, C., 'The development of participatory techniques: Facilitating children's views about decisions which affect them', in P. M. Christensen and A. James (eds), *Research with Children: Perspectives and Practices* (London: Routledge, 2008), pp. 125–55.

Pecora, P. J., 'Maximizing Educational Achievement of Youth in Foster Care and Alumni: Factors Associated with Success', *Children and Youth Services Review*, 34 (2012), 1121–9.

Rees, G., Brown, R., Smith, P. and Evans, R., 'Educational interventions for children and young people in care: A review of outcomes, implementation and acceptability', in D. Mannay, A. Rees and L. Roberts (eds), *Children and Young People 'Looked After'? Education, Intervention and the Everyday Culture of Care in Wales* (Cardiff: University of Wales Press, 2019), pp. 29–42.

Renold, E., *Girls, Boys and Junior Sexualities: Exploring Children's Gender and Sexual Relations in the Primary School* (Abingdon: Routledge, 2005).

Richardson, M. J., 'Embodied Intergenerationality: Family Position, Place and Masculinity', *Gender, Place & Culture: A Journal of Feminist Geography*, 22/2 (2015), 157–71.

Ross, N. J., Renold, E., Holland, S. and Hillman, A., 'Moving Stories: Using Mobile Methods to Explore the Everyday Lives of Young People in Public Care', *Qualitative Research*, 9/5 (2009), 605–23.

Sebba, J., Berridge, D., Luke, N., Fletcher, J., Bell, K. and Strand, S., *The Educational Progress of Looked After Children in England: Linking Care and Educational Data* (Oxford: Rees Centre for Research in Fostering and Education and University of Bristol, 2015).

Shaw, I. and Holland, S., *Doing Qualitative Social Work* (London: Sage, 2014).

Smith, P., 'A view from a Pupil Referral Unit: Using participatory methods with young people in an education setting', in D. Mannay, A. Rees and L. Roberts (eds), *Children and Young People 'Looked After'? Education, Intervention and the Everyday Culture of Care in Wales* (Cardiff: University of Wales Press, 2019), pp. 183–95.

Staples, E., Roberts, L., Lyttleton-Smith, J., Hallett, S. and CASCADE Voices, 'Enabling care-experienced young people's participation in research: CASCADE Voices', in D. Mannay, A. Rees and L. Roberts (eds) *Children and Young People 'Looked After'? Education, Intervention and the Everyday Culture of Care in Wales* (Cardiff: University of Wales Press, 2019), pp. 196–209.

Stein, M., *Young People Leaving Care: Supporting Pathways to Adulthood* (London: Jessica Kingsley, 2012).

Thorne, B., *Gender Play: Girls and Boys at School* (Buckingham: Open University Press, 1993).

Welbourne, P. and Leeson, C., 'The Education of Children in Care: A Research Review', *Journal of Youth Services*, 7/2 (2012), 128–43.

Welsh Government, *Children Looked After at 31 March by Local Authority, Gender and Age* (Cardiff: Welsh Government, 2015).

———, *Raising the Ambitions and Educational Attainment of Children Who Are Looked After in Wales* (Cardiff: Welsh Government, 2016).

Wilson, S. and Milne, E., 'Visual Activism and Social Justice: Using Visual Methods to make Young People's Complex Lives Visible across "Public" and "Private" Spaces', *Current Sociology*, 64/1 (2016), 140–56.

Winter, K., 'Widening our Knowledge Concerning Young Looked After Children: The Case for Research using Sociological Models of Childhood', *Child and Family Social Work*, 11 (2006), 55–64.

Woodcock Ross, T., *Specialist Communication Skills for Social Work: Focusing on Service Users' Needs* (Basingstoke: Palgrave Macmillan, 2011).

Zetlin, A., Weinberg, L. and Kimm, C., 'Improving Education Outcomes for Children in Foster Care: Intervention by an Education Liaison', *Journal of Education for Students Placed at Risk*, 9/4 (2004), 421–9.

14 | A view from a Pupil Referral Unit

Using participatory methods with young people in an education setting

Phil Smith

Introduction

THIS CHAPTER REFLECTS on the use of participatory research methods in relation to an ongoing research project based in the alternative education setting of a Pupil Referral Unit (PRU) in Wales. Participatory methods allow us to place the lived experiences of participants at the centre of research, and they align with contemporary notions of childhood, where children are viewed as the experts in their own lives (James et al., 1998). Arguably, such approaches provide a space for research *with* young people, rather than *on* them (Pauwels, 2011); reducing the 'us' and 'them' dualism between the researcher(s) and the researched (Pain, 2004, p. 656; see also Mannay and Staples, 2019 [Chapter 13 this volume]). In this sense, research becomes participant led, with the researcher acting as a facilitator, creating space for youth 'voice'.

In relation to education, these methods can support the school inspectorates' emphasis to include the views of pupils in decision-making processes. Fielding and Bragg (2003) outline the benefits of this approach for pupils, including an improvement in both academic and communication skills, and a renewed sense of agency and motivation with schooling. Similarly, Baroutsis et al. (2016) discuss how a sense of connectedness and belonging for pupils is important for their learning experience, and that by being active participants who are heard, and listened to, a sense of belonging in school can develop.

However, with a rise in participatory agendas and the practice of 'youth voice', it is important to be mindful of 'both the possibilities and limitations of initiatives aimed at "giving voice"' (Batsleer, 2011, p. 420). There is a need to recognise when participation work is merely 'ticking boxes and missing the point' (Batsleer, 2008, p. 141); becoming a tokenistic gesture which may silence young people, and reaffirm dominant voices. Participatory methods can have various connotations, and even when the research is constructed on the basis of young people's agendas, interests and concerns which are then acted on to some degree, the potential power imbalances inherent within these research relations should still be acknowledged.

Mannay (2016, p. 51) has argued that no study is ever carried out in a vacuum, whereby power relations cease to exist between the researcher and the researched. Similarly, using the work of Bernstein (1990, 2000), Arnot and Reay (2007) have emphasised the existence of power relations, challenging the idea that any voice can be captured outside this dynamic. Accordingly, a degree of structuring and moulding of 'voice' occurs through all research methodologies, and participatory research is not always necessarily more enabling for young people than other forms of research.

Reflexivity, and investing the time needed to carry out meaningful participatory research can be difficult when research projects are increasingly restricted by time (Mannay and Morgan, 2015). However, a failure to do so can seriously undermine a participatory approach, which needs to be adaptable to meet participant needs and unforeseen circumstances during the process. It is also important for researchers to openly discuss their fieldwork experiences, in terms of the purpose, the challenges faced, and the compromises made. Such transparency and reflection can offer opportunities to recognise the differences that exist within participatory projects, and to what extent a piece of work has indeed been participatory, or only partially so. Accordingly, this chapter embraces the messiness of the research process and takes an open and reflexive approach, which can foster a development of participatory techniques.

Pupil Referral Units: What we know

Currently in Wales, PRUs are the most commonly used form of education other than at school (EOTAS), supporting 44.3 per cent of the EOTAS pupil population during the 2016/17 academic year (National Stats Wales, 2017). Mainstream schools have often been unable to support the complex needs of the young people, and, as a last option or for exclusionary purposes, they refer pupils into PRUs as a temporary solution.

PRUs are tasked with supporting and improving both the well-being and learning of pupils who have been referred from mainstream schools, in order for them to be re-integrated into the mainstream at the earliest opportunity.

Reasons for a child or young person being referred to a PRU in Wales will vary, but a high proportion of pupils have been identified with a level of social, emotional and behavioural difficulties (SEBDs) (Estyn, 2015). Whilst pupils with these difficulties are over-represented in such settings, their voices are amongst the least represented when it comes to research (Michael and Frederickson, 2013; Clarke et al., 2011). Similarly, PRUs themselves are marginalised both in the research literature, and as a form of schooling in Wales (Children's Commissioner for Wales, 2014).

The pupil population

The number of pupils who receive their education from an institution other than a mainstream school is relatively low in Wales: only three per 1,000 pupils in Wales during the 2016/17 academic year (Welsh Government, 2017). Despite this, the needs of these pupils are likely to be great, with 88.5 per cent identified as having special educational needs (SEN) in addition to any SEBD, and 33 per cent eligible for free school meals (FSM), an indicator of social deprivation (Welsh Government, 2017). At the same time, young people in care will be more likely to attend PRUs as a result of often difficult and challenging circumstances during childhood (Brodie, 2001; Blyth and Milner, 1993).

It is important to note that for those young people who are removed from mainstream settings, the risk of further marginalisation in their lives is increased (McCluskey et al., 2016). The educational outcomes for pupils attending PRUs are routinely far lower than children in mainstream schools (Pirrie et al., 2009). As such, young people leaving these schools are at increased risk of unemployment, ill health and other forms of social exclusion (see Jackson and Cameron, 2012). Whilst PRUs comprise a relatively small proportion of the education section, they are an important site for examining the educational processes that can marginalise vulnerable children and young people. Moreover, since care-experienced children and young people are over-represented in PRUs, and are already at a disadvantage in terms of educational attainment and achievement (see Allnatt, 2019 [Chapter 6 this volume]), this makes these sites particularly important arenas for examination.

Background to the study

This current Economic and Social Research Council funded, three-year study explores the daily practices, routines and occupational understandings of the people who work in a PRU in Wales. Pupils were also involved in the research, so that they could express their views and experiences of attending a PRU and provide a more nuanced insight into the everyday life of this alternative education setting. Pupils at the PRU had been identified with a level of SEBDs, which had led to their referrals, and some children and young people were also in the care system.

My professional background is youth work, where young people are always the focal point of the work. Therefore, taking a participatory approach aligned with my previous practice, which emphasised a 'responsibility to ensure that young people are given the chance to express their views' (Gormally and Coburn, 2014, p. 872). Additionally, whilst research that captures the views of young people has proliferated, those with SEBDs remain some of the least heard within the literature (Michael and Frederickson, 2013). Consequently, it was important to acknowledge these social actors, who, with their own experiences and perceptions of the PRU, and through daily interaction with staff, mutually created the organisational culture of the setting (Day, 2004).

Whilst there have been some recent attempts to outline good practice within PRUs in Wales (Estyn, 2015), this study is specifically interested in how practitioners make sense of their own performed roles. Resonating with Pithouse's (1987, p. 46) research, on the occupational world of social work, the study positioned 'the daily setting . . . as the authentic and purposeful construction of members who competently employ their own assumptions and "theories" of what constitutes good work'. Additionally, there has been a renewed interest in the educational experiences of young people in care in Wales (Rees and Munro, 2019 [Chapter 5 this volume]; Mannay et al., 2015, 2017). Consequently, an exploratory study of PRUs in Wales is even more pertinent, given that those in care are much more likely to attend PRUs when compared with their peers (Blyth and Milner, 1993; Brodie, 2001; Sellman et al., 2002).

This study worked with all young people in the PRU, not just those categorised as 'looked after'; however, there are many parallels between the experiences of pupils in PRUs and those of young people in care. For example, both experience intense monitoring in their daily lives, including regular, one-to-one meetings with professionals, mainly to support their progress in relation to well-being needs and academic work. Accordingly, I wanted to limit as much as possible further scrutiny into these young people's lives. Adopting a participatory approach, with creative methods, allowed pupils to choose their own levels of involvement in the study, whilst in a familiar environment. The following sections provide an account of the fieldwork process, in an attempt to add further insights into the use of participatory methods with young people in education settings.

Research context

The research site discussed is a PRU in Wales, which supports young people with behavioural difficulties, whilst also offering a service to young people who are socially anxious or school phobic. In the initial few months of the research, I spent most of my time with the latter category of pupils, referred to as the 'nurture' group. As all the pupils had some level of identified need, such as being school phobic, it was essential that the PRU catered for these needs by adopting different approaches to practice. Whilst the overarching aim was to support pupils to re-enter mainstream schooling, the most pressing need was often to encourage regular attendance at the PRU.

Pupils were likely to associate negative experiences with schooling that had resulted in their referral to the PRU; consequently, encouraging pupils back into a school environment was not always an easy task. Strategies included a gradual approach for some pupils, with short hourly visits gradually extended to full days and finally a full schooling week. The setting was friendly, welcoming and informal and the number of pupils registered at the PRU was low (66), with average class sizes ranging between three and eight pupils at any one time.

With a total of thirty-five staff working at the PRU and the small class sizes, this meant that staff were able to get to know the pupils quickly, gaining a grasp of individual personalities and needs, and forming close relational bonds. The relatively informal approach to practice was also seen in relation to school uniform. Key Stage 4 (aged 14 to 16) and 5 (aged 16 to 18) pupils could wear their own clothing, and, in addition, many staff were known on a first-name basis by pupils. Whilst there were clearly rules in place, which were mostly adhered to by the pupils, these were also up for negotiation. From my observations, staff never punished pupils, in terms of shouting or giving out detentions. Any issues that were raised were generally negotiated and talked through, mutually. Whilst hierarchical roles existed between staff and pupils, these appeared to be less prominent than those found in mainstream settings, as previous research has demonstrated (see Meo and Parker, 2004).

Reflections on the fieldwork

Between November 2016 and March 2017 I volunteered for one full day a week in the 'nurture' side of the PRU, supporting the work of school-phobic and socially anxious pupils and taking an active part in lessons, including well-being and drama. During this time I got to know the pupils and staff relatively well, explaining my research role and discussing my fieldwork plans. In total, ten pupils took part in the research, and we produced data about their experiences within the PRU across six weeks during one of the well-being classes. The pupils were aged between 12 and 15 and included six girls and four boys; the period of time they had spent at the PRU ranged from three weeks to three years.

From past experience of working with young people in a youth work capacity, I was keenly aware of the importance of having a period of familiarisation before I began the research, to build rapport with pupils. By volunteering in the setting over a prolonged period of time, I hoped to gain a better understanding of the pupils' experiences, by developing relationships built on trust and familiarity. Pupils with communication difficulties and other learning needs were unlikely to open up to a stranger over a short one-off interview, therefore one-off research encounters were seen as an inappropriate technique to gain an understanding of the pupils and their schooled lives.

Working as a volunteer in the setting involved supporting both staff and pupils with their daily work, and taking an active part in lessons. This 'easing in' period allowed me to get to know both the pupils and staff, and to become more familiar with the setting. In doing so, I was able to consider and tailor my research methods with regard to their suitability for young people's needs as individuals, as well as the needs of the PRU setting itself, in terms of fitting my methods into the schooling day without causing too much disruption.

My role did not require me to formally teach pupils, therefore, the traditional teacher/pupil hierarchy was not a feature of the relationship between myself and the pupils. Consequently, I could build informal relationships relatively quickly, talking with pupils during break times, playing football in the yard, and discussing shared interests, such as sport and food. By consistently attending on Thursdays, I became a part of the PRU's weekly routine; and learnt about the community and its everyday practices.

The pupils displayed a variety of skills, strengths and needs. For example, whilst some of the pupils actively and confidently engaged in lessons such as drama, playing musical instruments and singing songs, others never took part in these sessions, sitting on the periphery. There were clear differences between the pupils in relation to their confidence and articulation; and this differentiation meant that techniques of data production had to be carefully considered. For example, Cahill (2007) has documented the uneven nature of participatory methods, where more confident pupils have dominated proceedings, inadvertently sidelining the voices of others. It was important to involve all pupils as equally as possible, whilst also respecting their right to remain silent, and this premise aligned with a mosaic approach (Clarke and Moss, 2001).

The mosaic approach

Originally conceived by Clarke and Moss (2001), the mosaic approach uses a creative, participatory framework, focusing on the lived experience of children and young people. It combines the vocal with the visual, allowing participants to express their opinions both verbally and symbolically by selecting from a number of methods such as informal interviews, walking tours, drawing and photography. Participants can also devise their own ways of sharing their opinions and experiences if preferred. This approach has been used successfully with young children, including those who were pre-verbal, and more recently with young people in care (Quarmby, 2014).

In the fieldwork, the mosaic approach acted as a framework, which could be adapted according to the young people's needs and interests; and the requirements and restrictions of the setting. Each pupil could carry out as many or as few activities as they liked over a number of weeks. Once each activity was completed, these were added to an individual booklet. These booklets were then used for a final elicitation interview, to further explore the understandings of each pupil's PRU experiences. It was important to recognise the value of more formal approaches to data production with young people, such as interviews, as these provided an opportunity to check and clarify understandings, and the meanings of the visual artefacts.

It was also essential not to make assumptions about creative or participatory methods being more suitable for research with young people. As Thomson (2007) contends, participatory models of research can be useful with children, adults and young people; but some participants prefer, or are more comfortable taking part in traditional forms of research, centralising an interview style. For example, there is evidence to suggest that being asked to draw or write in front of others can cause anxiety for young people, because of issues around artistic ability (see Mannay, 2016). As many young people in PRUs have been identified with special educational needs, including difficulties with reading and writing, I wanted to ensure that my research methods were sensitive towards any such anxieties. Therefore, participant choice was centralised, and, in addition to creative and visual approaches, informal interview discussions were available to participants as an option for data production, along with participant observation techniques.

Creating data

An arrangement was made with staff that one of the weekly well-being lessons was allocated to the research project. Along with support staff, myself and the pupils sat around one of the large tables and I reminded everyone about the purpose of the research, and that pupils could choose to sit out of any or all of the activities if they wished. The activities were generated from initial discussions about the ways in which pupils could represent their experiences, and young people wrote all their ideas down on pieces of paper in the middle of the table. Enabling pupils to design their own methods for data production was in keeping with a participatory approach, as it involved them in the design of the research, rather than simply adopting a partially participatory approach, which constrained their involvement to producing data (Mannay, 2016).

In the first session, many pupils were keen to make drawings and to write stories about their experiences. Whilst I was available to give any advice when invited, I left the pupils to their own devices for the majority of the session. Some participants wrote about their personal experiences of becoming pupils in the setting, whilst others drew pictures of their favourite things in the PRU, including staff and specific days they had enjoyed together. The staff were pleased with the artefacts produced by the pupils and the ways in which they communicated the positive impacts of their experiences at the PRU. Throughout this session I was conscious of staff presence, and how this could potentially limit some of the pupils' capacity to raise difficult issues or complaints about their PRU experiences. Some pupils nonetheless communicated negative experiences from their PRU schooling in this session, such as particular lessons or areas of the building they did not like. Additionally, I hoped that the final one-to-one elicitation interviews would become a space where pupils felt comfortable about discussing any further difficult experiences.

These research tasks appeared to support staff, reaffirming to them the importance and relevance of their daily work, and the strong bonds that existed between pupils and staff. For example, when one pupil showed a member of staff the story she had written, about how the PRU had supported her in changing her life around, the teacher became emotional, and expressed that they were very proud of the pupil. Importantly, these creative activities provided opportunities for participants to raise topics, which they may not have articulated in everyday conversations about their educational setting.

In one session, the pupils asked if they could take me on a group tour of the PRU, to show me the things they valued the most. We recorded the conversations along the way, and pupils also took photographs. We were accompanied by one of the well-being staff and a teaching assistant. Whilst I acknowledge the 'intrusive presence' of the researcher during the data production, attempting to step-back and allow pupils to lead the activity during the tour, this inadvertently left space for 'the "intrusive presence" of significant others' (Mannay, 2013, p. 136). Staff members were keen to offer advice and suggestions to the pupils about locations to visit and which photographs to take. Whilst I valued the support of staff in the sessions, their presence also meant that some pupils were steered through parts of the activities, inhibiting the participatory nature of the research and the voice of the young people. Additionally, as the recorded tours became a group activity rather than the individual approach originally anticipated, this meant that dominant pupil voices took centre stage in the resulting audio recording, silencing more reticent voices (Gallagher, 2008). Due to time constraints it was not possible to do future tours with individual pupils, which could have generated greater insights into the lived experiences of individual pupils.

Concluding and thinking forward

Overall, using participatory methods as part of this ongoing research project proved a useful way of gaining rich 'data' from a group of PRU pupils about their experiences of school. These creative methods allowed those pupils who often sat on the periphery of daily schooling activities to take part and produce their own work; which could have proved much more challenging through traditional research methods. Accordingly, the variety of methods used from the mosaic approach were useful in supporting these weekly group tasks in the limited amount of time available, with pupils who displayed a range of needs.

On the whole, the pupils appeared more comfortable working in groups: whilst this was useful, in that more pupils took part, it also meant that dominant voices took centre stage in certain tasks, marginalising other voices. Furthermore, as the sessions took place within class time and in the presence of staff, this made it increasingly difficult to escape the power dynamics of adult/child where the voices of young people were structured by adult voices. In this PRU, where supporting the needs of pupils was paramount to the vocation of staff, this meant that staff were likely to be a constant presence on some level during the research process. It is also worth considering that the potential for adults to structure the voices of young people may be particularly pertinent to those in care who routinely have interactions with adults in a range of settings in the course of their day-to-day lives, including social workers, therapeutic practitioners and bespoke education support teams.

This resonates with concerns held by Walmsley and Johnson (2003), who question whose story is actually being told within participatory research. I attempted to mitigate such concerns by providing a space for each pupil to talk openly about their experiences, reflecting on their creative artefacts in one-to-one and group elicitation interviews. Incorporating these interviews into the research plan provided a space for pupils to talk openly, away from staff members, and allowed me to pay attention to what may have been missed, as well as check that the pupils were happy with my interpretations of their creative outputs.

I also intend to work with pupils to explore how the research findings can be disseminated, in keeping with a participatory approach from design, to fieldwork, to dissemination. Attending the PRU Pupil Council will offer opportunities to discuss the research findings, and put forward changes for practice suggested by the participants. The power dynamics at play within school settings, and between young people and adults more generally within society, can act as a barrier to enacting change. For some young people in care, a sense of powerlessness over certain aspects of their lives is likely to be felt particularly acutely. However, within a PRU, which tends to be characterised by less intense and overt hierarchical relations between staff and pupils, and through the informal, mutually respectful relationships that exist between them, this provides opportunity for pupils to make suggestions, and, potentially, for these to be heard and responded to by adults. It is important to outline at the start of any participatory project that change cannot and does not always occur, but that any meaningful engagement with pupil voice does involve listening and acknowledgement, as well as acting to some degree on this voice. A failure to do so can seriously harm any future involvement of pupils in such practices.

As discussed at the outset of this chapter, marginalised young people often lack a sense of belonging and connectedness in relation to school, and particularly those who have been referred out of mainstream schools (Baroutsis et al., 2016). Including these pupils in decision making that affects their lives, and creating a space in which to have a voice and to be heard are, perhaps, then crucial for these young people, in terms of supporting them once more in gaining a connectedness with school. Despite the challenges which we as researchers working with children and young people must continue to recognise, these participatory techniques should be seen as a useful mechanism for fostering young people's engagement with school. What is more, they offer enormous potential to allow the voices of young people in care to be heard and represented in and through research, in relation to matters affecting their lives.

Acknowledgements

I would like to thank the Economic and Social Research Council for funding this research and all the young people who have kindly given up their time to openly participate and discuss their experiences of PRU schooling.

References

Allnatt, G., 'Transitions from care to higher education: A case study of a young person's journey', in D. Mannay, A. Rees and L. Roberts (eds), *Children and Young People 'Looked After'? Education, Intervention and the Everyday Culture of Care in Wales* (Cardiff: University of Wales Press, 2019), pp. 69–82.

Arnot, M. and Reay, D., 'A Sociology of Pedagogic Voice, Power, Inequality and Pupil Consultation', *Discourse: Studies in the Cultural Politics of Education*, 28 (2007), 311–25.

Baroutsis, A., Mills, M., McGregor, G., te Riele, K. and Hayes, D., 'Student Voice and the Community Forum: Finding Ways of "Being Heard" at an Alternative School for Disenfranchised Young People', *British Educational Research Journal*, 42/3 (2016), 438-53.

Batsleer, J., *Informal Learning in Youth Work* (London: Sage, 2008).

———, 'Voices from an Edge. Unsettling the Practices of Youth Voice and Participation: Arts-based Practice in The Blue Room, Manchester', *Pedagogy, Culture & Society*, 19/3 (2011), 419-34.

Bernstein, B., *Class Codes and Control: Vol. 4. The Structuring of Pedagogic Discourse* (London: Routledge, 1990).

———, *Pedagogy, Symbolic Control and Identity: Theory, Research and Critique* (rev. edn), (Lanham, MD: Rowman and Littlefield, 2000).

Blyth, E. and Milner, J., 'Exclusion From School: A First Step in Exclusion From Society?', *Children and Society*, 7/3 (1993), 255-68.

Brodie, I., *Children's Homes and School Exclusion: Redefining the Problem* (London: Jessica Kingsley Publishers Ltd, 2001).

Cahill, C., 'Doing Research with Young People: Participatory Research and the Rituals of Collective Work', *Children's Geographies*, 5/3 (2007), 297-312.

Children's Commissioner for Wales, *The Right to Learn: Supporting Children and Young People at Pupil Referral Units to Reach their Potential* (2014). Available at *https://www.childcomwales.org.uk/uploads/publications/456.pdf* (accessed 21/03/15).

Clarke, A. and Moss, P., *Listening to Young Children: The Mosaic Approach* (London: National Children's Bureau Enterprises Ltd, 2001).

Clarke, G., Boorman, G. and Nind, M., '"If They Don't Listen I Shout, and When I Shout They Listen": Hearing the Voices of Girls with Behavioural, Emotional and Social Difficulties', *British Educational Research Journal*, 37/5 (2011), 765-80.

Day, C., *A Passion for Teaching* (Oxon: Routledge Falmer, 2004).

Estyn, *Education Other Than at School: A Good Practice Survey* (2015). Available at *https://www.estyn.gov.wales/thematic-reports/education-other-school-good-practice-survey-june-2015* (accessed 04/04/16).

Fielding, M. and Bragg, S., *Students as Researchers: Making a Difference* (Cambridge: Pearson Publishing, 2003).

Gallagher, M., 'Power Is Not an Evil: Rethinking Power in Participatory Methods', *Children's Geographies*, 6/2 (2008), 137-51.

Gormally, S. and Coburn, A., 'Finding Nexus: Connecting Youth Work and Research Practices', *British Educational Research Journal*, 40/5 (2014), 869-85.

Jackson, S. and Cameron, C., 'Leaving Care: Looking Ahead and Aiming Higher', *Children and Youth Services Review*, 34 (2012), 1107-14.

James, A., Jenks, C. and Prout, A., *Theorising Childhood* (Cambridge: Polity Press, 1998).

Mannay, D., *Visual, Narrative and Creative Research Methods: Application, Reflection and Ethics* (Abingdon: Routledge, 2016).

———, '"Who Put That on There . . . Why Why Why?" Power Games and Participatory Techniques of Visual Data Production', *Visual Studies*, 28/2 (2013), 136–46.

———, Evans, R., Staples, E., Hallett, S., Roberts, L., Rees, A. and Andrews, D., 'The Consequences of Being Labelled "Looked-After": Exploring the Educational Experiences of Looked-after Children and Young People in Wales', *British Journal of Educational Research*, 43/4 (2017), 683–99.

——— and Morgan, M., 'Doing Ethnography or Applying a Qualitative Technique?: Reflections from the "Waiting Field"', *Qualitative Research*, 15/2 (2015), 166–82.

——— and Staples, E., 'Sandboxes, stickers and superheroes: Employing creative techniques to explore the aspirations and experiences of children and young people who are looked after', in D. Mannay, A. Rees and L. Roberts (eds), *Children and Young People 'Looked After'? Education, Intervention and the Everyday Culture of Care in Wales* (Cardiff: University of Wales Press, 2019), pp. 169–82.

———, Staples, E., Hallett, S., Roberts, L., Rees, A., Evans, R. and Andrews, D., *Understanding the Educational Experiences and Opinions, Attainment, Achievement and Aspirations of Looked After Children in Wales* (Cardiff: Welsh Government, 2015).

McCluskey, G., Riddell, S., Weedon, E. and Fordyce, M., 'Exclusion from School and Recognition of Difference', *Discourse: Studies in the Cultural Politics of Education*, 37/4 (2016), 529–39.

Meo, A. and Parker, A., 'Teachers, Teaching and Educational Exclusion: Pupil Referral Units and Pedagogic Practice', *International Journal of Inclusive Education*, 8/1 (2004), 103–20.

Michael, S. and Frederickson, N., 'Improving Pupil Referral Unit Outcomes: Pupil Perspectives', *Emotional and Behavioural Difficulties*, 18/4 (2013), 407–22.

Pain, R., 'Social Geography: Participatory Research', *Progress in Human Geography*, 28/5 (2004), 652–63.

Pauwels, L., 'An integrated conceptual framework for visual social research', in E. Margolis and L. Pauwels (eds), *The Sage Handbook of Visual Research Methods* (London: Sage, 2011), pp. 3–23.

Pirrie, A., Macleod, M., Cullen, A. and McCluskey, G., *Where Next for Pupils Excluded from Special Schools and Referral Units?* (2009). Available at *http://dera.ioe.ac.uk/11069/1/DCSF-RR163.pdf* (accessed 21/08/17).

Pithouse, A., *Social Work: The Organisation of an Invisible Trade* (Aldershot: Avebury, 1987).

Quarmby, T., 'Sport and Physical Activity in the Lives of Looked After Children: A "Hidden Group" in *Research, Policy and Practice*', *Sport, Education and Society*, 19/7 (2014), 944–58.

Rees, P. and Munro, A., 'Promoting the education of children in care: Reflections of children and carers who have experienced "success"', in D. Mannay, A. Rees and L. Roberts (eds), *Children and Young People 'Looked After'? Education,*

Intervention and the Everyday Culture of Care in Wales (Cardiff: University of Wales Press, 2019), pp. 56–68.

Sellman, E., Bedward, J., Cole, T. and Daniels, H., 'A Sociocultural Approach to Exclusion', *British Educational Research Journal*, 28/6 (2002), 889–900.

Thomson, F., 'Are Methodologies for Children Keeping Them in Their Place?', *Children's Geographies*, 5/3 (2007), 207–18.

Walmsley, J. and Johnson, K., *Inclusive Research with People with Learning Disabilities: Past, Present and Futures* (London: Jessica Kingsley Publishers, 2003).

Welsh Government, 2017, *Pupils Educated Other than at School, 2016/17* (2017). Available at *http://gov.wales/docs/statistics/2017/170803-pupils-educated-other-than-at-school-2016-17-en.pdf* (accessed 21/08/17).

15 | Enabling care-experienced young people's participation in research

CASCADE Voices

Eleanor Staples, Louise Roberts,
Jennifer Lyttleton-Smith, Sophie Hallett
and CASCADE Voices

Introduction

CASCADE VOICES is a collaboration between Voices from Care Cymru (VfCC), a user-led organisation that upholds the rights and welfare of children and young people with experience of public care, and CAS-CADE, the Children's Social Care Research and Development Centre, based at Cardiff University. The group is made up of care-experienced young people who have been trained in social research methods and it advises on all aspects of research, from design to dissemination. Its aim is to embed the voices of young people who have experience and expertise in relation to social care services within research on health and social care topics.

Membership is open to all care-experienced young people in Wales and for those who wish to be involved, CASCADE researchers provide training over two days. The training is run twice a year. This introduces young people to the purpose of social research and the importance of ethical practice, whilst also providing opportunities to try out some traditional and creative social research techniques. Following the training, young people are invited periodically (typically bi-monthly) to consult and collaborate on a wide range of projects. Any individual or organisation wishing to consult with the group is charged a fee that is passed on to VfCC to cover administrative costs and the young people's expenses. The group is an ongoing collaborative project; members remain involved for as long as they wish and there are no requirements in terms of attendance. Meetings are facilitated by a CASCADE researcher, supported by a member of staff from VfCC. The work of CASCADE Voices has included generating ideas that have turned into successful research bids, informing the conduct and design of research studies, reviewing research tools, acting as peer researchers, and contributing to analysis and dissemination.

This chapter will provide an account of the development, operation and challenges of CASCADE Voices. First it will detail its shared roots with the CASCADE research centre and its relationship with shifting understandings about children, childhood and youth as well as the unique political backdrop of the Welsh Government's formal commitment to children's rights. Following this, there will be a discussion of the way children's and young people's participation has been conceptualised, and what kind of participation is facilitated by CASCADE Voices. It will then provide an insight into how the group works; case study examples of its influence and engagement across stages will include instances of where this has worked well, where it has been less successful and what the learning has been. Finally, some of the ongoing practical and ethical tensions that we have encountered will be acknowledged.

Locating CASCADE Voices

CASCADE was established in 2014 by Professor Sally Holland and CASCADE Voices was a core component of the emerging research centre. CASCADE is dedicated to producing high-quality, internationally recognised research on issues across the spectrum of children's social care in order to contribute to improving the well-being and safety of children and their families living in challenging circumstances. It has sought to bridge divides between academic research, government policy and practitioner and service user need, to maximise the impact and influence of research evidence, and to enable wide audiences to access the results of research (see Mannay et al., 2019 [Chapter 16 this volume]). CASCADE Voices was designed to provide a link between the academic community and children and young people who had been on the receiving end of, often multiple, social care interventions and were thus 'experts by experience' (Preston-Shoot, 2007).

The development of CASCADE Voices must also be understood in relation to increased academic interest in children's and young people's participation. The new sociology of childhood positions children as active beings with agency, 'a move away from seeing children as passive recipients of adult socialization, to a recognition that children are social actors in their own right' (O'Kane, 2000, p. 136). Critical sociological thinking about children, childhood and youth has led to the recognition that there are inherent power relations at work when academic researchers construct discourses about children and young people without asking them for their views and experiences directly. As such, the development of CASCADE Voices recognises and responds to Oakley's (1994) notion of flawed 'adultist' concepts of childhood.

Furthermore, if research about children and young people does not engage with them as active, competent and knowing beings, the situation where 'young people are typically positioned by adults who create the professional and political agenda' (Clark and Statham, 2005, p. 45) will not change. Recognising young people as experts is one of the key principles of CASCADE Voices, which provides researchers with a mechanism for understanding the shape of care-experienced children's and young people's lives, and thus a better understanding of what they want and need from services which are designed to support them and others like them.

CASCADE Voices also developed against the backdrop of the Welsh Government's adoption of the United Nations Convention on the Rights of the Child (UNCRC) as the basis for policy making about children and young people in Wales. Early in the process of devolution, the Welsh Assembly Government was clear about its commitment to children's rights. In 2000 the policy document *Children and Young People: A Framework for Partnership* (WAG, 2000, p. 3) stated that the UNCRC had:

> encouraged a positive and optimistic image of children and young people as active holders of rights ... The Assembly believes that the Convention should provide a foundation of principle for dealing with children.

The UNCRC was formally adopted by the Welsh Assembly Government in 2004. The policy statement *Rights to Action* (Welsh Assembly Government, 2004) translated the UNCRC into seven aims for all children and young people in Wales upon which policies, programmes and services must be based in decision making, planning and funding. In addition, the UNCRC has strengthened the basis for children's and young people's direct participation in research studies (Holland et al., 2010). CASCADE Voices both ensures that participation is respectful and responsive to the needs of participants by ensuring that children are 'properly researched on' (Beazley et al., 2009, p. 370), promoting children's rights within research.

Additionally, CASCADE Voices upholds Convention rights in terms of being non-discriminatory (article 2), working in the child's best interest (article 3), providing the right to be heard (article 12) and freedom of expression (article 13). More recently, the Welsh Government's emphasis on co-production, recognising and drawing upon the expertise of individuals and communities in the design and delivery of public services, has culminated in the Social Services and Well-being (Wales) Act 2014. The notion of 'citizen-centred' services and doing 'with' rather than 'to' those who need support are key themes underpinning the Act and principles which also underpin CASCADE Voices. Health and Care Research Wales (2017, p. 2), the body which supports research capacity on behalf of the Welsh Government, also suggests that research opportunities should be afforded to the public:

> Co-production of health and social care research ensures the public of Wales are equal partners with researchers in the creation of new knowledge and truly have a voice in health and social care research activity.

Providing care-experienced young people with an opportunity to exercise a 'strong voice' within a university research centre means that research can be both relevant and respectful to the lived experiences of children and young people who have received social care interventions.

Participating how?

CASCADE Voices seeks to provide opportunities for young people to participate in research in a capacity beyond that of respondent, embedding their voice in the design, ethical safeguards, data collection tools and dissemination of research. However, participation is not a straightforward concept. It has been discussed, debated and described in many ways (Rocha, 1997; Jensen, 2000; Shier, 2001; Reddy and Ratna, 2002). Although it has been critiqued, refined and developed, Roger Hart's (1992) early conceptualisation of the 'ladder of participation' has been hugely influential in these debates. There is insufficient space to fully explicate Hart's model in this chapter; however, it is useful in demonstrating that involving children and young people, and enabling their participation, are not the same thing.

For example, Hart conceives of the bottom rung of the ladder of participation as 'manipulation'. This would include giving three-year old children placards to hold as part of a protest against the removal of funds from a pre-school. The cause is presented as being inspired by and involving children, but they cannot be said to have any meaningful understanding about it, or the ability to disagree: they are there to bolster their parents' protest. However well-meaning the activity or cause, we must think carefully about how we involve children and young people. In the context of research, we must ask whether children's and young people's involvement serves our ends and is manipulative, decorative or tokenistic (to use Hart's terminology) or actually provides an opportunity for meaningful participation.

In a more recent articulation of children's and young people's participation offered by Francis and Lorenzo (2002), CASCADE Voices can be characterised as participation through 'institutionalisation'; members of the group are trained in the institutional norms of social research in order to participate. This form of participation requires children and young people to fit into an established, adult model in order to participate and as such can be said to devalue their own cultural and social practices. However, researchers who strive for inclusive, emancipatory and participatory research with children and young people must still work within the specific parameters of academic research. Indeed, Kellett (2005, p. 9) states that 'while children's understanding and knowledge of childhood is evident, a genuine barrier to children engaging in research is their lack of knowledge and skills'. Consequently, by training CASCADE Voices members, and introducing them to the practices and language of social research, they are given an opportunity to participate in research as 'insiders' whilst also providing unique expertise through their experience of having lived in public care. In this way, the development of CASCADE Voices seeks to build on traditional models of children's participation and service user involvement. It offers opportunities for care-experienced young people to participate in research 'as instigators of ideas, research designers, interviewers, data analysts, authors, disseminators and users' (Walmsley and Johnson, 2003, p. 10).

A distinct feature of the group is its long-term, open-ended structure that provides opportunities for participation based upon young people's needs and commitments. Rather than one-off consultations or single project involvement, CASCADE Voices aims to provide members with opportunities for longer-term experiences and engagement with CASCADE, with multiple and varied chances for influence and involvement that can work flexibly around the young people's lives. As highlighted in Figure 15.1, this includes opportunities to contribute before, during and after the conduct of individual research projects.

The potential for young people to remain engaged with CASCADE Voices over extended periods of time and across a range of projects is open to critique. Beresford (2013) has previously noted a tendency to dismiss those who regularly engage in service user participation activities as the 'usual suspects'; where the experiences of a small sample of motivated individuals are repeatedly used to represent the many. Such a dismissal misrecognises the contributions that these individuals make, and while we understand the need for diverse experiences and varied voices, prominent academics and other 'experts' on care-experienced children and young people are not spoken about in these terms. We contend that the 'usual suspects' of CASCADE Voices have ideas, passion and expertise that have enhanced and informed numerous projects. With experience comes greater understanding and, often, enhanced critical skills relating to research that we have found in long-term CASCADE Voices members.

Figure 15.1: *Participation in different stages of the research process*

Before the research	During the research process	After the research
• Informing ideas for future projects • Informing research design and methods	• Ensuring ethical standards • Iterative consultation and discussion • Acting as peer researchers	• Informing policy and practice recommendations • Informing and engaging with dissemination • Assisting with impact projects

A final point about participation is that CASCADE Voices seeks to create mutually beneficial relationships. The group is advantageous to CASCADE but it is also intended to be a positive experience for young people, based upon principles of inclusion and empowerment. Young people who are care-experienced have often endured a succession of temporary relationships with professionals, carers and friends due to staff turnover or placement moves which are out of the control of children and young people themselves (Leeson, 2007). Instead of replicating another temporary experience, it was hoped that young people would view group membership as an opportunity to build and strengthen social networks, think creatively and critically, and debate and justify arguments. Accordingly, CASCADE Voices supports the continued development of individual skills which has potential for increasing young people's participation in other arenas; it provides a chance for group participation and the creation of friendships and networks; and it provides a conduit for care-experienced young people to participate in research.

How does the group work?

We have broadly categorised the five stages of research that members of CASCADE Voices are enabled to have some involvement in and provided case study examples to demonstrate how this works in practice.

1. Ideas

CASCADE's involvement with VfCC has been collaborative rather than consultative and this has resulted in several new ideas for research being developed into research bids. By building a relationship with an advocacy and support organisation that is not dependent on, or entirely motivated by, a specific research project, ideas for research are able to grow organically and collaboratively.

Case study one

Over time, group members had become concerned about the experiences of young people in and leaving care when they became parents. While some had positive experiences of parenthood, in too many instances young people had encountered significant difficulties and challenges, including instances of compulsory removal of a child from their care. In response, a fellowship application was developed that directly explored some of these concerns (see Roberts et al., 2017; Roberts, 2019 [Chapter 11 this volume]). This is an example of how the open-ended and continuing nature of CASCADE Voices allows ideas to develop through informal talk with young people, ideas that may not surface in a formal meeting.

2. Research design

A meeting of CASCADE Voices can be used to develop details of a project's research design or to collaborate on specific methods and research tools. Members of CASCADE Voices have demonstrated great awareness of certain opportunities and barriers to research, which is invaluable at the design stage. To collaborate and participate effectively in this stage of research (both in terms of the researcher getting what they need and the young people seeing how they are having an influence), members of the group must have undergone the research methods training offered by CASCADE.

Case study two

A study evaluating a training course for residential care practitioners included an element of research with young people. A CASCADE Voices meeting was convened to discuss the best ways to collect data with the young people. The group had a great deal of insight into residential care, even those who had not directly experienced it but shared the experiences of acquaintances, family and friends. They came up with some of the key issues that they felt the researcher should explore with young people and characteristics of an 'ideal worker' that could be tested with the participants. However, the main discussion centred on people's experiences of care, and problems they had encountered in care, rather than around which method would best explore young people's perceptions of their residential care workers. In this instance, while the research topic was familiar to the group, the research questions were very specific and related to measuring a discrete set of qualities or skills exhibited by residential care practitioners. The learning here was primarily that the facilitator should always ensure that the group is given a clear idea of the research questions before embarking on discussion of a topic, especially where the topic is care related. Subsequently, the overarching research design was completed without reference to CASCADE Voices. This was unfortunate as input at this stage would have been a valuable addition to the project, particularly because the difficulties encountered in the CASCADE Voices session were to some extent replicated in the data collection itself.

3. Data collection and analysis

Members of CASCADE Voices have acted as peer researchers for specific projects, collecting data with research participants. Peer researchers have been recruited using an application process and successful candidates received two days of additional training covering ethics, methods, confidentiality and safeguarding in more detail. Members of the group have also been asked to help identify and develop themes emerging from qualitative data. In terms of analysis, it is paramount that the conditions of anonymity are met so that participants' qualitative accounts are not recognisable and it is also important that the data is presented in accessible ways.

Case study three

In a study exploring the experiences of children and young people who are looked after in relation to education, peer researchers facilitated focus groups with young people in locations in north and south Wales (see Mannay et al., 2015, 2017). They used the interview schedule which we had devised during training as a guide, but due to their own expertise and the respect they garnered from participants, they managed to elicit discussions from the group that researchers would not have been able to. The peer researchers were also adept at managing breaks and bringing conversations back on track when they drifted off topic. Overall the peer researchers were able to produce very rich and nuanced data relating to young people's experiences of education and gained additional skills and confidence from being part of the project.

4. Iterative monitoring

The group members have been involved in projects in different ways and at different points. Sessions have been scheduled more frequently than the regular bi-monthly meetings where a project requires such input. An important point relating to this kind of involvement is that the group's financial or other compensation must be fully built into a bid so that it is properly resourced.

Case study four

A review of some statutory guidance undertaken by CASCADE involved a large amount of data collection with social care practitioners; it also involved consultation with the CASCADE Voices group (Hallett et al., 2017). At the start of the project, the group was convened as a focus group, to gather data about the subject-matter that the guidance related to and to gather feedback about various categories and terms used in the guidance.

The second workshop was not a data-collection activity; instead preliminary findings and recommendations from the wider research project were taken to the group for discussion and debate. By involving the group members at different stages of the project and in different capacities (as research participants and advisers), they were able to help shape the data collected as well as guide the way that this data was interpreted to form the recommendations of the review. This was fruitful, as in the second workshop the group saw how the research process worked and how their experiences had been recognised and incorporated in the preliminary findings.

5. Dissemination

CASCADE Voices have acted as advisers on appropriate forms that research outputs should take in order to be accessible to different audiences, and as co-producers of those outputs. Again, an important point here is that involvement in dissemination requires adequate resourcing, especially where outputs take alternative forms such as videos, plays, and artwork. As such, the group's involvement needs to be properly built into a bid in order to achieve some level of meaningful participation.

Case study five
As part of the study discussed earlier which explored young people's experiences of education, non-traditional research outputs were created, including short films (see Mannay et al., 2019 [Chapter 16 this volume]). Transcript extracts from the research were narrated by some CASCADE Voices group members and recorded in a professional recording studio. However, some of the data produced in the project required voice-overs, with younger children not represented within CASCADE Voices. These children, and some additional young people, were selected by the production company that the researchers were working with via drama workshops run at local schools. None of these narrators were care-experienced and there was a lack of diversity in terms of regional accents.

These videos featured successfully in events and were disseminated via social media so that global audiences of young people and key stakeholders could access vital messages for improving the educational experience of children in public care. However, the representational authenticity of the films varied and there was a clear difference in the affective quality and impact of some of the CASCADE Voices narratives in relation to those produced by non-care-experienced children and young people.

This issue highlights the conflict between producing outputs with the most 'impact' in a short amount of time and on a tight budget versus enabling more care-experienced children and young people an opportunity for participation in dissemination; perhaps by expanding opportunities both within and outside CASCADE Voices. The learning about how to negotiate and communicate with professionals from other backgrounds to ensure values of inclusion and participation are upheld has been significant, as has an understanding about the importance of adequate resourcing for dissemination work.

Ongoing challenges

Despite its high methodological and ethical aspirations, CASCADE Voices faces ongoing challenges and competing demands. First, there are concerns about the diversity of young people's voices that are heard via the group and how well they represent the heterogeneity of children and young people in and leaving public care. Theoretically, group membership is open to any care-experienced individual, but in practice members are most likely to be referred through VfCC. This means that group members are engaged with a supportive organisation and typically live within a small number of neighbouring authorities in south Wales. Additionally, the CASCADE researchers and VfCC staff who facilitate the group are not Welsh language speakers and we have not been able to offer the group, or any materials, in the Welsh language. As such, the group reaches a discrete set of young people who are supported by VfCC to attend meetings. In addition, while efforts are made to hold meetings during school holidays they are held during the day, on weekdays. This can make it difficult for those who work or are in full-time education or training to attend. Whilst attempts to meet in the evening have been made, the caring responsibilities of the researchers who facilitate the group make this difficult to sustain [1].

The strategic vision for CASCADE Voices is expansion, to make it accessible to young people living in rural and urban communities across Wales and to those who would like to access the group via the medium of Welsh. The voices of younger children and those with experience of a different range of children's social care services, such as disability and youth offending are also sought. Yet whilst this strategy will enable a broader range of perspectives to be included, it is somewhat at odds with the initial core values of forging long-term, meaningful relationships with care-experienced young people. As membership grows and diversifies, so too do the challenges of sustaining regular contact, a recognisable and safe group identity and opportunities for individual young people.

Challenges also remain in respect of recognising the contribution of the young people. A nominal cost is attached to typical bi-monthly meetings, which covers administration costs, travel expenses and refreshments for the young people attending. It seems somewhat disingenuous to speak of young people being valued and having expertise when they are reimbursed only for travel costs, especially when both CASCADE researchers and VfCC staff are salaried, but issuing payments to young people can be difficult because one-off payments are often prohibited for those in receipt of welfare benefits. Further, we remain cautious about paying young people in case it incentivises or pressures participation: we are attempting to avoid the power relations inherent in trading in money.

The TimeBanking model offers a potential compromise for recognising young people's involvement. TimeBanking is based upon principles of reciprocity, co-production, people as assets, and the egalitarian value that everybody's time is equal (Cahn, 2004) whilst providing a practical way to negotiate the issue of welfare benefit rules. Time becomes currency (Bretherton and Pleace, 2014) which everyone can acquire and spend, so giving an hour to take part in research can be recompensed with a Time Credit that can be spent doing an hour of an activity such as visiting the cinema, indoor climbing or training. However, Time Credits are not typically offered in exchange for expert collaboration, which arguably compounds, rather than challenges, notions that care-experienced young people are seen and treated differently within society. CASCADE researchers facilitate the group as part of a job, not in exchange for a Time Credit. As such, the group's basis for participation is very different to the researcher's, and this is an issue which we continue to wrestle with.

More broadly, CASCADE Voices is not institutionally funded and if the costs of facilitating CASCADE Voices become too high, either due to direct payments to young people or the cost of purchasing Time Credits, or even providing gift vouchers in exchange for participation, the group becomes unsustainable. Indeed, other researchers have documented that 'much of how inclusive research ideals are borne out comes down to questions of power and money' (Nind et al., 2016, p. 3). Resourcing and securing proper recognition for CASCADE Voices are significant and continuing challenges for the group.

Conclusion

This chapter highlighted the development and operation of CASCADE Voices. Our attempts to enable care-experienced young people's participation in research are in part borne out of a concern about the way that discourses and understandings about them have been constructed without them. As such, CASCADE Voices provides opportunities for individuals to participate in research but it also represents a gesture to redress 'the wrongs done when research has labelled, pathologized and colonised its subjects' (Nind et al., 2016, p. 6). We do not claim to have created a perfect model for doing this and whilst it is easy to note the group's achievements and strengths, of which there are many, we have also reflected on some of the challenges that we have encountered and continue to negotiate. Practical and ethical challenges remain, but it is hoped that the examples of the way that the group has engaged in and with research are instructive and inspiring for others who wish to engender children and young people's participation both in research and in other decision-making and community activities.

Acknowledgements

We would like to thank all of the young people who have participated in CASCADE Voices, past, present, and future. We would also like to thank Christopher Dunn and Rachael Vaughan from Voices from Care Cymru for their support and help with running CASCADE Voices and Darren Andrews, Anya Barton, Phil Smith and Suzanne Spooner who assisted with some of the group training.

Note

1.   To date, all CASCADE staff involved with the group have been women. This is perhaps unsurprising given that CASCADE's team is female dominated. Displaying and managing patience, compassion, warmth and calmness are all part of facilitating CASCADE Voices. This emotion-work has been argued to be expected of and practised by women to a greater extent than men in academic research but not valued in the same way as other aspects of research (Reay, 2004). The gendered division and misrecognition of emotional labour is not the domain of this chapter, but it is noted because we are seeking to provide a reflexive account of the group and its functioning.

References

Beazley, H., Bessell, S., Ennew, J. and Waterson, R., 'The Right to be Properly Researched: Research with Children in a Messy, Real World', *Children's Geographies*, 7/4 (2009), 365–78.

Beresford, P., *Beyond the Usual Suspects* (London: Shaping Our Lives, 2013). Available at *http://www.shapingourlives.org.uk/documents/BTUSReport.pdf* (accessed 10/3/17).

Bretherton, J. and Pleace, N., *An Evaluation of the Broadway Skills Exchange Time Bank* (York: University of York, 2014).

Cahn, E., *No More Throwaway People: The Co-Production Imperative* (Washington, D.C.: Essential Books, 2004).

Clark, P and Statham, J., 'Listening to Young Children: Experts in Their Own Lives', *Adoption & Fostering*, 29/1 (2005), 45–56.

Francis, M. and Lorenzo, R., 'Seven Realms of Children's Participation', *Journal of Environmental Psychology*, 22 (2002), 157–69.

Hallett, S., Crowley, A., Deerfield, K., Staples, E. and Rees, A., *Review of the Wales Safeguarding Children and Young People from Sexual Exploitation (CSE) Statutory Guidance* (Cardiff: Welsh Government, 2017).

Hart, R., *Children's Participation: From Tokenism to Citizenship: Innocenti Essays No. 4* (Florence: UNICEF, 1992).

Health and Care Research Wales, *Engaging and Involving the Public of Wales in Health and Social Care Research: Today's Research; Tomorrow's Care* (Cardiff:

Welsh Government, 2017). Available at *https://www.healthandcareresearch.gov. wales/uploads/Policy%20%26%20Strategy/principles_public_involvement_ eng.pdf* (accessed 22/02/17).

Holland, S., Renold, E., Ross, N. and Hillman, A., 'Power, Agency and Participatory Agendas: A Critical Exploration of Young People's Engagement in Participative Qualitative Research', *Childhood*, 17/3 (2010), 360–75.

Jensen, B. B., 'Participation, commitment and knowledge as components of pupils' action competence', in B. B. Jensen, K. Schnack and V. Simovska (eds), *Critical Environmental and Health Education: Research Issues and Challenges* (Copenhagen: Danish University Education, 2000), pp. 219–38.

Kellett, M., *How to Develop Children as Researchers* (London: Paul Chapman Educational Publishing, 2005).

Leeson, C., 'My Life in Care: Experiences of Non-participation in Decision Making Processes', *Child & Family Social Work*, 12 (2007), 268–77.

Mannay, D., Evans, R., Staples, E., Hallett, S., Roberts, L., Rees, A. and Andrews, D., 'The Consequences of Being Labelled "Looked-After": Exploring the Educational Experiences of Looked-after Children and Young People in Wales', *British Journal of Educational Research*, 43/4 (2017), 683–99.

———, Roberts, L., Staples, E. and Ministry of Life, 'Lights, camera, action: Translating research findings into policy and practice impacts with music, film and artwork', in D. Mannay, A. Rees and L. Roberts (eds), *Children and Young People 'Looked After'? Education, Intervention and the Everyday Culture of Care in Wales* (Cardiff: University of Wales Press, 2019), pp. 210–24.

———, Staples, E., Hallett, S., Roberts, L., Rees, A., Evans, R. and Andrews, D., *Understanding the Educational Experiences and Opinions, Attainment, Achievement and Aspirations of Looked After Children in Wales* (Cardiff: Welsh Government, 2015).

Nind, M., Armstrong, A., Cansdale, M., Hollis, A., Hooper, C., Parsons, S. and Power, A., 'TimeBanking: Towards a Co-produced Solution for Power and Money Issues in Inclusive Research', *International Journal of Social Research Methodology*, 20/4 (2016), 387–400.

Oakley, A., 'Women and children first and last', in B. Mayall (ed.), *Children's Childhoods: Observed and Experienced* (London: The Falmer Press, 1994), pp. 13–32.

O'Kane, C., 'The development of participatory techniques: Facilitating children's views about decisions which affect them', in P. Christensen and A. James (eds), *Research with Children: Perspectives and Practices* (London: Routledge Falmer, 2000), pp. 125–55.

Preston-Shoot, M., 'Whose Lives and Whose Learning? Whose Narratives and Whose Writing? Taking the Next Research and Literature Steps with Experts by Experience', *Evidence & Policy: A Journal of Research, Debate and Practice*, 3/3 (2007), 343–59.

Reay, D., 'Cultural Capitalists and Academic Habitus: Classed and Gendered Labour in UK Higher Education', *Women's Studies International Forum*, 27/1 (2004), 31–9.

Reddy, N. and Ratna, K., *A Journey in Children's Participation* (Bangalore: The Concerned for Working Children, 2002).

Roberts, L. '"A family of my own": When young people in and leaving state care become parents in Wales', in D. Mannay, A. Rees and L. Roberts (eds), *Children and Young People 'Looked After'? Education, Intervention and the Everyday Culture of Care in Wales* (Cardiff: University of Wales Press, 2019), pp. 140–52.

———, Meakings, S., Forrester, D., Smith, A. and Shelton, K., 'Care-leavers and Their Children Placed for Adoption', *Children and Youth Services Review*, 79 (2017), 355–61.

Rocha, E., 'A Ladder of Empowerment', *Journal of Planning, Education and Research*, 17 (1997), 31–44.

Shier, H., 'Pathways to Participation: Openings, Opportunities and Obligations – a New Model for Enhancing Children's Participation in Decision-Making, in Line with Article 12.1 of the United Nations Convention on the Rights of the Child, *Children and Society*, 15 (2001), 110–24.

UN General Assembly, *United Nations Convention on the Rights of the Child* (Geneva: United Nations, 1989).

Walmsley, J. and Johnson, K., *Inclusive Research with People with Learning Difficulties: Past, Present and Future* (London: Jessica Kingsley, 2003).

Welsh Assembly Government, *Children and Young People: A Framework for Partnership* (Cardiff: Welsh Assembly Government, 2000).

———, *Children and Young People: Rights to Action* (Cardiff: Welsh Assembly Government, 2004).

Welsh Government, *Social Services and Well-being (Wales) Act 2014* (Cardiff: Welsh Government, 2014).

16 | Lights, camera, action

Translating research findings into policy and practice impacts with music, film and artwork

Dawn Mannay, Louisa Roberts, Eleanor Staples and Ministry of Life

Introduction

THERE HAS BEEN A growing emphasis on research impact, particularly in relation to the Research Excellence Framework (REF) in the United Kingdom. The REF (2011) defines impact as 'any effect on, change or benefit to the economy, society, culture, public policy or services, health, the environment or quality of life, beyond academia'. In negotiating a demonstrable contribution to society (ESRC, 2017), researchers now need to consider alternative multimodal outputs that reflexively, ethically and creatively move beyond the academic article and standard report to communicate their findings. Accordingly, it is important that academics take 'audience and archive as a starting point' (Silver, 2016) and explore effective vehicles for dissemination, engagement and impact.

Creating multimodal, accessible materials is particularly important when research recommendations can only be actualised by a diverse range of stakeholders, who may not engage with more traditional outputs. This is pertinent to research with children who are looked after and care leavers because, despite a plethora of research (Brodie, 2010; Berridge, 2012; Stein, 2012; Welbourne and Leeson, 2012; Sebba et al., 2015) and policy making (see the Children Act 1989, the Children Act 2004, the Children and Young Persons Act 2008, and the Social Services and Well-being

(Wales) Act 2014), many of the reported issues, barriers and inequalities have remained a pervasive feature of the care experience.

This chapter discusses the ways in which findings from a study with care-experienced children, young people and young adults were translated into creative arts-based materials, including films, music videos and graphic art. The chapter questions the impact of purely written and verbal forms of dissemination and explores the impact of arts-based practice. This is followed by a discussion of how we worked collaboratively with the creative industries to articulate the messages from children and young people looked after; reflecting on the process and the impacts of the multimodal materials that were produced. The chapter argues that engaging diverse publics with research findings and recommendations necessitates a move beyond the academic article and report-based outputs.

Background

As Becker (2007, p. 285) contends, 'there is no best way to tell a story about society . . . the world gives us possibilities among which we chose'. However, typically research project completion involves the writing up of the findings and recommendations in a final report, which may be restricted to a 'small audience who are closely associated with the research project' (Timmins, 2015, p. 35). The publication of a report is often followed by related peer reviewed journal articles and other scholarly publications; however, arguably this dissemination strategy is restricted to an academic audience (Barnes at al., 2003). Accordingly, the implications of much of this work often appear to have little impact on practice, policy or communities (Finfgeld, 2003; Troman, 2001), limiting opportunities for change and improvement.

For Knowles and Burrows (2014, p. 242), 'we are increasingly subject to a range of administrative processes that demand that we can demonstrate that the research that we carry out, and the outputs that result from it, possess some utility to non-academics and that they possess causal powers to influence the world in some way or another'. Not discounting the argument that these demands can put pressure on academic staff and be seen as part of an audit culture where we are continually measured and evaluated (Strathern, 2000), as academics we are often personally invested in contributing to positive changes in the areas that we study. As Keen and Todres (2007) contend, 'qualitative research, done well, is worth disseminating', therefore, it is important to explore other modes of communicative practice.

Creative dissemination approaches 'can promote insight and new ways of knowing that communicate . . . research to both public and professional audiences' (Bruce et al., 2013, p. 23). In this way, arts-based approaches can make visible participants' experiences that are often left unarticulated or hidden, drawing the audience in as 'embodied, sensual beings in the living details' (Halford and Knowles, 2005) of the messages we seek to communicate. Additionally, they can be more accessible than traditional reports, which can act as a barrier for those who have difficulties with literacy, those who are unable to access costly prestigious academic journals, or those who simply do not have the capacity to invest their time in reading long and complex reports, strategies and academic articles. These barriers are central in the gap which often exists between educational research and everyday practice (see Vanderlinde and van Braak, 2010). Reflecting on these considerations, the following sections discuss how the research findings from a project with care-experienced children and young people were translated into a series of multimodal outputs to increase the reach, audience and impact of the key findings.

The study

The dissemination strategies discussed in this chapter were related to a Welsh Government commissioned study to explore the educational experiences, attainment and aspirations of care-experienced children and young people in Wales (Mannay et al., 2015, 2017a; see also Rees et al., 2019; Mannay and Staples, 2019 [Chapters 3 and 13 of this volume]). The original study reviewed literature on the educational experiences of the care-experienced population; conducted a full systematic review of effective educational interventions; and involved creative activities and qualitative interviews with sixty-seven participants who were or had been looked after.

As in the standard model (Timmins, 2015), the study generated a detailed report (Mannay et al., 2015) and led to journal publications (Evans et al., 2017; Mannay et al., 2017a, 2017b); it also generated further impact as the findings and recommendations informed policy strategy (Welsh Government, 2016). However, when reflecting on the literature reviewed in the project, we were dismayed by the number of times that recommendations, similar to our study's findings, had been made; but not met with the requisite changes in the lives of care-experienced children and young people. This raised concerns that, despite reporting our findings and recommendations through traditional approaches, they would have little impact in making positive changes on the ground – in schools, foster homes and social service provision.

Consequently, we worked within the project budget and sought extension funding to collaborate with the creative industries to produce alternative forms of reporting and engagement materials. This was achieved within the initial project by creating four short films and a magazine for young people with the support of funding from the Welsh Government. We then went on to secure a Cardiff University Engagement Team grant to produce artwork, music audios and videos, and bespoke art pieces representing the key project recommendations. Additionally, we applied to an Economic and Social Research Council's Impact and Acceleration Account, administered through Cardiff University. With this support we were able to consult further with children and young people, produce an animated short film, #messagestoschools, create an education charter, organise a poetry competition for children and young people, produce a music audio and music video, commission further art pieces, create a magazine for foster carers, and engage in a series of events and workshops for key stakeholders across Wales. The following section will consider the creation, production and impact of some these multimodal outputs [1].

Generating creative outputs

The researchers and creatives were committed to producing effective materials that would authentically represent children's and young people's accounts and effectively relay the findings and recommendations of the project. However, this brought challenges around who can and should be 'seen and heard' (Lomax, 2015, p. 493). The 'politics of recognition' argues that collaborative projects should provide a platform through which participants are both visible and recognisable in research outputs, so that they are present in the telling of their stories (Sweetman, 2009). This approach has proved successful in previous projects (see Sweetman and Hensser, 2010; Byrne et al., 2016), but we were wary of adopting an approach that exposed or identified the research participants.

This is not to say that children and young people would not have wanted to be 'seen and heard' or that we felt that they could not engage audiences and offer a genuine and nuanced account of their experiences. Indeed, they could have articulated their challenges and recommendations more effectively than the research team and creative industries. However, ethically we were primarily concerned with 'time immemorial' (Brady and Brown, 2013), and the issue that once visual data is made available it is very difficult to control and impossible to take back if children or young people changed their minds. Consequently, all of the creative outputs had the challenge of maintaining anonymity, which meant that they moved beyond a simple visual representation to a more complex re-visualisation (Mannay, 2016b).

In the initial films [2] we were able to draw on the extensive footage of the visual artefacts that children and young people had created (see Mannay and Staples, 2019 [Chapter 13 this volume]), as well as the movement of activities that were part of the research events. The vocal narrative of the film was constructed from the verbatim transcripts of children and young people but we were not able to use the audios of their actual voices because of issues of confidentiality. Our participatory approaches in the fieldwork are predicated on giving 'voice' (Gallacher and Gallagher, 2008); so we had concerns about creating voice-overs that could potentially silence the participants' points of emphasis and meaning making.

The films were voiced by school children trained by the creative team but there were tensions around the audibility conferred by those who spoke in Received Pronunciation [3], for the production team, and our preference for a diversity of local accents. The accounts of older young people were voiced by other care leavers, which added an element of authenticty [4]. Therefore, although the films were useful and generated impact, as discussed further in the following section, some friction remained. For the research team, who had conducted the interviews, the accounts from younger children did not always retain the right emphasis and tone in the voice-overs. Nevertheless, the films powerfully communicated the key messages and, in maintaining anonymity and confidentiality, it must be accepted that re-visualisation and re-vocalisation can only retain traces of the participants and enable a differential, and partial, form of authentic voice (see Mannay et al., forthcoming).

Music videos, music audios and graphic art pieces were generated to represent the key reflections and recommendations made by children and young people about their aspirations, experiences and suggestions for change [5]. Again the challenge was to 'communicate participants' narratives, retaining the power of these accounts but removing the associated images and wider contextualisation to maintain confidentiality' (Mannay, 2016a, p. 135). The lyrics for the songs were constructed directly from the accounts of children and young people; and feedback from care-experienced viewers, within and outside the research activities, has been positive in that they have commented that the music reflects their concerns and 'tells the truth' about their experiences. Arguably, the effectiveness of the music audios and videos reflects the experience of the artists and producers, who have worked for many years delivering events, workshops and courses with marginalised children and young people in Wales, including those with a care background. In this way, they were connected with many of the issues raised in the research because of the overlaps and resonances with their own work.

The graphic art pieces, were centralised in communicating some of the main themes from the project, and Figure 16.1 powerfully visualises the argument that children and young people are aspirational, but that their aspirations are often blocked and diminished through their experiences. Another image in the collection related to the ways in which being 'looked after' becomes a label that de-individualises and marks out children and young people. Lastly, one image explored how meetings during school time made children and young people highly visible in a way that they did not have control over; and how the issues discussed in meetings about care were often painful and stigmatising (see Mannay et al., 2015, 2017a).

It was a difficult task for the creative team and artist to represent

Figure 16.1: *Aspirations – Artist – DroneBoy Laundry*

complex narratives in single images and retain the richness of the data. They were not involved in the fieldwork and, in wanting to represent the transcripts they worked with, invested in best representing the participants' accounts and accentuating key messages, whilst being separated from the wider practices and provision base that the research team were endeavouring to work with and influence. As Lomax (2015, p. 500) argues, it is difficult to find a balance between participants' accounts 'while recognising the ways in which this may conflict with our own and others' expectations'. For example, drawing on accounts where young people had shared negative interactions with practitioners, one of the pieces of draft artwork visually represented these professionals as vilified characterisations.

Children and young people had presented negative descriptions of teachers and social workers; however, there were also positive accounts. While the artist was centred on creating research reciprocity for the participants (Richardson, 2015), we had competing pressures, attempting to strike a balance between getting the messages out from the accounts of children and young people and, at the same time, constructing a narrative that would engage, and not alienate, practitioners on the ground. Inevitably, this created some tensions in the working relationship, and engendered a reflection on both situated ethics and the 'complex and controversial landscape of dissemination, representation and visibility, which questions what we "do" and "should do" with visual outputs' (Mannay, 2016a, p. 3). Nevertheless, ultimately we were able to work collaboratively to co-construct images that both retained traces of the narrative accounts of participants and represented them in ways which could open up new dialogues with wider stakeholders. This is important as in attempting to create positive change, it is necessary to be mindful of the ways that the visual may be consumed by audiences (Lomax and Fink, 2010).

Additional materials were generated from further consultations with care-experienced young people and a poetry competition for children and young people looked after and care leavers [6]. Our original intention was to create a paper copy charter to disseminate the ideas from these consultations. However, in our discussions with young people they suggested that their #messagestoschools were represented in multimodal outputs, which led to the creation of a film and poster [7], and three art pieces [8]. Again, we felt it was important to work with film-makers who had a background in working with marginalised communities and in co-producing the script and animation scenes, these shared understandings contributed to the effectiveness and affective value of the film. The young person selected to create the voice-over also added an element of authenticity to the film: her local accent firmly embedded the narrative within the Welsh context, and, as a Welsh speaker, she was able to make two versions; and this bilingual approach was more respectful to the original research sample that had included first language Welsh speakers. A music video summarising the themes raised in the entries to the poetry competition was also made to provide another medium to share the key messages.

Three images were created by an artist [8] who had some direct experience of the care system. This biographical resonance meant that they were both personally invested in the wider project and its aims, and that they had a direct understanding of many of the issues that had been raised by care-experienced children and young people. One poster incorporated a treasure chest and map to communicate the need for children, young people and foster carers to know who their designated teacher [9] is in school, as this is not always clear and transparent (see Girling, 2019 [Chapter 10 this volume]). Another image encouraged teaching staff and other key practitioners to have high expectations for children and young people by featuring a runner and finishing line; this was important in relation to reports in the consultations and original research that children and young people felt that they were not considered as 'successful subjects' (see Mannay et al., 2017a).

The final image (see Figure 16.2) revisited the problematic nature of being made visible, and in particular being taken out of the classroom for meetings relating to care provision (see Mannay et al., 2015, 2017a). These images, and the earlier graphic art pieces were printed as posters and postcards, as well as being shared electronically in the films and music. In addition to this work, two magazines [10] were created, one for foster carers, *Greater Expectations*, and one for young people, *Thrive*. These provided an easily accessible account of the findings in a user friendly format, which mirrored traditional magazines with problem pages, stories, advice sections and activities. Again, the involvement of an organisation embedded in the care system, the Fostering Network, meant that the magazines produced were designed specifically for their intended audiences.

It was hoped that the artwork, magazines, music and film outputs would work together to engage a diverse audience and that the messages could contribute to changes in practice and thinking. The following section discusses the feedback from these outputs and how they have helped to generate impact from the project.

Generating impact

As Knowles and Burrows (2014) have noted, there are difficulties and pressures involved in demonstrating impact, and the ways in which this is measured, evaluated and audited. However, it is important to provide an account of how employing multimodal materials contributed to engagement, action and audiencing of the research findings beyond what was achieved by more traditional forms of academic and public policy dissemination. In a short chapter, we are unable to report on all aspects of how this work has been shared and used, but we will offer some examples.

In terms of reach, the *Greater Expectations* and *Thrive* magazines were both posted to 3,500 foster homes in Wales, taking the research findings into the home, rather than expecting foster carers and young people to find and engage with the research. The #messagestoschools hardcopy materials were also posted to all schools in Wales (n = 1,631). The film, music and artwork was made available online and to date the music videos

Figure 16.2: *Spotlight – Artist – Nathan Bond*

from the initial project have had 2,582 views on YouTube. The artwork was made into postcards and posters, which have been shared widely with key stakeholders for them to use in their work. We have taken these materials to a number of academic conferences and a series of invited events, as well as sharing them in twelve targeted learning conferences and further workshops with over 800 representatives from schools, fostering services and Local Authority stakeholders and practitioners.

This work also led to further funding from the Welsh Government to create an online 'community of practice'. This resource, ExChange: Care and Education [11], works on the principle that best practice can develop where experience and expertise are shared and collaboration encouraged; and the online hub hosts a range of materials, including those from this project, to create a 'one-stop-shop' for anyone with an interest in care and education. In terms of reframing public discussions and raising awareness the project engendered notable media interest and the songs were played on the radio and one of the films was shortlisted in the final of the Cardiff Mini Film Festival. These examples illustrate how the range of multimodal materials increased public interest and extended reach, in terms of dissemination; but it is also important to consider if this resulted in actual change.

Evidencing change in a measurable way is hugely problematic (Strathern, 2000); where we can document some aspects of reach, it is difficult to know if engagement leads to action. The Welsh Government (2107) annual review of its strategy for children looked after, one year on, reported examples of progress, including a 10 percentage point increase since 2012 in the Key Stage 4 performance of care-experienced young people. We are not claiming any direct causal effect from the materials we produced, and we appreciate how these improvements are the result of complex actions from multiple stakeholders. However, the strategy centralised recommendations from our research, and we are hopeful that our creative multimodal outputs have played some part in this progression.

We can report, with more certainty, on qualitative responses from key stakeholders. For example, in response to the films and music, practitioners on the ground have spoken to us, filled in feedback cards at events and completed online surveys distributed to workshop attendees and Local Authority practitioners. They have discussed how these materials moved them emotionally, and how they have motivated them to make changes in their professional practice, such as not taking children out of classrooms for meetings and having more faith in young people to succeed academically. Similarly, practitioners have told us how they have put up artwork in their offices to remind them and their colleagues about not labelling young people, the importance of scaffolding aspirations and why designated teachers need to be visible within the school system. Additionally, foster carers have reported on the usefulness of the magazines and films; and young people have spoken about feeling more empowered and how the materials have offered them some reassurance that their concerns are being listened to and acted upon. This is not quantifiable evidence; however, it illustrates the instrumental changes that can be made by individuals on the ground, which can ultimately contribute to future improvements for children and young people looked after.

Conclusion

Responding to Alexandra's (2015, p. 43) question, 'what impact does voice have if no one is listening?', the research team, project partners and creative industries sought to enable forms of political, personal and practice-based audiencing. In producing powerful visual and musical accounts, the venture has offered an opportunity for children's and young people's accounts and ideas for change to be expressed and communicated in multimodal formats, and, in doing so, suggested an agenda for further academic research, policy making and projects of social justice. Traditional formats of reports, academic articles and policy documents are necessary, and we realise their importance in negotiating change. However, they are not always enough, and it is important to consider alternative forms of creative engagement and dissemination. In writing this chapter, we hope that other researchers and practitioners will draw on and share the materials we have produced; and that they will also consider the ways in which they can work more creatively to contribute to improving the educational experiences and outcomes of children and young people both in the Welsh context and internationally.

Acknowledgements

We would like to acknowledge the children and young people who made this chapter possible. We would also like to thank the Welsh Government for commissioning the original study and, later, the ExChange: Care and Education resource; and for their ongoing support with disseminating the research findings. We are grateful to the Cardiff University Engagement Team funding, and the Economic and Social Research Council's Impact and Acceleration Account fund, administered by Cardiff University. It is also important to note the role of collaborating organisations in the impact and engagement activities facilitated by the Children's Social Care Research and Development Centre (CASCADE), namely Ministry of Life, Like an Egg, Hummingbird Audio Landscaping, Cat & Mouse, Voices from Care Cymru, the Fostering Network, DroneBoy Laundry, Nathan Bond, and the Care Forum Wales – Looked After Children Network.

Notes

1. The multimodal outputs from this project are hosted at *http://sites.cardiff. ac.uk/cascade/looked-after-children-and-education/*.
2. The initial films from the project were produced in association with the Fostering Network, Hummingbird Audio Landscaping and Cat & Mouse.
3. Received Pronunciation (RP) is the accent of Standard English in the United Kingdom and it is associated with educated speech and English as spoken in the south of England.

4. Young people involved with Voices from Care Cymru assisted with the voice-overs for the films.
5. All graphic art pieces, music audios and music videos were created in association with Ministry of Life and the artists DroneBoy Laundry and Nathan Bond.
6. The poetry competition was judged by the Children's Commissioner Office in Wales, Ministry of Life and award-winning Welsh poet Sophie McKeand, Young People's Laureate Wales. The consultations and poetry were used to create a #messagestoschools charter in collaboration with the Care Forum Wales Looked After Children Network. The related outputs included a charter poster (in English and in Welsh); three graphic art posters (in English and in Welsh); a 2.5-minute film (in English and in Welsh); and a music audio and a music video.
7. The #messagestoschools film and poster were created in association with Like an Egg and the film is available in English at *https:// e69c78e447 vimeo.com/214645169/* and in Welsh at *https://vimeo.com/219376741/3e31f68656.*
8. The #messagestoschools artwork was created by Nathan Bond.
9. There is a duty for governing bodies of all maintained schools to appoint a designated teacher for looked-after children on the school roll. The designated teacher should have lead responsibility for helping school staff understand the things which affect how looked-after children learn and achieve; and have lead responsibility for the development and implementation of the children's personal education plans within the school.
10. The magazines for young people and foster carers were created in conjunction with the Fostering Network.
11. The ExChange: Care and Education resource can be found at *http://www.exchangewales.org/careandeducation.*

References

Alexandra, D., 'Are we listening yet? Participatory knowledge production through media practice: encounters of political listening', in A. Gubrium, K. Harper and M. Otañez (eds), *Participatory Visual and Digital Research in Action* (Walnut Creek, CA: Left Coast Press, 2015), pp. 41–56.

Barnes, V., Clouder, D., Pritchard, J., Hughes, C. and Purkis, J., 'Deconstructing Dissemination: Dissemination as Qualitative Research', *Qualitative Research*, 3/2(2003), 147–64.

Becker, H. S., Telling About Society (Chicago: University of Chicago Press, 2007).

Berridge, D., 'Educating Young People in Care: What Have We Learned?', *Children and Youth Services Review*, 34/6 (2012), 1171–5.

Brady, G. and Brown, G., 'Rewarding But Let's Talk About the Challenges: Using Arts Based Methods in Research with Young Mothers', *Methodological Innovations Online*, 8/1 (2013), 99–112.

Brodie, I., *Improving Educational Outcomes for Looked After Children and Young People*, Centre for Excellence and Outcomes in Children and Young People's

Services (C4EO) (2010). Available at *archive.c4eo.org.uk/themes/vulnerablechildren/educationaloutcomes/files/improving_educational_outcomes_full_knowledge_review.pdf* (accessed 17/03/17).

Bruce A., Schick Makaroff, K. L., Sheilds, L., Beuthin, R., Molzahn, A. and Shermak, S., 'Lessons Learned About Art-based Approaches for Disseminating Knowledge', *Nurse Res*, 21/1 (2013), 23-8.

Byrne, E., Elliott, E. and Williams, G., 'Performing the Micro-Social: Using Theatre to Debate Research Findings on Everyday Life, Health and Wellbeing', *Sociological Review*, 64/4 (2016), 715-33.

Economic and Social Research Council., 'What is impact?' (2010). Available at *http://www.esrc.ac.uk/research/impact-toolkit/what-is-impact/* (accessed 17/03/17).

Evans, R., Brown, R., Rees, G. and Smith, P., 'Systematic Review of Educational Interventions for Looked-After Children and Young People: Recommendations for Intervention Development and Evaluation', *British Educational Research Journal*, 43/1 (2017) 68-94.

Finfgeld, D., 'Metasynthesis: The State of the Art – so Far', *Qualitative Health Research*, 13/7 (2003), 893-904.

Gallacher, L. A. and Gallagher, M., 'Methodological Immaturity in Childhood Research? Thinking through "Participatory Methods"', *Childhood*, 15 (2008), 499-516.

Girling, R., 'Yet another change: The experience of movement for children and young people looked after', in D. Mannay, A. Rees and L. Roberts (eds), *Children and Young People 'Looked After'? Education, Intervention and the Everyday Culture of Care in Wales* (Cardiff: University of Wales Press, 2019), pp. 127-39.

Halford, S. and Knowles, C., 'More Than Words: Some Reflections on Working Visually', *Sociological Research Online*, 10/1 (2005). Available at *http://www.socresonline.org.uk/10/1/knowleshalford.html* (accessed 17/01/18).

Keen, S. and Todres, L., 'Strategies for Disseminating Qualitative Research Findings: Three Exemplars', *Forum: Qualitative Social Research*, 8/3 (2007), Art. 17. Available at *http://nbn-resolving.de/urn:nbn:de:0114-fqs0703174* (accessed 01/03/18).

Knowles, C. and Burrows, R., 'The Impact of Impact', *Etnográfica*, 18/2 (2014), 237-54.

Lomax, H., 'Seen and Heard? Ethics and Agency in ParticipatoryVisual Research with Children, *Young People and Families*', *Families, Relationships and Societies*, 4/3 (2015), 493-502.

——— and Fink, J., 'Interpreting Images of Motherhood: The Contexts and Dynamics of Collective Viewing', *Sociological Research Online*, 15/3 (2010). Available at *www.socresonline.org.uk/15/3/2.html* (accessed 17/01/18).

Mannay, D., Visual, *Narrative and Creative Research Methods: Application, Reflection and Ethics* (Abingdon: Routledge, 2016a).

———, 'Landscapes of invisibility, visibility and re-visualisation: employing creative methods of data production and dissemination to generate ethical impacts with marginalised communities', presented at *33rd Annual Qualitative Analysis Conference*, Brock University, Canada, 11-13 May (2016b).

————, Evans, R., Staples, E., Hallett, S., Roberts, L., Rees, A. and Andrews, D., 'The Consequences of Being Labelled "Looked-After": Exploring the Educational Experiences of Looked-after Children and Young People in Wales', *British Journal of Educational Research*, 43/4 (2017a), 683–99.

————, Fink, H. and Lomax, H., 'Visual ethnography', in P. Atkinson, S. Delamont, M. Hardy and M. Williams (eds), *The SAGE Encyclopaedia of Social Research Methods* (London: Sage, forthcoming).

———— and Staples, E., 'Sandboxes, stickers and superheroes: Employing creative techniques to explore the aspirations and experiences of children and young people who are looked after', in D. Mannay, A. Rees and L. Roberts (eds), *Children and Young People 'Looked After'? Education, Intervention and the Everyday Culture of Care in Wales* (Cardiff: University of Wales Press, 2019), pp. 169–82.

————, Staples, E. and Edwards, V., 'Visual Methodologies, Sand and Psychoanalysis: Employing Creative Participatory Techniques to Explore the Educational Experiences of Mature Students and Children in Care', *Visual Studies*, 32 (2017b), 345–58.

————, Staples, E., Hallett, S., Roberts, L., Rees, A., Evans, R. and Andrews, D., *Understanding the Educational Experiences and Opinions, Attainment, Achievement and Aspirations of Looked After Children in Wales* (Cardiff: Welsh Government, 2015).

Rees, G., Brown, R., Smith, P. and Evans, R., 'Educational interventions for children and young people in care: A review of outcomes, implementation and acceptability', in D. Mannay, A. Rees and L. Roberts (eds), *Children and Young People 'Looked After'? Education, Intervention and the Everyday Culture of Care in Wales* (Cardiff: University of Wales Press, 2019), pp. 29–42.

REF, Assessment framework and guidance on submissions. REF 02.2011 (2011). Available at: *www.ref.ac.uk/pubs/2011-02/* (accessed 17/02/18).

Richardson, M., 'Theatre as Safe Space? Performing Intergenerational Narratives with Men of Irish Descent', *Social and Cultural Geography*, 16/6 (2015), 615–33.

Sebba, J., Berridge, D., Luke, N., Fletcher, J., Bell, K. and Strand, S. *The Educational Progress of Looked After Children in England: Linking Care and Educational Data* (Oxford, Rees Centre for Research in Fostering and Education and University of Bristol, 2015).

Silver, D., 'Telling "About Society" for Public Sociology'. Presented at *Visual Innovation: A Methods Workshop #Visual16*. BSA Postgraduate Forum & Visual Methods Study Group, Staffordshire University, 22 November 2016 (2016).

Stein, M., *Young People Leaving Care: Supporting Pathways to Adulthood* (London: Jessica Kingsley, 2012).

Strathern, M., *Audit Cultures: Anthropological Studies in Accountability, Ethics and the Academy* (London: Routledge, 2000).

Sweetman, P., 'Just anybody? Images, ethics and recognition', in J. Gillett (ed.), *Just Anybody* (Renja Leino, Winchester: Fotonet/The Winchester Gallery), pp. 7–9.

———— and Hensser, L., *City Portraits* – Research output: Non-textual form, Exhibition (2009). Available at *https://www.southampton.ac.uk/mediacentre/news/2010/jul/10_78.shtml* (accessed 17/01/18).

Timmins, F., 'Disseminating Nursing Research', *Nursing Standard*, 29/48 (2015), 34–9.

Troman, G., 'Tales from the interface: Disseminating ethnography for policy making', in G. Walford (ed.), *Ethnography and Education Policy* (London: JAI, 2001), pp. 251–73.

Vanderlinde, R. and van Braak, J., 'The Gap between Educational Research and Practice: Views of Teachers, School Leaders, Intermediaries and Researchers', *British Educational Research Journal*, 23/2 (2010), 299–316.

Welbourne, P. and Leeson, C., 'The Education of Children in Care: A Research Review', *Journal of Youth Services*, 7/2 (2012), 128–43.

Welsh Government, *Raising the Ambitions and Educational Attainment of Children Who Are Looked After in Wales* (Cardiff: Welsh Government, 2016).

————, *Raising the Ambitions and Educational Attainment of Children Who Are Looked After in Wales: One Year On* (Cardiff: Welsh Government, 2017).

IV
CONCLUSION

17 | Conclusion

Dawn Mannay, Alyson Rees and Louise Roberts

Introduction

THIS CONCLUDING CHAPTER is concerned with both revisiting and consolidating key messages from the intervening chapters, which dealt with diverse but connecting themes about *Children and Young People 'Looked After'? Education, Intervention and the Everyday Culture of Care in Wales*. The collection as a whole has offered the reader a broad and varied focus. It has considered the policy and practice landscape of Wales, and provided a unique insight into the lives of those in or connected to the care system in Wales. Moreover, the collection encapsulates a range of experiences, contexts and influences that reflect the diversity of children's and young people's lives. There can be a tendency to refer to children and young people in care as if they are a static, homogeneous group. In contrast, their individual characteristics, personalities, talents and abilities vary, as do their histories, circumstances, needs and relationships. As children and young people have told us, 'I shouldn't be labelled or underestimated just because I am "looked after". I am not just a number, I am me'[1]. This collection has sought to reflect this diversity.

The three sections, 'Education and Policy Intervention', 'The Culture of Care and the Everyday Lives of Children and Young People' and

'Participatory, Qualitative and Collaborative Approaches', are embedded in the Welsh context. However, the issues raised and the recommendations posed have direct relevance for readers in the United Kingdom, and points of interest and resonance for international audiences. Additionally, by directly addressing the nature and scope of social research, and the impact of social relations on this research, the volume will be relevant to practitioners and researchers across a range of academic disciplines and fields of interest.

We are proud of the contributions brought together here, and feel that the volume is a valuable addition to the fields of social care, social work and the social sciences. At the same time, it is clear that there is still much for those interested in children and young people, policy and practice, and the everyday culture of care, to learn and to do. Consequently, this chapter both reflects back and looks forward to consider the directions that future explorations and practices might take. This process of reflexivity and moving forward is arranged by returning in turn to each core theme, 'Education and Policy Intervention', 'The Culture of Care and the Everyday Lives of Children and Young People' and 'Participatory, Qualitative and Collaborative Approaches'.

Education and policy intervention

The opening chapter effectively set out the broader landscape of care in Wales by presenting national and localised rates of children and young people 'looked after' (Elliott, 2019). One important message from this was that nationally in Wales, and in other countries, the number of children and young people entering the care system is rising. This emphasises an importance, and an urgency, to draw on research and experience to develop the most effective strategies to ensure that care-experienced children and young people have the necessary support throughout their educational journeys.

It also raises a number of challenges as many of those working in children's services and within the education system have reported that they are already weighed down with scrutiny, targets, management control, high staff turnover and heavy caseloads (Munro, 2012; Care Council for Wales, 2014; Diaz, 2018; Parkins, 2018); and some foster carers are leaving the profession due to increased surveillance and the threat of allegations (Plumridge and Sebba, 2016). These issues impact on the ability of social workers, teachers, foster carers and other practitioners to work effectively and creatively with children and young people. Additionally, as Elliott (2019) points out, there is a growing evidence base for a relationship between deprivation and rates of children looked after, which suggests that the most marginalised communities are more at risk of being involved in the care system (see also Roberts, 2019).

In considering what actions could be taken to address ongoing educational inequalities, Gwyther Rees, Rachel Brown, Phil Smith and Rhiannon Evans (2019) offered a discussion of their detailed systematic review of educational interventions for children and young people in care. The evidence base proved both limited and mixed, suggesting that continued efforts are required to develop and evaluate supportive interventions which are theoretically sound; and that there are no simple fixes to address either current problems, or those envisaged by the increasing numbers of children and young people entering the care system. Rebecca Pratchett and Paul Rees (2019) also raised further concerns in their conclusions that educational outcomes of care-experienced populations remain significantly below those of the non-looked-after population; arguing that continued efforts to support educational achievement are necessary.

However, despite the uncertainties around the effectiveness of intervention programmes and research illustrating pervasive gaps in educational outcomes, there have been a number of recent positive policy developments and investments in training, guidance and support programmes in Wales. For example, research findings around the education of care-experienced children and young people (see Mannay et al., 2015; The Fostering Network, 2015) informed the Welsh Government's strategy 'Raising the ambitions and educational attainment of children who are looked after' (Welsh Government, 2016). An evaluation of the strategy in its first year illustrated some improvements in the educational attainment and qualification outcomes for care-experienced children and young people (Welsh Government, 2017). There has also been a greater acknowledgement of the role of teaching staff and 'Making a difference – a guide for the designated person for looked after children' (see Welsh Government, 2017), has provided practical and research informed guidance for educators with a responsibility for care-experienced students.

The strategy also led to the implementation and evaluation of the pilot Fostering Well-being Programme in Cwm Taf, south Wales[2]. The Fostering Network runs this programme based on the Head, Heart, Hands model of social pedagogy (Petrie et al., 2009), which takes a holistic understanding of well-being. However, it also includes a major focus on working together to achieve educational improvements for care-experienced children and young people. Additionally, the Welsh Government commissioned a free to access, online community of practice to act as an interactive repository for guidance, support and research materials around care and education [3]. Furthermore, the Welsh Government has appointed a series of ongoing consultations with children and young people. These consultations will potentially provide some indication of the continuities and changes in care and educational experiences for children and young people in Wales, and the extent to which the current strategy can contribute to further improvements.

Nevertheless, despite the importance of education, Paul Rees and Amy Munro (2019) offered an alternative conceptualisation of 'success', arguing that an isolated concern to improve educational performance for children and young people in care is unhelpful as 'success' is inextricably bound to a range of intra- and inter-personal factors in children's and young people's lives, both within and beyond education. Highlighting themes that are echoed throughout the collection (see, for example, Rees 2019; Girling, 2019). Children's and young people's emotional well-being and their relationships with key people in their lives were reported as fundamental to notions of happiness and success. Gemma Allnatt (2019) also complicated ideas of 'success', contending that even seemingly outwardly successful educational subjects who have entered higher education face a number of barriers in their journeys, characterised by housing instability and a lack of social support systems.

Again, there has been policy development in this area, which may have benefited more recent higher education students with similar biographies to the participants in Allnatt's study. For example, 'When I'm Ready' came into force in April 2016 in Wales, in response to campaigns about the need for children and young people in care to have the right to emotional and relationship based support beyond the age of 18 years. 'When I'm Ready' offered children and young people looked after in Wales the right to remain living in foster care once they reach 18 years of age (Fostering Network, 2016). The scheme was set up by the Welsh Government in 2015 and made legal by the Social Services and Well-being (Wales) Act under Post 18 Living arrangements (Welsh Government, 2016b).

However, the scheme has been criticised because, unlike young people in foster care, young people are not able to stay in their residential care home past the age of 18 under the 'When I'm Ready' arrangement (see Children's Commissioner for Wales, 2017). Therefore, it will be interesting to see the extent to which the ongoing Welsh Government consultations with care-experienced young people will be able to provide an insight into whether 'When I'm Ready' has provided the anticipated increase in relationship-based support for young people post-18. It is important not to disregard the central importance of education for care-experienced children and young people. Schools and other educational institutions can provide a touchstone of familiarity, offer support and guidance, and enable gateways to further opportunities. At the same time, they are embedded in wider sociocultural structures that are also important sites of inquiry, as explored in the following section.

The culture of care and the everyday lives of children and young people

The second theme of the book offered an insight into the everyday lives and experiences of care-experienced children and young people, which have the potential to exacerbate or alleviate the disadvantages they face both within and beyond the sphere of education. Study within or about the private space of the home is contentious (Lincoln, 2012), and it can be difficult for researchers to 'delve into the life of the everyday of their participants' and 'walk their walk, and talk their talk' (Russell and Barley, 2016). Nevertheless, it can be advantageous to gain an insight to these hidden worlds (Mannay et al., 2017), and Alyson Rees' (2019) chapter provided a 'worm's eye view' into the lives and caring practices of 'stable' foster families. The chapter highlighted the importance of successfully navigating dominant discourses of risk within children and family social work, to ensure children and young people who are 'looked after' enjoy an unfettered sense of being cared for, caring about, being part of, and taking part in family life.

Notions of risk were also centralised in Holly Gordon's (2019) consideration of outside play and the natural environment for children and young people in care, which proposed a risk-competent approach to supporting children and young people's access to the natural environment. These two contributions reported the salience of both touch and outdoor play for children and young people. However, discourses of 'risk' continually threaten the potential benefits of these practices. For example, the threat of allegations (Plumridge and Sebba, 2016) and systems of surveillance permeated with value judgements and an overweening 'safety' culture (see Rosier, 2009; Dowty, 2008), act to close down the very relationships and spaces in which children and young people can grow and develop. Arguably, this 'risk-averse' climate where a comforting arm around a shoulder induces anxieties about fear of prosecution, and running, playing and climbing, outdoors, unless heavily organised and monitored, is conceptualised as dangerous, is especially harmful for care-experienced children and young people, and those charged with their care.

Conceptualisations of risk, harm and benefit are also features of the complex and highly emotive issue of birth family contact. Joanne Pye and Paul Rees (2019) worked with children and young people, birth parents, carers, contact workers and social workers, to identify the constituents of 'positive contact'. Highlighting the differing and sometimes contrasting experiences and perspectives of stakeholders involved in contact arrangements, the importance of open and considered communication between each party was put forward as a way to engender best practice, and foster 'positive contact'. The associated barriers were often attributed to lack of time, training, resources and experience, which link back to the arguments posed earlier in the book about the growing numbers of children in care and the strain on children's services (Elliott, 2019; Munro, 2012; Care Council for Wales, 2014; Diaz, 2018). This suggests that alongside policy strategies, social work and social services need to be adequately resourced and that future investment is vital to ensure quality services, which are both informed and effective in serving care-experienced children and young people, as well as their families and carers. This theme has been explored further in the English context in relation to the impacts of austerity and cuts to local service provision (see Cann and Lawson, 2016).

Rebecca Girling's poignant chapter on residential care brought to the fore the often unexplored expectations on children and young people to seamlessly adjust to new living arrangements, to form new relationships and adapt to the norms and rules of their new surroundings. Choice, understanding and control were central to young people's reflections of change and movement, and Girling argued that increased recognition should be afforded to the psychological as well as the physical aspects of movement and change. The failings in residential care have been addressed to some extent with increased regulation, such as the Children's Homes (Wales) Regulations (National Assembly for Wales, 2002). However, the emphasis on education, health, protection, hazards and safety, food and adequate staffing, does not easily facilitate a significant focus on the affective elements of movement. There exists an enormous wealth of research on how emotion operates in specific social and cultural contexts (Loughran and Mannay, 2018), and arguably this could be considered in further studies exploring the impacts of time, place and movement for care-experienced children and young people.

Leaving care may signal the end of a care journey, but the effects of being a child and young person 'looked after' are pervasive and far reaching. As Berger (1972, p. 370) contends:

> The present tense of the verb to be refers only to the present: but nevertheless with the first person singular in front of it, it absorbs the past, which is inseparable from it. 'I am' includes all that has made me so. It is more than a statement of immediate fact: it is already biographical.

It is important then to think about the transition to adulthood, and to parenthood for young people in and leaving the care system, and Louise Roberts (2019) effectively illustrated how the long shadow of care history permeates the present. Motherhood and mothering are conceived in relation to hierarchies through which those living in poverty or in marginalised areas often become characterised by 'otherhood' and 'othering'; a positioning that leaves them vulnerable to overt and indirect forms of criticism, surveillance and policing (Brady and Brown, 2013; Mannay et al. 2018). Arguably, for care-experienced parents these experiences are intensified, with additional forms of monitoring and often the absence of the support that other parents would receive from wider family networks.

There have been recent initiatives to prevent women who have experienced the compulsory removal of a child from experiencing a repeat pregnancy in the short term, whilst successive child removal remains the most likely outcome. For example, the 'Reflect' project is currently being evaluated by Louise Roberts, Nina Maxwell and Claire Palmer [4]. However, a pressing concern is breaking intergenerational cycles of care placements, which involve holistic, dedicated support for young people in care and care leavers, so that they are in a better position to have and retain a family of their own. In terms of parenthood, but also a range of other areas discussed across the collection, there are calls for effective systems of support, guidance and resourcing, so that care-experienced children and young people can enjoy a more equal playing field, which will enable them to secure positive futures.

Participatory, qualitative and collaborative approaches

The final section of the book focused specifically on research methodologies. This is important as our research designs and techniques frame what can be known, and in turn what can be acted upon to inform policy change and practice development. It is worth, first, considering the methodological lessons from the opening parts. The initial contributions here provided convincing arguments for better reporting of quantitative data around localised patterns of increases in the number of children and young people in care (Elliott, 2019), and more robust systems of measurement in studies applying random controlled trials, so that they can provide more clarity around the extent to which any interventions produced positive impacts (Rees at al., 2019). Quantitative and experimental approaches are fundamental in allocating resources, measuring the impacts of interventions and advising policy and practice initiatives. They can also provide the baseline information for more qualitative forms of inquiry, which are explored in the closing set of chapters.

Key considerations in effective qualitative inquiry are ethical practice, positionality and reflexivity, which are explored by all of the authors. Drawing on Amanda Coffey's (1999, p. 22) argument that 'who is a stranger or a member, an outsider or an insider, a knower or an ignoramus is all relative and much more blurred than conventional accounts might have us believe', Claire Palmer's (2019) chapter detailed her positioning in qualitative interviews with adoptive parents of older care-experienced children. The chapter offered a range of insights into engagement and experiences across the adoption process, which emphasised the value of following up baseline statistics with in-depth discussions with participants. Palmer also drew upon her own experiences to critically reflect on the influence of the self on the research encounter, which has resonance for social researchers but may also be of interest to practitioners and carers in recognising their relational responses to others.

In the following two chapters, Dawn Mannay and Eleanor Staples (2019) and Phil Smith (2019) continued with the theme of the fieldwork relationship and reflected on the benefits of creative methods when undertaking research with care-experienced children and young people. Aligning with the Welsh Government's formal commitment to children's rights, which has strengthened the national basis for children's and young people's participation in research studies (Welsh Assembly Government, 2004), the authors centralised the importance of enabling space for children and young people to direct conversations and reflect on their experiences. Mannay and Staples explored the benefits of creative research but noted that their participatory approach was restricted to the fieldwork process, whilst Smith reflected on the ways in which adult voices can still permeate the accounts of young people, despite his emphasis on enabling the multimodal project to be participant led.

Eleanor Staples, Louise Roberts, Jennifer Lyttleton-Smith, Sophie Hallett and CASCADE Voices (2019), widened the discussion to reflect on collaborative partnership and coproduction. Finding ways to involve participants in all elements of the research process is an important consideration for researchers (see Children's Commissioner for Wales, 2017), and this chapter explored how this could be achieved, and the barriers to this involvement. In this way, the chapter acts as an exemplar, illustrating how young people can be involved in posing research questions, designing projects, conducting fieldwork as peer researchers, evaluating outcomes, and disseminating findings. This approach moved beyond a form of decorative or tokenistic involvement (Hart, 1992) and provided an opportunity for meaningful participation, where children and young people were positioned as the experts in their own lives (James and James, 2004), from whom researchers, practitioners and policy makers have much to learn.

In the final chapter, Dawn Mannay, Louisa Roberts, Eleanor Staples and Ministry of Life (2019) focused on the significance of impact, 'extending the social researcher's responsibility from outputs to outcomes' (Brady et al., 2007, p. 123). For Silverman (1999, p. 273):

> The idea that social research might influence public policy
> provides an inspiration for many young social scientists.
> In most English speaking countries, the sad truth is that
> things have never worked in this way.

However, although this may be true of many studies, this does not have to be the case and there is now a greater appreciation of, and expectation for, a relationship between social research and change. Academics have begun to share how they have challenged the assumption that academic research has little meaning for the lives of 'real' people (see Letherby et al., 2007), and the project built on this earlier work. The use of innovative multimodal outputs including film, artwork and music [5] were discussed as modes to engage diverse audiences, and have real impacts on not only policy but also on everyday ground-level practice. By involving both care-experienced children and young people, and those who care for them, in research that centralises their voices and experiences, and having a commitment to communicating research findings, there is a genuine potential to contribute to positive improvements and new ways of working.

Final reflections

This collection has sought to recognise the distinct features of the policy and practice landscape in Wales for children and young people who are looked after. The chapters have highlighted the pervasive disparity of outcomes in and beyond education, and the profound significance of relationships on the lived experiences, development and well-being of care-experienced children and young people. It has also reflected on the reach and impact of research studies that have gone some way towards not only raising the voice of children and young people in care but ensuring that there are opportunities for these voices to be heard, and acted upon. Importantly, the studies have also illustrated the support of third sector organisations, charities, research partners, Local Authorities and the Welsh Government, who shared the authors' vision for impact and change. This underlines the benefits of researchers understanding their national policy context, building relationships and reputations over time, and working collaboratively with policy maker and partners to achieve common goals (see Lenihan, 2018).

We are heartened by the breadth, scope and quality of research showcased within this collection and its potential to make valuable and informed contributions to ongoing efforts to address inequality and disadvantage for children and young people in Wales, and internationally, who are 'looked after'. Yet it is also clear that there is more to do. There are gaps in our knowledge base both with regard to care-experienced children and young people and their education, but also concerning their wider life and relationships. Further research is required in a number of areas, to illuminate the ways in which enrichment and improvements can be made with and for the lives of children and young people looked after.

In editing this collection, we have gained a wealth of knowledge, developed more nuanced understandings of the lives of children and young people who are or have been 'looked after', and at the same time gained a deeper appreciation of different disciplinary research approaches and applications. We hope that readers have enjoyed a comparable experience in journeying through the valuable and moving accounts offered across *Children and Young People 'Looked After'? Education, Intervention and the Everyday Culture of Care in Wales*. Moreover, we hope that some readers are inspired to draw on these examples and take up the challenge to continue to address the inequalities faced by children and young people in Wales, and globally. In closing the collection, we return to an earlier quote to re-emphasise an important take-home message from a young person: 'I shouldn't be labelled or underestimated just because I am "looked after". I am not just a number, I am me.'

Notes

1. This quote is taken from the #messagestoschools work, which involved a poetry competition and consultations with children and young people. More details about the project can be found at *http://www.exchangewales.org/ messagestoschools*.

2. More information on the Fostering Well-being Programme in Cwm Taf, south Wales is available at *https://www.thefosteringnetwork.org.uk/media-release/2017/wellbeing-fostered-children-in-wales-be-improved-thanks-innovative-project*.

3. ExChange: Care and Education: *http://www.exchangewales.org/careand education*.

4. More information about the Reflect project is available at *http://sites.cardiff. ac.uk/cascade/research/research-projects/reflect/*.

5. Multimodal outputs are available at *http://www.exchangewales.org/laceproject*.

References

Allnatt, G., 'Transitions from care to higher education: A case study of a young person's journey', in D. Mannay, A. Rees and L. Roberts (eds), *Children and Young People 'Looked After'? Education, Intervention and the Everyday Culture of Care in Wales* (Cardiff: University of Wales Press, 2019), pp. 69–82.

Berger, J., *About Looking: Writers and Readers* (London: Penguin, 1972).

Brady, G. and Brown, G., 'Rewarding but Let's Talk About the Challenges: Using Arts Based Methods in Research with Young Mothers', *Methodological Innovations Online*, 8/1 (2013), 99–112.

———, Bywaters, P., Knyspel, M., Letherby, G. and Steventon, G., 'Outcomes', in G. Letherby and P. Bywaters (eds), *Extending Social Research: Application, Implementation and Publication* (Buckingham: Open University Press, 2007), pp. 123–41.

Cann, R. and Lawson, K., *Cuts: The View from Foster Carers: The Impact of Austerity Measures on Fostered Children and the Families that Care for Them* (London: The Fostering Network, 2016).

Care Council for Wales, *The Profile of Social Workers in Wales: Report from the Care Council for Wales Register of Social Care Workers June 2014* (Cardiff: Care Council for Wales, 2014). Available at *https://socialcare.wales/cms_ assets/file-uploads/The-Profile-of-Social-Workers-in-Wales-2014.pdf* (accessed 14/03/18).

Children's Commissioner for Wales, *Hidden Ambitions: Achieving the Best for Young People Leaving Care* (Llansamlet: Children's Commissioner for Wales, 2017).

Coffey, A., *The Ethnographic Self: Fieldwork and the Representation of Identity* (London: Sage, 1999).

Diaz, C., *A Study into Children and Young People's Participation in Their Children in Care Reviews and the Role of the Independent Reviewing Officer* (PhD thesis, Cardiff University, 2018).

Dowty, T., 'Pixie-dust and Privacy: What's happening to Children's Rights in England?', *Children & Society*, 22/5 (2008), 393–9.

Elliott, M., 'Charting the rise of children and young people looked after in Wales', in D. Mannay, A. Rees and L. Roberts (eds), *Children and Young People 'Looked After'? Education, Intervention and the Everyday Culture of Care in Wales* (Cardiff: University of Wales Press, 2019), pp. 15–28.

Fostering Network, The, *What is Needed to Enable Looked After Children to Achieve in Education?* (Cardiff: The Fostering Network, 2015).

———, *When I am Ready* (Cardiff: The Fostering Network, 2016). Available at https://www.thefosteringnetwork.org.uk/policy-practice/practice-information/when-I-am-ready (accessed 20/03/18).

Girling, R., 'Yet Another Change: The Experience of Movement for Children and Young People Looked After', in D. Mannay, A. Rees and L. Roberts (eds), *Children and Young People 'Looked After'? Education, Intervention and the Everyday Culture of Care in Wales* (Cardiff: University of Wales Press, 2019), pp. 127–39.

Gordon, H., 'The natural environment and its benefits for children and young people looked after', in D. Mannay, A. Rees and L. Roberts (eds), *Children and Young People 'Looked After'? Education, Intervention and the Everyday Culture of Care in Wales* (Cardiff: University of Wales Press, 2019), pp. 99–112.

Hart, R. A., *Children's Participation: From Tokenism to Citizenship* (Florence: UNICEF Innocenti Centre, 1992).

James, A. and James, A. L., *Constructing Childhood: Theory, Policy and Social Practice* (London: Palgrave Macmillan, 2004).

Lenihan, A., *Pathways to Impact in the Welsh Government and the National Assembly for Wales: A Practical Guide for Researchers* (2018). Available at https://campaignforsocialscience.org.uk/pathwaystoimpact/# (accessed 06/03/18).

Letherby, G., Brady, G. M. and Brown, G. C., 'Working with the community: research and action', in C. J. Clay, M. Madden and L. Potts (eds), *Towards Understanding Community: People and Places* (London: Palgrave Macmillan, 2007), pp. 123–36.

Lincoln, S., *Youth Culture and Private Space* (Basingstoke: Palgrave Macmillan, 2012).

Loughran, T. and Mannay, D. (eds), *Emotion and the Researcher: Sites, Subjectivities and Relationships*, Studies in Qualitative Methodology, Vol. 16 (Bingley: Emerald, 2018).

Mannay, D., Creaghan, J., Gallagher, D., Marzella, R., Mason, S., Morgan, M. and Grant, A., 'Negotiating Closed Doors and Constraining Deadlines: The Potential of Visual Ethnography to Effectually Explore Private and Public Spaces of Motherhood and Parenting', *Journal of Contemporary Ethnography* (2017). Available at http://journals.sagepub.com/doi/10.1177/0891241617744858 (accessed 15/03/18).

————, Creaghan, J., Gallagher, D., Mason, S., Morgan, M. and Grant, A., '"Watching what I'm doing, watching how I'm doing it": Exploring the everyday experiences of surveillance and silenced voices among marginalised mothers in Welsh low-income locales', in T. Taylor and K. Bloch (eds), *Marginalized Mothers, Mothering from the Margins*, Advances in Gender Research, Vol. 25 (Bingley: Emerald, 2018).

————, Staples, E., Hallett, S., Roberts, L., Rees, A., Evans, R. E. and Andrews, D., *Understanding the Educational Experiences and Opinions, Attainment, Achievement and Aspirations of Looked After Children in Wales* (Cardiff: Welsh Government, 2015).

————, and Staples, E., 'Sandboxes, stickers and superheroes: Employing creative techniques to explore the aspirations and experiences of children and young people who are looked after', in D. Mannay, A. Rees and L. Roberts (eds), *Children and Young People 'Looked After'? Education, Intervention and the Everyday Culture of Care in Wales* (Cardiff: University of Wales Press, 2019), pp. 169–82.

————, Roberts, L., Staples, E. and Ministry of Life, 'Lights, camera, action: Translating research findings into policy and practice impacts with music, film and artwork', in D. Mannay, A. Rees and L. Roberts (eds), *Children and Young People 'Looked After'? Education, Intervention and the Everyday Culture of Care in Wales* (Cardiff: University of Wales Press, 2019), pp. 210–24.

Munro, E., *Munro Review of Child Protection: Progress Report* (2012). Available at https://www.gov.uk/government/publications/progress-report-moving-towards-a-child-centred-system (accessed 14/03/18).

National Assembly for Wales, *The Children's Homes (Wales) Regulations – Welsh Statutory Instruments 2002 No. 327* (Cardiff: National Assembly for Wales, 2002).

Palmer, C., 'Positionality and reflexivity: Conducting qualitative interviews with parents who adopt children from foster care', in D. Mannay, A. Rees and L. Roberts (eds), *Children and Young People 'Looked After'? Education, Intervention and the Everyday Culture of Care in Wales* (Cardiff: University of Wales Press, 2019), pp. 155–68.

Parkins, A., *An Exploration of Teacher's Subjective Experiences of Wellbeing and Teaching in Wales* (unpublished MA dissertation, Cardiff University, 2018).

Petrie, P. and Cameron, C., Hepstinall, E., McQuail, S., Simon, A. and Wigfall, V., *A Holistic Personal Approach to Work with Children and Young People Across Services: European Models for Practice, Training, Education and Qualification: Briefing Paper* (London: Thomas Coram Research Unit, 2009).

Plumridge, G. and Sebba, J., *The Impact of Unproven Allegations on Foster Carers* (Oxford: University of Oxford, 2016).

Pratchett, R. and Rees, P., 'Exploring the educational attainment and achievement of children who are "looked after" in formal kinship care', in D. Mannay, A. Rees and L. Roberts (eds), *Children and Young People 'Looked After'? Education, Intervention and the Everyday Culture of Care in Wales* (Cardiff: University of Wales Press, 2019), pp. 43–55.

Pye, J. and Rees, P., 'Factors that promote positive supervised birth family contact for children in care', in D. Mannay, A. Rees and L. Roberts (eds), *Children and Young People 'Looked After'? Education, Intervention and the Everyday Culture of Care in Wales* (Cardiff: University of Wales Press, 2019), pp. 112–26.

Rees, A., 'The daily lived experiences of foster care: The centrality of food and touch in family life', in D. Mannay, A. Rees and L. Roberts (eds), *Children and Young People 'Looked After'? Education, Intervention and the Everyday Culture of Care in Wales* (Cardiff: University of Wales Press, 2019), pp. 85–98.

Rees, G., Brown, R., Smith, P. and Evans, R., 'Educational interventions for children and young people in care: A review of outcomes, implementation and acceptability', in D. Mannay, A. Rees and L. Roberts (eds), *Children and Young People 'Looked After'? Education, Intervention and the Everyday Culture of Care in Wales* (Cardiff: University of Wales Press, 2019), pp. 29–42.

Rees, P. and Munro, A., 'Promoting the education of children in care: Reflections of children and carers who have experienced "success"', in D. Mannay, A. Rees and L. Roberts (eds), *Children and Young People 'Looked After'? Education, Intervention and the Everyday Culture of Care in Wales* (Cardiff: University of Wales Press, 2019), pp. 56–68.

Roberts, L. '"A family of my own": When young people in and leaving state care become parents in Wales', in D. Mannay, A. Rees and L. Roberts (eds), *Children and Young People 'Looked After'? Education, Intervention and the Everyday Culture of Care in Wales* (Cardiff: University of Wales Press, 2019), pp. 140–52.

Rosier, K., 'Children as problems, problems of children', in J. Qvortrup, W. Corsaro and M. Honig (eds), *The Palgrave Handbook of Childhood Studies* (Basingstoke: Macmillan, 2009), pp. 256–72.

Russell, L. and Barley, R., 'Ethics, Education and Ethnography; Working with Young People and Children', presented at *Engaging Children and Young People: Creative Methods and Research Ethics* (Huddersfield: University of Huddersfield, 2016).

Silverman, D., *Doing Qualitative Research* (London: Sage, 1999).

Smith, P., 'A view from a Pupil Referral Unit: Using participatory methods with young people in an education setting', in D. Mannay, A. Rees and L. Roberts (eds), *Children and Young People 'Looked After'? Education, Intervention and the Everyday Culture of Care in Wales* (Cardiff: University of Wales Press, 2019), pp. 183–95.

Staples, E., Roberts, L., Lyttleton-Smith, J., Hallett, S. and CASCADE Voices, 'Enabling care-experienced young people's participation in research: CASCADE Voices', in D. Mannay, A. Rees and L. Roberts (eds), *Children and Young People 'Looked After'? Education, Intervention and the Everyday Culture of Care in Wales* (Cardiff: University of Wales Press, 2019), pp. 196–209.

Welsh Assembly Government, *Children and Young People: Rights to Action* (Cardiff: Welsh Assembly Government, 2004).

Welsh Government, *Raising the Ambitions and Educational Attainment of Children Who are Looked After in Wales* (Cardiff: Welsh Government, 2016a).

———, *When I'm Ready Good Practice Guide* (Cardiff: Welsh Government, 2016b).

———, *Raising the Ambitions and Educational Attainment of Children Who are Looked After in Wales – One Year On* (Cardiff: Welsh Government, 2017).

Index